EXISTENTIALISM AND RELIGIOUS BELIEF

EXISTENTIALISM AND RELIGIOUS BELIEF

ROGER HAZELTON

EDITOR

EXISTENTIALISM
AND
RELIGIOUS
BELIEF

by DAVID E. ROBERTS

The King's Library

New York

Oxford University Press

1957

CONTENTS

EDITOR'S PREFACE

EDITOR'S PREFACE

DAVID ROBERTS had brought this book well along toward completion before his untimely death in January 1955. The introduction was in rather sketchy form, one or two of the chapters were not quite finished, and a concluding section was lacking. As editor, I have sought to make good these omissions without in any way impairing the integrity of the total volume. Some rewriting has been necessary, particularly in order to make suitable transitions, but this has been kept to a minimum. The brief introductory and concluding portions represent an effort on my part to rework and expand material written by Professor Roberts for other purposes, in so far as this could be brought to bear upon the theme of the present book.

This volume shows the author at his characteristic best—unusually able to enter into the perspective of another's thought, extremely careful though never merely cautious in expounding it, always forthright and pointed in making his own judgments on the same issues. As David Roberts was among the very first American thinkers to take existentialism into account, so it cannot be doubted that his interpretation of the movement's leading figures will endure and prove immensely useful for years to come.

Dr. Roberts had wished to acknowledge his indebtedness to several colleagues and former students at Union Theological Seminary, among them Richard Kroner, Paul Tillich, Reinhold Niebuhr, Edmond LaB. Cherbonnier, Malcolm L. Diamond, and Marion Shows, for help in connection with the preparation of this manuscript. Thanks are also due to the editors of the *Review of Religion, Theology Today,* and *Religion in Life* for the use, in part, of articles contributed by Professor Roberts to their pages. Two distinguished lectureships on which he spoke, the Ayer at Colgate-Rochester Divinity School and the Greene at Andover Newton Theological School, contributed as well to the growth of this significant volume.

I venture to add, as editor, my own words of appreciation—to Robert McAfee Brown and Albert C. Outler for invaluable advice, to Betty Gardner for help with the index and the proofs, and to Wilbur D. Ruggles and Marion Hausner of the Oxford University Press, with whom it has been a delightful privilege to work.

Roger Hazelton

January 1957
Newton Centre, Massachusetts

EXISTENTIALISM AND RELIGIOUS BELIEF

EXISTENTIALISM AND RELIGIOUS BELIEF

INTRODUCTION

WHAT IS EXISTENTIALISM, and why should Christians pay any attention to it? There is no simple answer to this question because each of the writers whom we shall discuss gives his own account of what he is trying to do, and not all of these accounts are mutually compatible. Therefore we shall have to listen to what these thinkers actually have to say before we can even put forward an adequate definition of existentialism.

And one word of warning must be issued immediately. In recent years the word 'existentialism' has gained popular currency mainly through the works of Jean-Paul Sartre. People in Europe and America have seen his plays and read his novels and essays, and the idea has gotten abroad that existentialism means his particular brand of nihilism. Existentialism began, however, as a frankly Christian mode of thinking, and I shall hope to show that what is valid and illuminating in it can be held in perspective within the Christian faith. Yet I believe that these same emphases, when sundered from such faith, become particularly vivid expressions of the spiritual disintegration of our age.

Thus a study of existential philosophy brings into sharp focus the basic struggle between contemporary Christianity and so-called 'secularism.' The movement includes figures who represent both extremes, and many positions intermediate between them. Gabriel Marcel, the French Roman Catholic; Nicolas Berdyaev, the Russian Orthodox lay theologian; Martin Buber, the Jewish philosopher;

and many Protestant thinkers have found in this sort of reflection a powerful impetus driving them toward the affirmation and expression of religious faith. At the other extreme stand Martin Heidegger, the influential German philosopher who was unfortunately associated with the Nazis, and Sartre, who played a role in the French underground resistance. Both of these men are avowed atheists, and they are close together philosophically even though they stood at opposite poles politically during the war. Karl Jaspers provides a very interesting example of an intermediate position. He is not an atheist—on the contrary he is a deeply religious person; yet he holds aloof from his Protestant heritage and determinedly attacks the very center of Christian belief.

In all its forms, however, existentialism should be of compelling interest to the Christian thinker today. For it protests against those intellectual and social forces which are destroying freedom. It calls men away from stifling abstractions and automatic conformity. It drives us back to the most basic, inner problems: what it means to be a self, how we ought to use our freedom, how we can find and keep the courage to face death. And even more important, it bids each individual thinker wrestle with these problems until he has grown into personal authenticity, instead of simply taking his answers from someone else.

Yet in my opinion existentialism cannot serve as a self-sufficient philosophy. Its chief value is that of a corrective. By clearing away philosophical underbrush it brings us face to face with the urgency of ultimate questions. But it does not answer them. It may lead a man to the point where he sees the momentousness of a decision for or against faith in God. But the over-all value of existentialism depends upon the outcome. Where it leads to Christian faith, it offers a promising basis for a concordat between philosophy and theology. Indeed, anyone who takes Biblical revelation seriously must approach philosophical problems in a fashion which incorporates certain existential elements whether he uses this term or not. Yet even where existentialism leads to atheistic conclusions, it is of great importance that we understand it, for it offers a particularly poignant exposition of the predicament of modern man. Here we see individuals facing tragedy without any hope of salvation. We see them standing in utter loneliness and staring at bleak emptiness. And as Christians we need to understand these atheists because, unlike more complacent modern thinkers, they are honest enough to voice that sense of despair which is so widespread in our world. They speak, in fact, for millions of our contemporaries for whom God is dead. They tear away the masks of optimism, self-confidence, and indifference. They help us to understand how the will-to-power issues from hopelessness, how dictators can compel men to renounce their freedom for the sake of specious security, how emptiness lurks behind our amusements and our vices, and how men become enraged at a civilization which makes them cogs in a well-oiled economic and political machine.

Still, existentialism is difficult to define, even provisionally, because most of the writers I have mentioned are deliberately unsystematic. They are not in the slightest degree interested in purveying a set of findings like the answers to arithmetic problems which can be found at the back of the book. Rather are they interested in arousing the reader to a spiritual struggle. Hence the result of this kind of philosophy is what it does to you, not some answer which can be appropriated without going through the agony of figuring things out for yourself.

This is why these men so often produce plays, novels, journals, fugitive essays or meditations. For them, entering into the truth involves a profound kind of self-examination. The most significant thing, they feel, is a change in the man—his motives, feelings, and hopes—instead of an increase in his fund of knowledge. Such a method constitutes an explicit protest against traditional philosophizing by insisting that the personal commitments of a thinker be incorporated into his definition of truth. In fact, it accuses all objective philosophies of divorcing reason from life by trying to evade such human polarities as freedom-and-destiny, anxiety-and-courage, isolation-and-community, guilt-and-forgiveness, instead of recognizing that these polarities must remain perpetually at the center of vital thinking.

Ordinarily the student of philosophy assumes that his task is to master certain concepts and to get them straightened out rationally so that they will be free from inconsistency. He hopes thereby to arrive eventually at an explanation of nature, man, and God. But existentialism passionately protests that the truly great questions of life cannot really be answered by means of scientific information plus clear thinking. For example, I may learn and accept certain theories about immortality without moving one step toward fitness for eternal life. Or I may learn and accept arguments for the existence of God without making one step toward trusting Him in such a way as to incorporate His love in my own life.

The task which lies before us may seem, therefore, to be a contradictory one. We propose to survey and scrutinize existentialism, whereas a real grasp of it demands being on the inside rather than looking curiously at it from the outside. If the ghost of Kierkegaard were present, he would doubtless say that this book is a professor's project. Only the academic mind, he might say, could possibly be so stupid. And yet I cannot believe that this problem is totally insoluble. Is our danger very different from that of a teacher of literature? He can of course turn the study of Shakespeare or Dante into deadly pedantry, but need not. Admittedly, the problem of how to combine intense personal commitment with a critical detachment becomes most acute at the level of religious belief. But surely it is altogether possible to listen to another man's confession of faith (or unfaith) sympathetically, without feeling compelled to swallow it wholesale. And I, for one, can see no real contradiction in studying the general characteristics of existentialism, so long as it is remembered that acquiring information about it is very different from entering personally into the spiritual engagement which it exhibits. Therefore I shall make bold to suggest, in a preliminary way, a few of these general characteristics of existentialism.

First, it is a protest against all forms of rationalism which find it easy to assume that reality can be grasped primarily or exclusively by intellectual means. It is an emphatic denial of the assumption that construction of a logical system is the most adequate way to reach the truth.

In the second place, existentialism is a protest against all views which tend to regard man as if he were a thing, that is, only an assortment of functions and reactions. This means that in the sphere of philosophical theory existentialism stands against mechanism and naturalism; and in the sphere of social theory it stands against all patterns of human organization in which the mass mentality stifles the spontaneity and uniqueness of the individual person. Incidentally, this refusal to accept the dictates of mass-mindedness applies quite as much to the automatic conformities of a democratic, capitalistic society as it does to the obvious regimentation of a totalitarian ordering of life.

Thirdly, existentialism makes a drastic distinction between subjective and objective truth, and it gives priority to the former as against the latter. This word 'subjective' may be easily misunderstood. In ordinary speech when we say that someone has given a highly subjective interpretation, we imply that it is biased, prejudiced, and unreliable. When, however, existentialists speak of 'subjectivity' they have in mind something very different from this. They are not denying that through science, common sense, and logic men are able to arrive at genuinely objective truth. But they insist that in connection with ultimate matters it is impossible to lay aside the impassioned concerns of the human individual. They are calling our attention to the fact that in the search for ultimate truth the whole man, and not only his intellect or reason, is caught up and involved. His emotions and his will must be aroused and engaged so that he can live the truth he sees. The fundamental difference, then, is that between *knowing about* the truth in some theoretical, detached way and *being grasped* by the truth in a decisively personal manner. While the objective standpoint gets as far as it possibly can from the feelings, hopes, or fears of the individual human being, the subjective point of view puts the individual with his commitments and passions in the very center of the picture. And only

7

by the latter approach, say the existentialists, can a man be so grasped and changed inwardly as to deepen and clarify his relationship to reality, even as a thinker.

In the fourth place, existentialism regards man as fundamentally ambiguous. This is very closely linked to its predominant stress on freedom. It sees the human situation as filled with contradictions and tensions which cannot be resolved by means of exact or consistent thinking. These contradictions are not due simply to the present limitations of our knowledge, and they will not be overcome merely by obtaining further scientific information or philosophical explanation because they reflect the stubborn fact that man is split down the middle—at war with himself. He is free, yes; he is conscious of responsibility, of remorse, of guilt for what he has done. Yet his whole life is enmeshed within a natural and social order which profoundly and inevitably determines him, making him what in fact he is. He is finite; but he is capable of rising above the limits of any particular situation through his action or his imagination. His life is bounded in time and is moving forward toward death; yet he has a strange kinship with eternity because he can rise above the present and see its relation to the past and the future. From top to bottom, as it were, man is a contradictory creature. Viewed from the outside, he is but an episode in the vast process of nature. Viewed from the inside, each man is a universe in himself.

Hence there can be no simple answers to what man should do with his freedom. In one sense, he must himself create the answer by using his freedom to find out just what he wants to become. He will not avoid this dilemma by returning to the level of the animal who does not ask metaphysical and religious questions. Nor can he avoid it by accepting some ethical or religious system which purports to give him infallible guidance as to what he should do. For man himself has a hand in producing these systems, and does so for reasons which the systems cannot altogether conceal. All of us try to run away from this predicament. Everything would be simple if we could become either like animals or like God. As an animal, or as God, man would be liberated from the agonizing torments of moral conflict and inner strife. But so long as we remain human we must enter into the mystery of what it means to be a finite self possessing freedom.

It is quite obvious that some at least of these characteristics of existentialism are as old as human thought. For example, the Bible constantly tells us that only through a conversion of the whole man can we enter into the truth. One might then inquire why existentialists should be permitted to claim a monopoly on something which has been affirmed by virtually every Christian thinker. Yet writers like Pascal or Kierkegaard would gladly agree that there is no such thing as existentialism taken by itself. They would say that they were not trying to start something new, but were seeking to call men back to an inner realization of what Biblical revelation always has meant and always will mean. The crucial issue is not whether a philosophical outlook takes account of subjectivity, freedom, and inner conflict; every such outlook pays some attention to what these words stand for. The crucial issue is whether one regards these as central or peripheral. Many philosophers work them into a context which denatures them. They are woven into a fabric of thought where all contradiction is finally smoothed out into intelligibility and harmony. The genuinely existential thinker, on the contrary, regards contradiction as not merely the Alpha but the Omega; thought must not only begin here but must return to the given ambiguity of the human situation, and do so continually. In the end, moreover, thought cannot get beyond it.

One further word of clarification is necessary before taking up our study of individual existentialists. All stirring firsthand experience may be termed 'existential' in a fairly broad sense; for example, falling in love, being seized by some group loyalty such as patriotism, or possessing any type of moral earnestness. But this usage is so vague that the word becomes almost completely meaningless. In this regard it is helpful to focus upon the fact that man alone can ask ultimate questions, let alone answer them. Also, of course, we can ask pertinent questions about the weight or worth of a particular experience like serving our country or making a certain decision. Yet beyond such particular meanings and values we may ask why there is a world at all, why man exists at all, and whether our lives are at bottom meaningful or meaningless. These questions can be raised in a speculative and detached way, but whenever we come to face them with passionate earnestness, fully aware of the solemn risks and tremendous opportunities involved in them, we are entering into an 'existential attitude' in the narrower and stricter sense.

Now such an attitude has its potential weaknesses as well as its strengths. One may carry the contrast between subjective and objective to such a point that value or science or logic is unwisely deprecated. In theology, the contrast can be drawn so sharply that faith and reason are driven unwholesomely asunder. Let us be clear that wherever existentialism undercuts the elements of rational structure which are indispensable to both metaphysics and Christian theology, it must be rejected. Properly employed, however, this mode of thinking rightly opens the way to a reformulation of philosophy and Christian doctrine which can render them vital and dramatic instead of rigid and sterile.

Another potential weakness can be detected at that point where the isolated individual becomes so preoccupied with *his* freedom, *his* struggle, *his* inner conflicts, that he is shut off from fruitful contacts with nature, society, and God. Here again existentialism is primarily valuable as an antidote, but poisonous as an exclusive diet. As an antidote, it issues a not unimpressive protest against those tyrannical and legalistic elements which may be found in every society and every institution. But unless it is able to carry the human being in the direction of a restored and purified conception of community, it becomes a destructive and not a truly prophetic voice. So far as Christianity is concerned, this means that the acid test of an existentialist is his attitude toward the Church; and on this score some but not all of them betray a grave weakness.

Finally, stress upon freedom can lead toward either faith in God or downright atheism. That is why the movement which we are to study is divided roughly into two camps. One group is trying to make an atheistic acceptance of freedom and despair serve as the only possible answer. The other group is finding that the implications of human responsibility lead inescapably to a revival of religious faith. A deepened sense of human need and failure can lead toward readiness for faith in God. A keen recognition of our inability to heal ourselves through strenuous moral effort or through sustained theoretical knowledge can awaken us to the meaning of divine forgiveness. But on the other hand, the awareness of freedom may lead to the conviction that man must make himself self-sufficient, self-authenticating. It may prompt us to feel that dependence on God is no more than a form of slavery. It may cause us to take our last stand on a Stoic courage which is able to stare at emptiness, tragedy, and death unafraid. Thus existentialism has produced both the most penetrating forms of Christian faith and the most nihilistic types of human self-assertion. In the chapters that follow we shall find both of these alternatives, although our main concern will be to estimate the bearings of the movement known as existentialism upon the patterns of religious belief in our time.

PASCAL

PASCAL

THE MOST IMPORTANT PRECURSOR of modern existentialism was Blaise Pascal who lived from 1623 to 1662. Many contrasting forces entered into his spiritual struggle. As a Roman Catholic who never broke with the Church, he was linked to the heritage of medieval authority and certainty. Yet as a brilliant physicist and mathematician he was in the vanguard of the scientific revolution of the seventeenth century. Through his association with Jansenism, Pascal discovered in the Augustinian view of grace and predestination what seemed to him the plain truth about man and a faithful interpretation of the Bible; hence he stressed the polarity between faith and reason in a way that came quite close to Protestantism. Yet the task which lay nearest his heart was that of apologetics rather than doctrinal theology. The fragments which we know as Pascal's *Pensées* were notes for a vindication of Christianity addressed to those worldly-minded and skeptical contemporaries whom he knew so well.

He suffered from physical frailty and also from agonizing inner conflicts; he underwent a radical conversion which turned him away from the God of the philosophers toward the God of the Bible, and he kept a record of this experience sewn into the lining of his jacket. Near the end of his life he renounced his distinguished scientific career together with the sort of religious controversy that had prompted him to defend Port-Royal against the Jesuits in his *Provincial Letters*, with the proposed intention of devoting himself to self-discipline and to works of charity for the rest of his days.

15

1. The Genius

The story of Pascal's intellectual precocity is fascinating, but we can do no more than summarize it here. In his early teens, after his father had withheld books on mathematics on the ground that Blaise should first study Latin and Greek, he worked out the thirty-second proposition of Euclid (the sum of the interior angles of a triangle is equal to two right angles) for himself. By the time he was sixteen he had published a brief essay on conic sections. Within the next four years he invented a calculating machine in order to help his father, who at the time was a government agent in Rouen. This machine consisted of eight wheels set alongside each other in a box. Each wheel was roughly comparable to a modern telephone dial, and when it had been turned through a complete revolution of ten digits it turned the wheel to the left one-tenth of a revolution. The device could add, subtract, multiply, and divide, and it embodied the basic principles on which later calculating machines have been constructed.

When Pascal was twenty-three the entire family—his father, his two sisters, Gilberte and Jacqueline, and himself—was converted to Jansenism. Cornelius Jansen, who had been Bishop of Ypres, devoted his theological career to re-emphasizing the anti-Pelagian side of Augustine's work. Holding that free will has been lost through the Fall and Original Sin, he stressed the belief that salvation is due wholly to grace. This brought Jansen into conflict with the Jesuits, whose theology, based mainly on the thought of Molina, maintained that through free will man could so turn toward God and use grace as to contribute to his own salvation. The Jesuits sought to suppress Jansen's important work, the *Augustinus*, but by the time of Pascal's first conversion in 1646 it had been in print for six years. In order to understand Pascal's religious development, we must also take account of the convent of Port-Royal with which his fate was to be intertwined. This convent was located fourteen miles southwest of Paris, although it later acquired quarters in the

16

city itself. Under the leadership of Angelique Arnauld, who had been appointed abbess when she was a young girl and whose brother, Antoine, became the chief intellectual leader of Jansenism, the convent had undergone a reform, which was furthered by the co-operation of its spiritual director, Saint-Cyran. Saint-Cyran was a friend of Jansen, corresponded with him, and shared with him the hope that a great revival based upon sound doctrine and strict practice could be brought about in the Church. Port-Royal became the center of Jansenism and attracted a group of young men called *solitaires* who combined a regimen of meditation with manual work.

One of the first effects of Pascal's conversion was a regrettable incident which may be symptomatic of his life-long struggle with intellectual pride. A Dr. Forton (Saint-Ange), who had been appointed to a benefice in Rouen, published several books in which he attempted to demonstrate Christian doctrines by rational means. Pascal and some young friends cross-examined Dr. Forton, accused him of heresy, and stirred up a local ecclesiastical controversy. Nevertheless, while in his twenties Pascal's main interests were scientific rather than religious. He devoted himself to studies in physics and mathematics, which he avidly pursued despite the various physical afflictions that plagued him throughout most of his brief life. He had learned of an experiment whereby Torricelli had created a vacuum. This experiment was revolutionary because the prevailing view, following Aristotle, held that nature abhors a vacuum. Pascal witnessed a repetition of Torricelli's experiment in which a tube filled with mercury was placed in a basin half-filled with mercury. When the column of mercury descended to a given height, there could be no question that the space at the top of the tube was a vacuum, although all sorts of fanciful explanations were advanced to avoid this conclusion. Shortly thereafter Pascal proposed to test the hypothesis that the height of the mercury is related to atmospheric pressure by having a Torricellian tube carried from the bottom to the top of a mountain. Descartes, who was near the end of his great career, and who had recently conversed with the youthful Pascal, later claimed that he suggested this experiment

17

to him. The ensuing controversy may partially explain Pascal's aversion to Cartesianism, although the philosophical differences between the two men would have been sharp even if they had never engaged in a personal dispute.

Pascal published a pamphlet on his experiments concerning 'the void,' which evoked a protest from a Jesuit, Père Noël, who sought to defend the authority of Aristotle. Besides his appeal to authority, the Jesuit depended heavily on metaphysical arguments to show the impossibility of a nothingness. Pascal's reply was important because it laid down the principle that in connection with a question of fact in physics appeals to authority and metaphysics are irrelevant. Soon after he took another step toward showing the relation of air pressure to the phenomena he was studying. By inserting a small tube in the empty space at the top of a large tube, he was able to observe that mercury in the smaller tube descended completely as soon as the membrane which kept it air-tight was pierced. This occurred because, in the surrounding vacuum, there was no air pressure to hold the mercury in the smaller tube at a given height. Then, as Pascal gradually admitted air into the top of the larger tube, the mercury in the smaller tube rose proportionally. His brother-in-law, Florin Périer, who was living in Pascal's native town of Clermont, subsequently carried out Pascal's instructions for the famous Puy-de-Dôme experiment. With a party of learned men as observers, he climbed to the top of a mountain four thousand feet high and demonstrated that the column of mercury went down as the altitude increased because of the lessening of air pressure. On the basis of such work Pascal foresaw the usefulness of the barometer, and in his study of liquids he discovered the principles which the hydraulic press employs. Although he rarely turned to creative work in the field of mathematics, his few contributions give some hint of what he might have accomplished if he had devoted his life to it. Besides the essay on conic sections, published when he was sixteen, he was a pioneer in the theory of probability, and near the end of his life, in order to distract his attention while suffering from a toothache, he investigated the problem of the cycloid. His work in connection with the latter influenced Leibniz in developing the differential and integral calculus.

For some time Pascal's sister Jacqueline had wanted to go to Port-Royal as a nun, but had been prevented by her aged father who wished her to care for him. When the father died, it seemed that she could at last enter upon her vocation, but at this time Pascal was badly in need of money and unwilling to yield Jacqueline's share of the estate to Port-Royal. Yet unless Jacqueline could bring a dowry with her into the convent, she would have to become merely a lay sister doing the most menial work. It was only when his pride was stung by the fact that the convent agreed to make an exception, admitting Jacqueline as a 'charity case,' that Pascal was finally forced to do the decent thing and yield her part of the estate. This incident reflects the fact that although he regarded himself as a sincerely religious person, favorable to Jansenist views in theology, he was at this stage (around the age of thirty) torn between worldly ambitions and his Christian convictions. Through his friendship with the duc de Roannez and Mme de Sablé he was gradually making his way into society. He became acquainted with the various types of mentality which he was later to picture in the *Pensées* when he discussed human life apart from belief in God. They range from skepticism, epicureanism, and vice to a high code of honor and good taste. It was undoubtedly valuable, from the standpoint of deepening his knowledge of human nature, that Pascal was drawn out of his shell of purely intellectual activity. He had never gone to school, he had lived a sickly, sheltered existence, he was a somewhat arrogant young genius, and association with witty, disillusioned people must have done much to humanize him. Without such experience, it is doubtful whether he could have written about theological questions in the *Provincial Letters* with a clarity and humor which easily arrested the attention of the sophisticated segments of the population. During this 'worldly' period Pascal probably fell in love, and the girl may have been the sister of the duc de Roannez.[1] Perhaps his renunciation of the world is connected with the fact that his love was hopeless because the girl was so far above his own station.

2. The Memorial

Whatever the influences leading up to it may be, we can date the turning point in Pascal's life precisely, for he wrote a record of it which he kept sewn inside his jacket and which was discovered only after his death. Actually two papers were found: one an ordinary sheet which may contain the notes he wrote down immediately after his mystical experience. The second was a copy on parchment including a few additional lines. At the top of the paper stands a cross, and then follows:

The year of grace 1654,
Monday, 23 November, day of Saint Clement, pope and martyr, and of others in the martyrology.
Eve of Saint Chrysogonus, martyr, and others,
From about half past ten in the evening until about half past twelve,
.... FIRE ....
God of Abraham, God of Isaac, God of Jacob, not of the philosophers and scholars.
Certitude, certitude, feeling, joy, peace.
God of Jesus Christ.
Deum meum et Deum vestrum.
Thy God will be my God.
Forgetfulness of the world and of everything, except GOD.
He is to be found only by the ways taught in the Gospel. *Greatness* of the human soul.
O righteous Father, the world hath not known thee, but I have known thee.
Joy, joy, joy, tears of joy.
I have been separated from him.
Dereliquerunt me fontem aquae vivae.
My God, wilt thou forsake me?
Let me not be separated from him eternally.
This is the eternal life, that they know thee as the only true God, and the one whom thou hast sent, Jesus Christ.

20

Jesus Christ,
Jesus Christ.
I have been separated from him; I have fled him, renounced him, crucified him,
Let me never be separated from him.
He is preserved only by the ways taught in the Gospel.
Renunciation, total and sweet.
[The parchment adds:]
Total submission to Jesus Christ and to my director.
Eternally in joy for a day's trial on earth.
Non obliviscar sermones tuos. Amen.[2]

We know from a letter of Jacqueline to Gilberte that in the period immediately preceding this event Pascal had been living in solitude and in a condition of spiritual emptiness. He had already been seized by 'a great scorn of the world and an unbearable disgust for all the people who are in it'; he had been re-reading volumes already familiar to him by Montaigne and Epictetus, but had found no solace in the skepticism of the one or the stoicism of the other; he felt remote from God and could not overcome the feeling, no matter how sincerely he tried.

The association of the Memorial with the third chapter of Exodus is unmistakable, although of course we cannot recapture precisely what the experience meant to Pascal at the time. It is the God of the burning bush, I AM THAT I AM, Who reveals Himself with the promise to lead him out of bondage. Here, in direct encounter, Pascal experiences the difference between reason and the heart. The efforts of his own mind to solve the problem of human existence have left him in a bondage like that of the children of Israel in Egypt. The pathway of philosophy and science has led to a dead end, and the pathway of worldly ambition has brought only misery. But now, through no effort of his own, certainty and joy are given to him. Henceforth Pascal will never forget the misery of man when separated from God, and the grandeur of the human soul when it receives the knowledge and forgiveness of God. It is in Jesus Christ that he finds assurance. God did not forsake Pascal even though he had forsaken God. By a total renunciation of the world and of self, he now finds release from misery and comes to know the joy of certitude.

Shortly after this experience he spent a few weeks at Port-Royal. His conversion was attributed by others to a sermon preached by M. Singlin, the spiritual director referred to in the parchment, and apparently Pascal was content to keep his encounter with the God of Fire as a personal secret until his death. Although he did not stay at Port-Royal continually, he visited it frequently during the next year (1655). There he wrote a meditation on 'The Mystery of Jesus' [*] which develops the central theme of the Memorial. In this meditation he stresses the solitude of Jesus in the garden of Gethsemane, enduring agony while His friends sleep. 'Jesus will be in agony even to the end of the world. We must not sleep during that time.' 'Jesus tears Himself away from His disciples to enter into His agony; we must tear ourselves away from our nearest and dearest to imitate Him.' And then Pascal puts into the mouth of Jesus the words: 'Console thyself; thou wouldst not seek me, if thou hadst not found me.'

From the moment of his conversion onward, the note of renunciation is dominant; and toward the end of his life we find Pascal putting aside all intellectual pursuits and going so far as to submerge normal feelings of affection toward his own family and friends in his effort to imitate Christ.

3. *The* Provincial Letters

Only a few months after his conversion, Pascal found himself involved in the controversy between the Jansenists and the Jesuits which resulted in his *Provincial Letters*. On the one side Jansenism took a position which came perilously close to Calvinism. Following St. Augustine, it was held that as a result of the Fall sin is universal so that man can do nothing through free will to contribute to his own salvation. On those few who are predestined to salvation, God bestows 'efficacious grace' which is irresistible and has nothing to do with their merit. On the other side the Jesuits, following their leading theologian Molina (1535-1601), the author of *Harmony of Free*

Will and Free Grace, held that all men receive 'sufficient grace' which enables them to pray for and to *merit* 'efficacious grace.' This teaching makes the outcome of the workings of divine grace depend in part on how man employs his freedom, and it regards the meritorious man as able, in a real sense, to earn salvation. Between the two conflicting parties stood the Dominicans who, following St. Thomas, had something in common with each extreme. They agreed with the Jesuits that all men receive sufficient grace and that through the right use of free will men are capable of doing good. But, as Pascal pointed out, the word 'sufficient' as used by the Thomists was ambiguous; they regarded the grace in question as sufficient to make man responsible, but not sufficient to save him. So far as salvation is concerned the Thomist position agreed with Jansenism (i.e. Augustinianism) to the extent of admitting that the elect are saved only by efficacious grace.

As has frequently been true in the history of controversies over grace and freedom, the practical results were paradoxical. Logically it would seem that Jansenism should lead to a sort of moral indifference in view of its belief that no human effort can have the slightest bearing upon salvation. Molinism should lead to a severe moralism in which man seeks through his own free decision to follow an exacting pathway toward perfection and everlasting life. Actually the opposite was the case. Jansenism demanded renunciation of the world and a strict devotional life which sought to eradicate every form of sensuality, ambition, and pride. The Jesuits, on the other hand, set forth the most convenient and attractive ways in which harmony could be brought about between worldly morality and Christian faith.

Shortly after Pascal's conversion, the Jansenists at Port-Royal found themselves in a very difficult situation. Five propositions supposedly based upon the *Augustinus* had already been condemned by the Pope. Arnauld had denied that these propositions were actually in the book and called attention to the distinction between a question of fact and a question of doctrine. So far as the latter was concerned, the Jansenists declared that they were willing to renounce any teaching which the Pope condemned as heretical; but they remained adamant on the question of fact, holding that on such a matter the Pope could err. In attempting to defend the position that grace, being wholly at God's disposal, may be withdrawn even from a 'just' man, Arnauld cited the fact that St. Peter (the first Pope!) had denied Christ. For such temerity he found himself in imminent danger of being condemned as a heretic, and in view of his position of leadership in the movement this might mean the destruction of Jansenism. Furthermore, the court Arnauld was facing at the Sorbonne was packed against him by the Jesuits, and his efforts to appeal to public opinion were so erudite that they made very little impression. At this point Pascal was asked to help, and his *Provincial Letters* were the result. Their dramatic, witty discussion of the issues dealt the Jesuits a blow from which they have never fully recovered. At the same time the *Letters* created a style which has influenced the writing of French prose ever since.

Writing under the pseudonym of Louis de Montalte, which Morris Bishop suggests is an anagram on the phrase *'Talentum Deo Soli,'* [4] Pascal takes on the role of a plain man who is trying to get to the bottom of a theological controversy which turns out to be largely verbal. He tries to show that on the crucial issue the Thomists are really on the side of the Jansenists, so that their apparent agreement with the Molinists concerning sufficient grace is misleading inasmuch as the two groups use the same word to stand for quite different meanings. After Arnauld was censured, the third letter boldly proves that, since the Jansenist theologian has unimpeachable support in both Augustine and Chrysostom for his remarks about St. Peter's fall from grace, the attack is really aimed at Arnauld personally rather than at his opinions. His real crime is that he refuses to submit, not that his beliefs are heretical.

In the fourth letter, however, Pascal goes beyond technicalities and begins to take up theological questions on their own merits. He aims his polemic against the Molinist assumption—which on the surface seems so compatible with common sense—that a man cannot be regarded as sinning unless, knowing the good and having the power to perform it, he nevertheless deliberately turns away from it. By means of quotation from Jesuit source books the letter shows how, if this assumption is correct, one can avoid sin simply by avoiding thoughts of God, duty, and remorse. To the Jesuit contention that the sinner, as he consciously turns against the light, *must* have some remorse, Pascal replies: 'I hold myself bound in conscience . . . to inform you that there are thousands of people . . . who sin without regret—who sin with delight—who make a boast of sinning.' And when his opponent insists that his principle applies at least to good men, Pascal adds: 'The example of the saints is not a whit more in your favor. Who doubts that they often fall into sins of surprise, without being conscious of them?' In fact a genuinely good man will rarely sin by consciously and deliberately turning toward evil; rather, he is betrayed by forces he does not discern. The Jesuit position was that an action cannot be voluntarily good or evil unless the agent has reflected on the moral values at stake. Pascal shows that this would place most evil actions under the category 'involuntary' because they are carried out without careful moral reflection of any kind; and he insists that the 'ignorance' attending such heedlessness does not make the action either involuntary or innocent.

Here, as always, Pascal was deeply torn by conflict between his respect for the religious authority of the Pope and his devotion to truth; but he was encouraged to go ahead by an event which occurred after the publication of the first four letters. His little niece, Marguerite Périer, was miraculously cured of a disease of the eye by being touched with a thorn from Christ's crown which was being carried in a procession at Port-Royal. As a result of the miracle the persecution of Port-Royal stopped for the time being, still other cures took place by means of the Holy Thorn, and thus Pascal felt that the Jansenist cause had received confirmation from a source of authority higher than the Pope. So fortified, he turned his attack directly against the ethical system of the Jesuits. Aided by Arnauld and other Jansenist scholars who helped him go through such works as Escobar's *Moral Theology,* Pascal exposed the dangers of casuistry at its worst. He shows how, in accordance with the doctrine of probabilism, a priest may follow an opinion or a practice so long as it has the support of only one 'grave' theologian, even though the priest personally believes that the opinion or the practice is wrong. He cites a passage where a monk is permitted to put aside his religious habits in order to remain incognito when he goes to a house of prostitution. He quotes one Jesuit writer, Father Bauny, as saying: 'Absolution is not to be refused to such as continue in the proximate occasions of sin, if they are so situated that they cannot give them up without becoming the common talk of the world, or subjecting themselves to personal inconvenience.' [5]

Again, he shows how 'several casuists have contrived to relieve the wealthiest from the obligation of alms-giving . . . by giving such an interpretation to the word *superfluity* that it will seldom or never happen that any one is troubled with such an article.' [6] By exploiting the Jesuit doctrine concerning the direction of intention, a servant can help his master commit a crime so long as the servant takes as his aim the payment he will receive and does not favor the commission of the crime itself; a man can fight a duel so long as he simply goes for a walk at the appointed place and hour and then defends himself without directly accepting the challenge; a man can commit murder so long as his intention is directed toward the defense of his honor instead of toward revenge. Indeed, by the time Pascal has finished quoting from Jesuit sources, this ethical system is exposed as falling far below the ordinary legal standards of the day. The confessor is caricatured as exerting himself to find precedents and exceptions whereby he can suit his direction to the convenience and station of the person who comes to him. If the individual is devout and strict, the priest's advice will reflect that fact; but if the man is a wealthy, immoral worldling, then the priest 'tolerates some degree of relaxation.' As Pascal's Jesuit friend says in the sixth letter: 'The truth is, sir, we are forced to it. Men have arrived at such a pitch of corruption nowadays that unable to make them come to us, we must e'en go to them, otherwise they would cast us off altogether.' [7] 'They would be almost all of them excluded from our confessionals,' he continues in the seventh letter, 'had not our fathers relaxed a little from the strictness of religion, to accommodate themselves to the weakness of humanity. Anxious to keep on good terms both with the Gospel . . . and with the men of the world . . . they needed all the wisdom they possessed to devise expedients for so nicely adjusting matters as to . . . reconcile two things apparently so opposite.' [8] To which Pascal replies: 'I should certainly have considered the thing perfectly impracticable, if I had not known, from what I have seen of your fathers, that they are capable of doing with ease what is impossible to other men.' [9]

In short, under the guise of adapting Christianity to 'modern' conditions by following up-to-date theologians instead of the New Testament and the Fathers, the Jesuit system has devised ways of violating Christian morality while still giving lip-service to it. As a final example, consider this quotation from Escobar: 'We call it killing in treachery, when the person who is slain had no reason to suspect such a fate. He, therefore, that slays his *enemy* cannot be said to kill him in treachery, even although the blow should be given insidiously and behind his back.' Pascal replies: 'I grant you that this is something quite new to me, and I should gather from that definition that few, if any, were ever killed in treachery; for people seldom take it into their heads to assassinate any but their enemies.' [10] His readers could hardly escape the force of his summary comment: 'It would be better to have to do with persons who have no religion at all, than with those who have been taught on this system.' [11]

On through the tenth letter, the damning evidence piles up. In place of the central Christian conviction that contrition is an indispensable condition of divine forgiveness, the casuists, according to Pascal, have taught that mere 'attrition,' i.e. a selfish fear of damnation, is sufficient together with the sacraments for salvation. Through sanctioning the use of ambiguous statements they permit a man to deceive by tacitly interpreting a word as meaning something quite different from what his hearers will take it to mean. For example, he may swear that he did not do a certain thing by silently entering

27

the proviso that he did not do it on a given day, or before he was born. And whatever can be said in extenuation of the Jesuits—for it is true that Pascal concentrated upon the most flagrant abuses of casuistry instead of trying to look at the system as a whole—surely he was right in feeling that the attempt to earn salvation by means of compromises, rules, and excuses was utterly remote from the Gospel. Whether the ethical system was relatively high or relatively low as compared with ordinary standards of justice and prudence is beside the point. By fixing attention upon how men could *earn* salvation, it turned away from the central fact of the Gospel, namely that salvation comes to us as a free gift of God's love. By trying to figure out ways in which one could remain a Christian in good standing while suffering as little inconvenience and sacrifice as possible, it forgot that in responding truly to God's offer of forgiveness in Christ a man is lifted above calculation in the knowledge that even the utmost in self-sacrifice cannot 'repay' God for what He has done for us.

Because the *Provincial Letters* began to elicit furious replies from the Jesuits, with accusations to the effect that Louis de Montalte had misinterpreted and misquoted, Pascal devoted the eleventh through the sixteenth letters to a vindication of his methods and his citations. Despite the fact that a great deal of public support had been won for the Jansenists, the new Pope, Alexander VII, finally condemned them on 16 October 1656. Therefore in the final letters Pascal is placed in the position of having to show how he can remain loyal to the Pope while at the same time believing that the Pope had made a mistake. He does this by means of two arguments. First, he points out that the Jansenists are willing to condemn any teaching that the Pope regards as heretical. The whole dispute, however, centers around the question as to whether Jansen actually taught these heresies, and Pascal insists that the Pope has been misled on this point by his Jesuit advisers. But no matter who is right on the question of fact, the Jansenists cannot be censured for holding their ground because they are loyal to the Pope in matters of faith. In the second place, Pascal wishes to show that the central teaching of

Jansenism concerning efficacious grace is in line with the orthodox teaching of Thomism, and he accuses the Jesuits of trying to have Jansenism declared heretical now so that later they can attack everything Jansen taught. Inasmuch as he undoubtedly taught the doctrine of efficacious grace, the Jesuits will thus be able to undermine orthodoxy by a flank attack. They cannot afford to come into head-on collision with Thomism, yet by using Jansenism as a red-herring they hope to gain ground for their own semi-Pelagianism, which is incompatible with the teachings of St. Augustine and St. Thomas, without doing the foolhardy thing of attacking these great doctors of the Church openly. Whether or not Pascal was right in suspecting a devious plot, he cleverly turned the tables on his opponents by suggesting that they were the real heretics. Both the exigencies of the debate and the development of his own reflections have moved his version of 'Jansenism' away from Calvinism and toward Thomism.

Pascal has been criticized for stating at the beginning of the seventeenth letter that he was 'not of Port-Royal'—as though he were anxious to preserve himself from the charge of heresy even at the cost of admitting by implication that his friends were heretical. But that was not his intention. He was quite sincere in making the statement, for what he meant was that he had never been one of the *solitaires*. He wishes to stress the fact that his protest, in the first instance, is that of an independent individual. 'I have no sort of connection with any community except the Catholic, Apostolic and Roman Church, in the bosom of which I desire to live and die, in communion with the pope, the head of the Church, and beyond the pale of which I am persuaded there is no salvation.' [12] Besides asserting his own orthodoxy, he vigorously seeks to show that his Jansenist friends are also innocent of the charge of heresy.[13]

4. Grace and Freedom

Father Annat, chief spokesman for the Jesuits in reply to the *Provincial Letters*, had pointed out that the doctrine of efficacious grace can be construed either in a Calvinist or a Thomist fashion.

29

According to the first interpretation, the human will cannot resist it; according to the second, 'efficacious grace of itself governs the will in such a way that it still has the power of resisting it.' [14] Pascal's reply, given in the eighteenth letter, is that if the only thing Father Annat wants to have condemned is Calvinism, then every Jansenist is ready to agree. He even quotes three passages from Jansen himself to show that the bishop 'differs from Calvin, and agrees with the Thomists' on the very question of the irresistibility of grace.

As the discussion unfolds we find Pascal seeking to hold together two apparently contradictory truths. This method was to play a major role in the design for his Apology in defense of the Christian faith. 'Man, of his own nature, has always the power of sinning and of resisting grace . . . notwithstanding this, when it pleases God to visit him with his mercy, he makes the soul do what he wills, and in the manner he wills it to be done, while, at the same time, the infallibility of the divine operation does not in any way destroy the natural liberty of man . . . [According to St. Augustine] God transforms the heart of man, by shedding abroad in it a heavenly sweetness, which, surmounting the delights of the flesh, and inducing him to feel, on the one hand, his own mortality and nothingness, and to discover, on the other hand, the majesty and eternity of God, makes him conceive a distaste for the pleasures of sin . . . Finding his chieftest joy in the God who charms him, his soul is drawn towards him infallibly, but of its own accord, by a motion perfectly free, spontaneous, love-impelled; so that it would be its torment and punishment to be separated from him . . . The person has always the power of forsaking his God, and . . . he may . . . actually forsake him, provided he choose to do it. But how *could* he choose such a course, seeing that the will always inclines to that which is most agreeable to it, and that in the case we now suppose, nothing can be more agreeable than the possession of that *one good,* which comprises in itself all other good things? As St. Augustine says, "Our actions are necessarily determined by that which affords us the greatest pleasure."

'Such is the manner in which God regulates the free will of man without encroaching on its freedom, and in which the free will, which always may, but never will, resist his grace, turns to God with a movement as voluntary as it is irresistible, whensoever he is pleased to draw it to himself by the sweet constraint of his efficacious inspirations.

'These, father, are the divine principles of St. Augustine and St. Thomas, according to which it is equally true that *we have the power of resisting grace,* contrary to Calvin's opinion, and that, nevertheless . . . "God forms within us the motion of our will, and effectually disposes of our hearts" . . . By means of this distinction we demolish the profane sentiment of Luther . . . that "we co-operate in no way whatever towards our salvation, any more than inanimate things"; and, by the same mode of reasoning, we overthrow the equally profane sentiment of the school of Molina, who will not allow that it is by the strength of divine grace that we are enabled to co-operate with it in the work of our salvation.

'The only way of reconciling these apparent contrarieties, which ascribe our good actions at one time to God, and at another time to ourselves, is to keep in view the distinction, as stated by St. Augustine, that "our actions are ours in respect of the free will which produces them; but that they are also of God, in respect of his grace which enables our free will to produce them." ' [15]

In this passage Pascal scores a devastating point against his Jesuit opponents by listing Molinism and Calvinism as opposite extremes, both of which miss the paradoxical truth holding human freedom and divine sovereignty together. But here he is not interested primarily in lampooning or in displaying cleverness in debate. He is fighting resolutely for the truth, and he has now come upon a truth which seems to conflict with logic. In his own experience, Pascal had become convinced that both responsibility and determinism are inescapable facts. Yet *how* they are conjoined never became clear to him by means of thought alone. Rather, what he is now trying to express in the language of theology must first of all have become real to him in the encounter described in his Memorial. There he experienced directly how God is sovereign *through* and not in spite

31

of man's freedom. The determinism he confronted in the God of Fire was not mechanical or fatalistic. Instead of overriding his will, God transformed it. Notice that in this long quotation Pascal is not interested in developing an abstract theory of the relations between human freedom and divine grace. He knows that the only point at which they are actually conjoined is in the life of the converted man. Doubtless he believed that man's true good and the divine will coincide all the time. But he recognizes that our hearts must be so changed that we want fellowship with God voluntarily, as our highest blessedness, before we can detect the coincidence. The converted man remains free because he can still turn against God. But he does not will to do so. He freely casts away sin and God graciously takes away sin. Man *wills* to have a new heart and God *gives* it in one and the same act. The response is man's doing, but what evokes the response is God's doing. Man makes a genuine contribution to his own salvation; yet without God he could do nothing, for God enables us to will what we could not possibly will without Him.

In two ways, Pascal's outlook has significant bearing upon problems which will occupy our attention repeatedly in the course of this book. In the first place, we shall often observe how existentialists are concerned to affirm the reality of human freedom and responsibility against every scientific or philosophical theory which denies them. Pascal was a scientist, and scientific determinism undoubtedly played a role in inclining him favorably toward Jansen's theological determinism. But Pascal was impelled by his own experience to recognize that the union between freedom and determinism must be grasped at a level higher than science can provide.

In the second place, we shall find some existentialists arguing that the reality of freedom is incompatible with belief in God, while others hold that it is grounded in God. Pascal's own position clarifies this latter issue because he sees so clearly that freedom does not mean that man can turn in any direction he chooses. He discerned how all of our actions are evoked in response to something which influences us whether this be a physical object, another person, or

God. Even the rebellious man who says 'I'll do exactly as I please' is determined by what he wants most. Hence for Pascal there *need be* no conflict between human freedom and divine grace. Undeniably, so long as a man is willfully intent upon gaining his own ends, furthering his own ambitions, and mastering his own destiny, fellowship with God is impossible. In such circumstances he is either enraged by the fact that there is a supreme blessedness which he cannot attain all by himself, or he glories in his independence, rejects God, and honestly does not believe that such blessedness is real. Pascal knew that in order to reach such a man God must lay hold of him *despite* his will. This means that God must go against the way such a man is employing his freedom, but not against his freedom itself. The true distinction, then, is not between freedom and determinism. It is between being determined by that which leads to genuine freedom, and being determined by that which leads to actual slavery. Pascal had learned that the 'autonomy' which means remoteness from God is in reality only bondage.

He fails to discuss, however, how God determines the wills of those who remain estranged from Him. He moves beyond rigid Jansenism in holding that Christ died for all men and not only for the elect; and he holds that man can help make himself ready and willing to receive God's gift. Indeed, the purpose of the first part of the Apology is to arouse men from indifference toward their eternal destiny, to expose the folly of sin, and to replace both despair and arrogance with a humble readiness for faith. But, as we have already seen, Pascal does not regard sin primarily as a deliberate choice of evil. Men are attracted to it in ways which often lie outside consciousness and reflection. Indeed all men, because of the Fall, are estranged from God. Now if His offer of forgiveness in Christ can overcome this estrangement in the case of some, turning them from determination by sin to determination by blessedness, why not in the case of all? It would be wrong to conclude that because Pascal looks upon *good* actions as produced conjointly by human freedom and divine grace, he must therefore hold that *bad* actions are in the same sense produced by both God and man.

33

How, then, are we to explain the fact that some men remain in sin and reject God's redemption if He wills otherwise and is at the same time sovereign? The answer cannot be, from Pascal's standpoint, that they persist in turning their free wills deliberately toward evil; nor can it be that they are fatalistically caused by God to fall into inevitable damnation. Both his concept of responsibility and his concept of divine sovereignty lie between these extremes. Men are self-excluded from fellowship with divine love by what they are, and this cannot be construed exclusively as a product either of free choice or of necessity. Divine sovereignty is to be understood as operating *through* what men make of themselves, not apart from it, for only so can men be dealt with as persons and not as puppets. Since the offer of fellowship can be actualized only through a human response of trust and love, it is a fact that man can exclude himself from salvation. This means that God wills a state of affairs in which some men reject His will.

Is this a contradiction? Pascal does not deny that the problem with which we are dealing is mysterious. But how could the sovereignty of God be safeguarded by denying that God deals with men as they are? He continues to sustain men in existence even though they have forsaken Him; He wills that they shall live and act as what they are—forsakers. But this does not mean that He causes them to be forsakers or that He has forsaken them. If some men separate themselves from Him eternally, this reflects the fact that it is only a living soul and not an automaton which can enter into salvation. Sovereignty which operates by coercion can accomplish many things; sovereignty which operates by necessity can insure order; but the one thing such sovereignty cannot capture—and emancipate —is a man himself, his will, his heart.

5. The Apology—the Greatness and Misery of Man

Pascal, having discovered through the *Provincial Letters* that he could write about religious questions in a manner which was convincing to unbelievers as well as to Christians, turned his attention to a project which had long been in the back of his mind, namely an Apology in defense of the Christian faith. In the latter part of 1657 and the early part of 1658 he devoted himself to reading the Bible, to meditating upon devotional writings such as the *Imitation of Christ*, and some of the works of St. Theresa and St. Francis de Sales. He also consulted apologetic books by Raymond Sebond, Charron, and Grotius, and a volume called *Pugio Fidei*. And he continued to study the works which had already become so familiar to him—St. Augustine, the Stoics, Montaigne. In all of his reading and thinking, as Cailliet has shown, the Bible remained his primary source. At first he wrote nothing down because he was able to rely on his prodigious memory. But as he became increasingly ill, he found it necessary to jot down notes. Some of these are so brief and cryptic that they are unintelligible to us. In certain instances they may even state, as though it were his own, a position which he really intended to refute. Other ideas or 'thoughts' were more fully developed and might well have been incorporated, virtually unaltered, into the completed work.

We possess only an outline for the work as a whole. It was to have consisted of two parts, the first dealing with man's misery apart from God, the second with man's blessedness when restored to God. Pascal was a forerunner of existentialism because he begins with the human situation as viewed from within, instead of something objective (nature or Ideas); the force of his appeal depends upon arousing concern for those conflicts which cannot be resolved by reason; and its convincingness depends upon awakening the whole man to his true self and not upon logical demonstration. Moreover, Pascal was a forerunner of *Christian* existentialism because he believes that man's confidence in his own self-sufficiency must be shattered and a sense of need awakened before the Christian message of forgiveness can be presented meaningfully. Part One was to have been addressed to the 'worldly' mentality which Pascal had come to know well—the skeptic, the atheist, the Stoic, the Epicurean. Part Two, after the bankruptcy of these philosophies had been shown, would have expounded Biblical revelation as furnishing the answer which man seeks but cannot, through his own rational powers, create. Possibly Pascal even had in mind a progression of three stages, roughly corresponding to Kierkegaard's sequence, moving from skepticism through monotheism to faith in the Incarnation.

His starting point is the greatness and misery of man. He assumes that man's relationship with God has been seriously disturbed but not utterly destroyed. Hence the first task is a recovery *in feeling* of the linkage which remains. After arousing man from complacency by calling attention to the contradictoriness of his nature, Pascal is willing to let a person go as far as possible toward finding a remedy through his own philosophical or religious exertions, for he is confident that these attempts will come to a dead end. Then, and only then, will an individual be able to read the Bible existentially as if it contained God's word for *him*. It would not be far wrong to summarize Pascal's preparatory program as moving out of complacency into despair. Let us examine this program in some detail.

Setting forth in quest of self-knowledge, man compares himself with nature and immediately discovers a staggering disproportion between his reality and the world which surrounds him. He cannot understand himself as having been produced 'somehow' by nature, for nature provides no answer as to how man has come to be here, what he should do, and what will happen to him when he dies. Whereas the world consists of 'things,' man is a subject; therefore he cannot hope to comprehend his own nature by means of the sort of knowledge whereby he apprehends the external world.

Pascal writes: 'Let man consider what he is in comparison with all existence; let him regard himself as lost in this remote corner of nature; and from the little cell in which he finds himself lodged, I mean the universe, let him estimate at their true value the earth, kingdoms, cities, and himself. What is a man in the Infinite? But to show him another prodigy equally astonishing, let him examine the most delicate things he knows . . . I will paint for him not only the visible universe, but all that he can conceive of nature's immensity in the womb of [the] atom. Let him see therein an infinity of universes, each of which has its firmament, its planets, its earth, in the same proportion as in the visible world . . . Let him lose himself in wonders as amazing in their littleness as the others in their vastness . . . He who regards himself in this light will be afraid of himself, and, observing himself sustained in the body given him by nature between those two abysses of the Infinite and Nothing, will tremble at the sight of these marvels . . .

'For in fact what is man in nature? A Nothing in comparison with the Infinite, an All in comparison with the Nothing, a mean between nothing and everything. Since he is infinitely removed from comprehending the extremes, the end of things and their beginning are hopelessly hidden from him in an impenetrable secret . . . The nature of our existence hides from us the knowledge of first beginnings which are born of the Nothing; and the littleness of our being conceals from us the sight of the Infinite.

'Our intellect holds the same position in the world of thought as our body occupies in the expanse of nature . . .

'This is our true state; this is what makes us incapable of certain knowledge and of absolute ignorance. We sail within a vast sphere, ever drifting in uncertainty, driven from end to end. When we think to attach ourselves to any point and to fasten to it, it wavers and leaves us; and if we follow it, it eludes our grasp, slips past us, and vanishes for ever. Nothing stays for us. This is our natural condition, and yet most contrary to our inclination; we burn with desire to find solid ground and an ultimate sure foundation whereon to build a tower reaching to the Infinite. But our whole groundwork cracks, and the earth opens to abysses . . .

'If man made himself the first object of study, he would see how incapable he is of going further. How can a part know the whole? . . . Man is related to all he knows . . . To know man, then, it is necessary to know [the whole which binds everything together, for it is] impossible to know the parts without knowing the whole, and to know the whole without knowing the parts in detail . . . What completes our incapability of knowing things is the fact that they are simple, and that we are composed of two opposite natures, different in kind, soul and body . . . If any one maintain that we

37

are simply corporeal, this would far more exclude us from the knowledge of things, there being nothing so inconceivable as to say that matter knows itself . . . Instead of receiving the ideas of . . . things in their purity, we colour them with our own qualities, and stamp with our composite being all the simple things which we contemplate . . . Man is to himself the most wonderful object in nature; for he cannot conceive what the body is, still less what the mind is, and least of all how a body should be united to a mind.' [16]

When we turn away from external nature and contemplate man inwardly, what then do we find? A creature riddled with contradiction, uncertainty, folly, and misery. If this creature sets himself to get at the truth by 'pure reason,' he discovers that reason is surrounded by countless self-deceptions and limitations. There are, of course, truths which can be grasped by mathematical minds 'provided all things are explained to them by means of definitions and axioms; otherwise they are inaccurate and insufferable, for they are only right when the principles are quite clear.' But there are other truths which can be grasped only by the penetrative mind. 'They are scarcely seen; they are felt rather than seen; there is the greatest difficulty in making them felt by those who do not of themselves perceive them . . . We must see the matter at once, at one glance, and not by a process of reasoning . . . ' [17] And since the two aptitudes, mathematical and intuitive, are rarely combined in the same person, most men are able to see one kind of truth only at the cost of being blind to the other.

Reason is also frequently at the mercy of imagination, custom, and will. Imagination 'is that deceitful part in man, that mistress of error and falsity, the more deceptive that she is not always so . . . I do not speak of fools, I speak of the wisest men; and it is among them that the imagination has the great gift of persuasion. Reason protests in vain; it cannot set a true value on things. This arrogant power, the enemy of reason, who likes to rule and dominate it, has established in man a second nature to show how all-powerful she is. She makes men happy and sad, healthy and sick, rich and poor; she compels reason to believe, doubt and deny; she blunts the senses, or quickens them; she has her fools and sages; and nothing vexes us more than to see that she fills her devotees with a satisfaction far more full and entire than does reason . . . What but this faculty of imagination dispenses reputation, awards respect and veneration to persons, works, laws, and the great? How insufficient are all the riches of the earth without her consent! . . . If the greatest philosopher in the world find himself upon a plank wider than actually necessary, but hanging over a precipice, his imagination will prevail, though his reason convince him of his safety.' [18] Custom can so ingrain prejudices and assumptions that error is passed on from generation to generation, each believing it merely because it is familiar, when a direct appeal to evidence could easily remove the error. 'The will is one of the chief factors in belief . . . because things are true or false according to the aspect in which we look at them. The will, which prefers one aspect to another, turns away the mind from considering the qualities of all that it does not like to see; and thus the mind, moving in accord with the will, stops to consider the aspect which it likes, and so judges by what it sees.' [19]

The most serious obstacle to reaching the truth about ourselves is self-love. Man 'wants to be great, and sees himself small. He wants to be happy, and he sees himself miserable. He wants to be perfect, and he sees himself full of imperfections . . . This embarrassment in which he finds himself produces in him the most unrighteous and criminal passion that can be imagined; for he conceives a mortal enmity against that truth which reproves him, and which convinces him of his faults . . . He devotes all his attention to hiding his faults both from others and from himself, and he cannot endure either that others should point them out to him, or that they should see them. Truly it is an evil to be full of faults; but it is a still greater evil . . . to be unwilling to recognise them . . . [Yet] is it not true that we hate truth and those who tell it us, and that we like them to be deceived in our favour, and prefer to be esteemed by them as being other than what we are? . . . Hence it happens that if any have some interest in being loved by us, they are averse to render us a service which they know to be disagreeable. They treat us as we wish to be treated. We hate the truth, and they hide it from us. We desire flattery, and they flatter us. We like to be deceived, and they deceive us. So each degree of good fortune which raises us in the world removes us farther from truth, because we are most afraid of wounding those whose affection is most useful and whose dislike is most dangerous . . . Human life is thus only a perpetual illusion . . . No one speaks of us in our presence as he does of us in our absence. Human society is founded on mutual deceit; few friendships would endure if each knew what his friend said of him in his absence, although he then spoke in sincerity and without passion. Man is then only disguise, falsehood, and hypocrisy, both in himself and in regard to others. He does not wish any one to tell him the truth; he avoids telling it to others . . . ' [20]

Thus as soon as we venture out along the pathway of self-knowledge, what we discover is that man is desperately trying to avoid self-knowledge. The need to escape oneself explains why many people are miserable when they are not preoccupied with work or amusements or vices. They are afraid to be alone, lest they get a glimpse of their own emptiness. When a man is left with nothing but himself to face, he falls usually into boredom, melancholy, or despair. He is ceaselessly unhappy because he cannot exist in himself in the present. He may hate his enslavement to gambling, sexual adventure, war, and compulsive work, but he hates the alternative even more—facing himself in solitude. Everyone declares that he is looking for security; yet no one can reach security except through self-knowledge, and this is the very thing we are striving to avoid. By burying ourselves in work, by turning restlessly from one diversion to the next, by refusing to think of the passage of time and the inescapability of death we constantly run away from the one thing which might at last lead to peace and joy. For if we could face ourselves, with all our faults, we would then be so shaken out of complacency, triviality, indifference, and pretense that a deep longing for strength and truth would be aroused within us. Not until man is aware of his deepest need is he ready to discern and grasp what can meet his deepest need.

PASCAL

Nevertheless, all these miseries are symptoms of man's greatness, for do they not all spring from his capacities for thought, freedom, and imagination? 'Man is but a reed, the most feeble thing in nature; but he is a thinking reed. The entire universe need not arm itself to crush him. A vapour, a drop of water suffices to kill him. But, if the universe were to crush him, man would still be more noble than that which the universe has over him; the universe knows nothing of this.' [21] Man's greatness consists in the fact that he is created in the image of God and for fellowship with God. If this be true, we can see why his restlessness cannot be remedied until he finds his way back to the Infinite and Eternal, which is his only true good. All distractions are unsatisfying because they evade that self-knowledge which is attained only when we see ourselves—our creation, our present existence, and our destiny—in relationship to God.

Hence there are only two reasonable attitudes: to serve God because one knows Him, or to seek Him with all one's heart because one does not know Him. To be indifferent, to seek no answer to one's doubts, to take pride in skepticism and indifference—all this is radically dehumanizing; anyone who cares so little about the meaning of his own life cannot have much respect for the significance of others. Yet instead of abandoning such hardened men to their fate, Pascal clings to the conviction that they can be aroused. Perhaps the form of the Wager Argument, which we shall examine presently, reflects his supposition that only a direct appeal to self-concern *can* arouse them. He knows that a desire to find truth is never sufficient in itself; it is only an initial step, and does not necessarily lead to Christian faith. But it is indispensable as a first step, and unless a man has taken it, he can hardly appreciate the difference between proof and faith.

This can be set down as Pascal's first thesis: in his misery and greatness, man is a contradiction, a mystery, a torment to himself. 'What a chimera then is man! What a novelty! What a monster, what a chaos, what a contradiction, what a prodigy! Judge of all things, imbecile worm of the earth; depositary of truth, a sink of uncertainty and error; the pride and refuse of the universe!' And

41

as this passage continues it suggests his second and third convictions—that man's attempts to overcome the contradiction through philosophy and religion fail but that Christian faith, which is a gift of grace, can overcome it, not by furnishing intellectual answers, but by so converting the heart that man can again be at one with himself and with God. 'Who will unravel this tangle? Nature confutes the sceptics, and reason confutes the dogmatists. What then will you become, O men! who try to find out by your natural reason what is your true condition? You cannot avoid one of these sects, nor adhere to one of them. Know then, proud man, what a paradox you are to yourself. Humble yourself, weak reason; be silent, foolish nature; learn that man infinitely transcends man, and learn from your Master your true condition, of which you are ignorant. Hear God.' [22]

On the basis of the record of a conversation with M. de Saci in 1655 we know that Pascal, just after his mystical experience, formulated his views as to why philosophy cannot fathom the contradictoriness of human nature whereas Christian faith can do so. He finds two contrasting truths about man stated by Epictetus and Montaigne. The former rightly sees that God is man's sovereign good and the source of justice, but because Epictetus, 'ignorant of [man's] corruption,' has treated human nature 'as sound, needing no redeemer . . . this leads him to the highest pitch of pride.' He assumes, in short, that man can bring his life voluntarily into conformity with the goodness of God. On the other hand, Montaigne, regarding the reality of God as uncertain, holds that the true good for man is also uncertain and that we are incapable of reaching it. He is so thoroughgoing in his skepticism that he will not even assert *it* dogmatically; he makes a mockery of all assurances and beliefs by finding a perfect Pyrrhonian balance between affirmation and denial. Pascal admits that he 'cannot see without pleasure, in this author, haughty reason so invincibly reduced by its own weapons.' Montaigne accurately describes the wretchedness of man apart from God, but because he regards the wretchedness as irremediable and despairs of 'attaining a real good,' his philosophy issues in moral

42

relativism and slackness. A true view of man cannot be reached by synthetically combining these two outlooks. The one overlooks man's impotence, his bondage to sin. The other overlooks man's original righteousness, which is the mark of his greatness and his redeemability. When Epictetus and Montaigne are thus set in juxtaposition they simply cancel each other out. It is impossible on the level of their reflections to affirm the essential goodness and the essential wretchedness of human nature simultaneously. What is needed is a view of man which overcomes the errors of both by means of a truth that is higher than either.

For Pascal, this is the Gospel. Christianity holds together two truths which otherwise fall apart. First, man is created capable of knowing God; second, man is so corrupted that he is shut off from knowing God. The former, taken by itself, overlooks man's misery. It produces the arrogance of the philosopher who thinks he can know God without first being cleansed of sin; and Christianity is the corrective to this because it knows that the grandeur of man can be fulfilled only through dependence upon grace. The latter truth, taken by itself, overlooks salvation and thus produces despair. Here again, Christianity is the corrective because it believes in God's power to triumph over sin. Only in the light of Christ, the God-man, can these two opposite truths be held together. In Him they are united; for it is impossible to know Jesus Christ without knowing both man's misery as a sinner and his grandeur as a redeemed child of God. Christian faith acknowledges human weakness without falling into despair, and human greatness without falling into pride.

Let us examine some of the passages in which this theme, so central to Pascal's whole intention, is developed. 'Wretchedness being deduced from greatness, and greatness from wretchedness, some have inferred man's wretchedness all the more because they have taken his greatness as a proof of it, and others have inferred his greatness with all the more force, because they have inferred it from his very wretchedness. All that the one party has been able to say in proof of his greatness has only served as an argument of his wretchedness to the others, because the greater our fall, the more wretched we are, and *vice versa*. The one party is brought back to the other in an endless circle, it being certain that in proportion as men possess light they discover both the greatness and the wretchedness of man. In a word, man knows that he is wretched. He is therefore wretched, because he is so; but he is really great because he knows it.' [23]

'The greatness and the wretchedness of man are so evident that the true religion must necessarily teach us both that there is in man some great source of greatness, and a great source of wretchedness. It must then give us a reason for these astonishing contradictions. In order to make man happy, it must prove to him that there is a God; that we ought to love Him; that our true happiness is to be in Him, and our sole evil to be separated from Him; it must recognise that we are full of darkness which hinders us from knowing and loving Him; and that thus, as our duties compel us to love God, and our lusts turn us away from Him, we are full of unrighteousness. It must give us an explanation of our opposition to God and to our own good. It must teach us the remedies for these infirmities, and the means of obtaining these remedies. Let us therefore examine all the religions of the world, and see if there be any other than the Christian which is sufficient for this purpose. Shall it be that of the philosophers, who put forward as the chief good, the good which is in ourselves? Is this the true good? Have they found the remedy for our ills? . . . Is man's pride cured by placing him on an equality with God? [On the other hand] have those who have made us equal to the brutes . . . produced the remedy for our lusts? What religion, then, will teach us to cure pride and lust? . . . All other religions have not been able to do so. Let us see what the wisdom of God will do.

'"Expect neither truth," she says, "nor consolation from men. I am she who formed you, and who alone can teach you what you are. But you are now no longer in the state in which I formed you. I created man holy, innocent, perfect. I filled him with light and intelligence. I communicated to him my glory and my wonders. The eye of man saw then the majesty of God. He was not then in the darkness which blinds him, nor subject to mortality and the woes which afflict him. But he has not been able to sustain so great glory without falling into pride. He wanted to make himself his own centre, and independent of my help. He withdrew himself from my rule; and, on his making himself equal to me by the desire of finding his happiness in himself, I abandoned him to himself. And setting in revolt the creatures that were subject to him, I made them his enemies; so that man is now become like the brutes, and so estranged from me that there scarce remains to him a dim vision of his Author. So far has all his knowledge been extinguished or disturbed! The senses, independent of reason, and often the masters of reason, have led him into pursuit of pleasure . . . Such is the state in which men now are. There remains to them some feeble instinct of the happiness of their former state; and they are plunged in the evils of their blindness and their lust, which have become their second nature. From this principle which I disclose to you, you can recognise the cause of those contradictions which have astonished all men, and have divided them into parties holding so different views . . .

' "It is vain, O men, that you seek within yourselves the remedy for your ills. All your light can only reach the knowledge that not in yourselves will you find truth or good. The philosophers have promised you that, and you have been unable to do it. They neither know what is your true good, nor what is your true state. How could they have given remedies for your ills, when they did not even know them? Your chief maladies are pride, which takes you away from God, and lust, which binds you to earth; and they have done nothing else but cherish one or other of these diseases. If they gave you God as an end, it was only to administer to your pride; they made you think that you are by nature like Him, and conformed to Him. And those who saw the absurdity of this claim put you on another precipice, by making you understand that your nature was like that of the brutes, and led you to seek your good in the lusts which are shared by the animals . . ."

'God has willed to redeem men, and to open salvation to those who seek it. But men render themselves so unworthy of it, that it is right that God should refuse to some, because of their obduracy, what He grants to others from a compassion which is not due them. If he had willed to overcome the obstinacy of the most hardened, He could have done so by revealing Himself so manifestly to them that they could not have doubted . . . [But] it is not in this manner that He has willed to appear in His advent of mercy, because, as so many make themselves unworthy of His mercy, He has willed to leave them in the loss of the good which they do not want. It was not then right that He should appear in a manner manifestly divine, and completely capable of convincing all men; but it was also not right that He should come in so hidden a manner that He could not be known by those who should sincerely seek Him. He has willed to make Himself quite recognisable by those; and thus, willing to appear openly to those who seek Him with all their heart, and to be hidden from those who flee from Him with all their heart, He so regulates the knowledge of Himself that He has given signs of Himself, visible to those who seek Him, and not to those who seek Him not.' [24]

'Christianity is strange. It bids man recognise that he is vile, even abominable, and bids him desire to be like God. Without such a counterpoise, this dignity would make him horribly vain, or this humiliation would make him terribly abject.' [25]

If we look upon these passages as demonstrative arguments, they are of course very defective. Epictetus and Montaigne do not, after all, exhaust the possibilities of a philosophical interpretation of human nature. Furthermore, throughout the *Pensées* Pascal assumes that the non-Christian religions are inadequate even though he knows very little about them. Above all, the passages take for granted what is supposedly being demonstrated. His criticism of Stoic views of human goodness presupposes the doctrine of Original Sin. His criticism of Montaigne's skepticism presupposes the doctrine of salvation by grace. Only if one has already accepted Pascal's remedy is his diagnosis convincing. How can such arguments ever have been intended to appeal to 'men of the world' when their truth can be evident only to one who already in some sense accepts Christian faith?

The first answer, of course, is that Pascal was not attempting to set forth proofs in the ordinary sense at all. He sought to find common ground with 'men of the world' by eliciting recognition of the contradiction between misery and greatness which is man's actual condition. Thereby he hoped to arouse yearning for a wholeness which would not merely reconcile conflicting ideas but would heal the split within man himself. His concern with sin and salvation centered not on doctrine as much as on the personal relationship between man and God which doctrine seeks to express. Pascal's approach was right, at least to the extent that estrangement and reconciliation must be dealt with not by argument but by insight. A change in feeling and motivation must occur; a shift from evasion and despair to openness and trust must be brought about. Otherwise changes in one's ideas are ineffectual. This is true in relations between human beings, in so far as healing and reconciliation take place. Pascal saw that it is also true of man's relationship with God; and his view of Christ is determined not by the schematic neatness with which belief in the Saviour fits into the total pattern, but by Pascal's own encounter with divine power as mediated through Christ's suffering.

6. Faith and Reason

What sort of 'apologetics,' though, is this? Most of the apologetic works Pascal read, and most of those which have been written since his time, take natural theology as their point of departure. We have already seen why Pascal cannot attach primary importance, so far as belief in God is concerned, to the objective truths of science and cosmology. From them we cannot arrive at an adequate understanding of human nature—i.e. of man as subject; the information they provide cannot answer questions about the origin, meaning, and destiny of human existence. Experience had also convinced him that the only way to reach a skeptic, once a point of

47

contact has been established by awakening him to his baffling condition of misery and grandeur, is to present the full implications of the Gospel instead of trying to remain exclusively at the level of reason. 'For those in whom . . . light is extinguished, and in whom we purpose to rekindle it, persons destitute of faith and grace, who, seeking with all their light whatever they see in nature that can bring them to this knowledge, find only obscurity and darkness; to tell them that they have only to look at the smallest things which surround them, and they will see God openly, to give them, as a complete proof of this great and important matter, the course of the moon and planets, and to claim to have concluded the proof with such an argument, is to give them ground for believing that the proofs of our religion are very weak. And I see by reason and experience that nothing is more calculated to arouse their contempt.' [26]

Arguments for the existence of God do not make a dent on atheists, and Pascal sees why. We cannot really achieve demonstrable certainty, analogous to that of mathematics, concerning the reality of God. Descartes tried to follow the geometrical method in this area and his whole case can be summarized by saying that unless God exists, the universe is not an intelligible harmony. But such reasoning falls on deaf ears if one has become deeply aware of the inner contradictions which Pascal stresses; for thinking, by itself, is impotent to overcome this inner warfare. Descartes' method ignores the central problem because it cannot possibly cope with it. Rational proofs fail to convince the unbeliever because they do not arouse that awareness of need which in turn gives rise to a passionate search for fellowship with God. So long as deity is merely an idea to be entertained we are dealing with a philosophical idol, not with the God of Abraham, Isaac, and Jacob.

Furthermore, to try to reach some kind of general knowledge of God apart from Jesus Christ is useless and sterile even for the theist. It suggests that there is some way of knowing God other than through yielding our hearts to His grace. And it often issues in well-meaning but misleading attempts to bring about a synthesis between philosophy and faith by pointing out that both have ethical monotheism in common. Such a synthesis is misleading because if philosophy assumes that knowledge of God is possible without a mediator, while faith assumes the opposite, then the God they both talk about is not really the same. Finally, the theistic proofs can never be coercive because in this visible world the goodness of creation is intermingled with corruption; hence, although God is omnipresent, He is not directly evident. Through nature, in short, we can dimly discern enough of the presence of the hidden God to know that we have lost true knowledge of Him, but natural theology cannot provide any sort of resting place. Its main function, for Pascal, is the negative one of making man so aware of the inadequacy of philosophical knowledge of God that he sees the need for a mediator.[27]

His position, therefore, must be understood in the light of this contrast between reason and the heart. Clearly Pascal did not regard the two as utterly opposed, for he insists that both kinds of truth are reached only by conquering willful desire. It is obvious that rational demonstration must be free from emotional bias. But he also holds that the truths of the heart are at the opposite pole from believing whatever I happen to want to believe; a man's whole nature must be transformed by God before such truths can be grasped. Hence when he declares that rational proofs in support of Christianity avail little, and that the individual must be aroused by his sense of need to a passionate yearning, Pascal is *not* saying that religious truth must fulfill my personal desire. On the contrary, he is declaring that my personal desires must be so altered that they come into conformity with religious truth.[28] Faith and reason belong to different orders, but they need not come into conflict. Warfare breaks out only when one tries to make totalitarian claims which exclude the other. Actually, both are indispensable. Rational demonstration is capable of employing principles which are basically similar in all men. But only faith can reach what is unique in each man; its appeal is concrete instead of general, and it is addressed to the whole person instead of just to the intellect. Paradoxically, there is also a sense in which reason is special while faith is universal. For ability to follow a rational demonstration may require some degree of training in abstract thinking, but the questions faith deals with are familiar to everyone, including the most ignorant. What is called for in the latter case is not erudition and brilliance, but simplicity and humility.

To speak thus of the contrast between faith and reason is an oversimplification, however. Actually Pascal used three orders of knowing. In the *Provincial Letters,* while attempting to drive home the contrast between questions of fact and questions of doctrine, he writes: 'In what way . . . are we to learn the truth of facts? It must be by the eyes . . . which are the legitimate judges of such matters, as reason is the proper judge of things natural and intelligible, and faith of things supernatural and revealed . . . The senses, reason, and faith, have each their separate objects, and their own degrees of certainty . . . So far from faith destroying the certainty of the senses, to call in question the faithful report of the senses would lead to the destruction of faith . . . Whatever the proposition may be that is submitted to our examination, we must first determine its nature, to ascertain to which of those three principles it ought to be referred. If it relate to a supernatural truth, we must judge of it neither by the senses nor by reason, but by Scripture and the decisions of the Church. Should it concern an unrevealed truth, and something within the reach of natural reason, reason must be its proper judge. And if it embrace a point of fact, we must yield to the testimony of the senses, to which it naturally belongs to take cognizance of such matters.' [29] And in the *Pensées* he writes: 'From all bodies together, we cannot obtain one little thought; this is impossible, and of another order. From all bodies and minds, we cannot produce a feeling of true charity; this is impossible, and of another and supernatural order.' [30]

This doctrine of the three orders is the clue to many things in Pascal. By means of it he seeks to reconcile his scientific knowledge with his Christian convictions concerning miracle. It forms part of the basis on which he attempts to work out a consistent view of the literal and the symbolic meanings to be found in the Bible. It determines the kinds of evidence which can be brought forward in defense of Christianity. Whether or not he adhered to his own teaching consistently, the principle of the three orders is a decidedly fruitful one. Scientific and logical questions cannot be settled by appealing to faith, and facts and logic are no substitute for the insight of the loving heart.

Before turning to a further consideration of Pascal's case for Christianity, however, we must examine the famous Wager Argument whereby he sought to prod men of the world into taking the leap of faith. It must be confessed that the form of the argument is repellent. Set in the context of a complicated discussion concerning gamblers' odds on gaining an infinitely happy life against a finite number of chances of loss, it seems to appeal to a calculating form of selfishness and to sanction hypocrisy. The valuable point in the Argument is that it stresses, as Kierkegaard and William James (in his essay 'The Will to Believe') also emphasize, that religious faith involves inescapable decision in the face of inescapable uncertainty. Pascal even tends to obscure this point by writing as though the advantage lies so heavily on the side of faith that nothing is really being risked. The passage, *Pensée*, no. 233, is too long to quote in full, but a few crucial sentences call for special scrutiny. 'If there is a God, He is infinitely incomprehensible . . . We are . . . incapable of knowing either what He is or if He is . . . Who then will blame Christians for not being able to give a reason for their belief? . . . They declare . . . that it is a foolishness . . . If they proved it, they would not keep their word; it is in lacking proofs that they are not lacking in sense . . . "God is, or He is not." But to which side shall we incline? Reason can decide nothing here . . . According to reason, you can defend neither of the propositions. (But then, why make a choice at all?) You must wager. It is not optional . . . Since you must choose, let us see which interests you least. You have two things to lose, the true and the good; and two things to stake, your reason . . . and your happiness . . . Your reason is no more shocked in choosing one rather than the other, since you must of necessity choose . . . But your happiness? Let us weigh the gain and the loss in wagering that God is. Let us estimate these two chances. If you gain, you gain all; if you lose, you lose nothing. Wager, then, without hesitation that He is . . . You would like to attain faith, and do not know the way; you would like to cure yourself of unbelief, and ask the remedy for it. Learn of those who have been bound like you, and who now stake all their possessions. These are people who know the way which you would follow, and who are cured of an ill of which you would be cured. Follow the way by which they began; by acting as if they believed, taking the holy water, having masses said, et cetera. Even this will naturally make you believe, and deaden your acuteness.'

One hopes that in the final version of the Apology this passage would have been modified considerably so that it would clearly appeal to the heart rather than (seemingly) to the calculating intellect. A man at a gambling table who must wager is probably an awkward symbol for the fact that detachment is impossible where the meaning of human existence is at stake. And the advice to 'act as if one believed, taking the holy water, having masses said, et cetera' is an unfortunate way of suggesting the truth which Pascal may have had in mind—namely that in the midst of uncertainty or unbelief it is more relevant to expose oneself to attitudes which might yield religious devotion and insight than to be preoccupied with the rational sufficiency or insufficiency of theistic proofs.

This latter point is consistent with Pascal's general conviction that the main obstacle to faith is not honest doubt but arrogant self-will. Putting the Wager Argument in the most favorable light possible, then, we can say it appeals to self-interest in order to force the complacent or skeptical man out of indifference. It brushes aside proofs and brings the discussion into the area of personal commitment because the real reason for irreligion is a refusal to take one's own defects seriously. Behind a pose of intellectual integrity, the doubter is actually incapable of surrendering his heart; he is annoyed at the fact that the basic questions of life call for decision and cannot be answered by the methods in which he is expert. The Argument seeks to break through the defenses of this pose.

7. The Evidence for Christianity

Pascal realized that until a man has taken the leap of faith, the kind of evidence that is put forth in defense of Christianity will not be convincing. For its truth is of the third order, and if it is to be apprehended at all it must be through the heart, i.e. the whole man in a person-to-Person relationship. This does not mean that faith is simply created by feeling. Christianity does rest upon 'objective' evidence, but this consists in historical events not metaphysical principles. Therefore we must present it as a story, a message, instead of trying to demonstrate it as a theory. Biblical revelation is certain, not in the sense that it cannot be doubted but in the sense that it becomes convincing when tested in life. It is entirely reasonable for philosophy to acknowledge its limits at this point; and if it does not set itself up as a substitute for redemption, or as making redemption unnecessary, then the knowledge it has to offer can find fruition rather than rejection within the mind of the Christian believer.

Pascal's treatment of Biblical evidence strikes us in many respects as archaic. He distinguishes between carnal and spiritual Jews, holding that the former looked forward to the Messiah as a worldly conqueror whereas the latter anticipated through prophecy the Advent of Jesus Christ. The true witness to Christ in the Old Testament is therefore typological and figurative, and its significance can be rightly grasped only by the spiritually minded. This approach to the Old Testament reflects Pascal's general conviction that Scripture hides and reveals God simultaneously. It is like a mirror where each man finds what he has in the depths of his heart. The hiddenness of God makes us aware of our corruption, our estrangement from Him. The presence of God makes Him accessible to those who desire to see, and makes all men inexcusable, since it is only the resistance of their own wills that prevents them from accepting the gift of grace. The connection between prophecy and Christ remains utterly obscure so long as one rejects mystery entirely; for this connection does not constitute a philosophical *demonstration* (a) that God reveals Himself uniquely in the Bible and (b) that the Bible must be understood in Christo-centric terms. Pascal of course realizes that his position is circular. Unless one acknowledges the Biblical mysteries of Original Sin and the hiddenness of God, he cannot fathom his own nature and his own relationship to God. Only one who already accepts Biblical faith can recognize in Scripture a true account of his present condition and of how he came to be as he is. From such a perspective the Christian can see why all attempts to reach a conception of God on the analogy of man's present sinful nature are doomed to failure; he can understand why rational knowledge must end in frustration since it cannot remove the obstacle which separates man from God. But if a man does not realize that he is a contradictory and incomprehensible chimera, neither the problem nor the remedy can make any impression on him.

Hence the prophecies enlighten some and baffle others in accordance with the condition of their hearts. Those who expect a conqueror are baffled when the Messiah comes as a servant. But for those who can read it with the eyes of charity, the entire Bible has a comprehensive and consistent meaning; it is held together from beginning to end by the figure of Christ. 'To understand Scripture, we must have a meaning in which all the contrary passages are reconciled . . . In Jesus Christ all the contradictions are reconciled.' [31] His deity is hidden to those whose eyes are blinded, not only before the Advent, but during His earthly career and in the centuries which have succeeded it. Instead of making the significance of His person obvious and self-evident to all, He comes as one born in obscurity, living in poverty and dying in ignominy. Thus God's mode of working is and remains strange to men. His love makes us aware of how remote we are from pure love, and yet, at the same time, it awakens in us a realization that we *can* respond to Him in kind, through love. Thus His offer of forgiveness is addressed to us in such a way that the whole man is engaged—in either acceptance or rejection.

Pascal believed that the miracles of Jesus and of the early Church are further evidence that God's power is incomprehensible. In general he takes the attitude that since these events show the living reconciliation of man's vileness with his capacity to be like God, and portray the only truth which can hold together the fact of estrangement and the hope of triumph, therefore it is also possible to believe in the miracles recounted in the record of God's saving work. If God can perform the miracle of breaking through my self-will, then it is not impossible to believe that through One who lives in the truth He can also foretell the future, govern the seas, heal the sick, and raise the dead. Pascal realizes that miracles by themselves do not prove the truth of a doctrine, but he holds that if a man shows by his teachings and his life that he is faithful to God's unfathomable workings in other respects, we can believe his attestation to miracles, when conjoined with such truth, as a further manifestation of the same incomprehensible power. Moreover, he regards it as a miracle that the Church itself has survived, from precarious beginnings, through persecution, and despite the rise and fall of empires. Finally, Pascal saw that when dealing with historical events, our approach must differ from that of the pure scientist. Perhaps odds could be computed on the chances of assembling one of Cicero's orations by scrambling type together in a haphazard fashion, but these odds have no bearing on the actual composition of such a speech when thought and purpose intervene. When we look at the Biblical record, therefore, our task cannot be merely one of asking whether certain events occurred; the authenticity of the account must be approached not in light of what we regard in general as probable but in light of the fact that here God was at work and the witnesses who wrote the record were trustworthy men.

So far as the determination of historical facts are concerned, Pascal's argument now seems to us filled with special pleading. Without doubting the sincerity of Biblical writers—on the contrary, taking for granted that they shared the mentality of their times and reported faithfully from within it—we can still insist on interpreting their statements concerning facts in the light of subsequently acquired knowledge of the physical world. But at least one of Pascal's points is still sound. He saw that where the spiritual significance of events is concerned, the fact that Biblical writers were men of faith addressing fellow-believers strengthens their claim to credibility instead of undermining it.

At the end of the Apology, after having examined in detail all that could be said about prophecy, miracle, and the continuity of the Church as providing confirmatory evidence for one who has made the leap of faith, Pascal would still have clung to his central conviction that only the Cross, which remains unfathomable, can so overcome self-will that a man is really convinced. It is grace, not reason, which establishes Christianity within the heart; and it is selfishness, not reason, which prompts a man to reject it.

8. The End of Pascal's Life: Conclusions

While preparing his notes for the Apology, Pascal was succumbing to the illness which killed him at the age of thirty-nine. At one point during this period he arranged for a competition with other mathematicians, with a prize attached, in connection with problems of the cycloid. As a result of an unfortunate misunderstanding, Pascal was accused of unfairness in administering the contest. But this was merely an episode for his attention was now given over almost wholly to religion. The pressure on Port-Royal had increased and the nuns were forced to sign a statement renouncing the five propositions; although the Jansenists made an attempt to append an introductory explanation which clung to the distinction between fact and doctrine, the introductory statement itself was condemned. His sister Jacqueline died of grief at having signed the statement, and Pascal was so ashamed of having taken part in the effort to formulate a compromise that he was driven to an extreme position of defiance against the Pope. This led to a rupture between himself and his friends at Port-Royal. In the midst of an argument with them he fainted, partly from illness and partly from grief over the fact that

his closest allies would not defend God's truth. He resolved to renounce everything intellectual and to devote himself exclusively to
a life of ascetic discipline and simplicity. Even in this last period,
however, he could not destroy the practical workings of his mind.
He conceived the plan of an omnibus to provide transportation for
the poor people of Paris, and these conveyances were actually put
into operation before his death. He gave all his money to charitable
causes. He upbraided his sister Gilberte for showing normal affection toward her children. He became virtually obsessed with the
idea that no human being should be attached to him, and he to no
one, in order that love for God in Christ might be sole and supreme.
He even wore an iron girdle with sharp points which he drove into
his side with his elbows whenever he felt himself unduly moved
by pleasure or temptation. He took a poor family into his house, and
when the son came down with smallpox, Pascal moved out rather
than disturb the boy, despite the fact that he himself was desperately ill.

In his closing days he was attended by a parish priest named
Beurrier, and the latter's Memoirs gave rise to a dispute which
has never been settled. What probably happened is this. Father
Beurrier, who was a simple man, reported faithfully that Pascal
regarded himself as a sincere and orthodox Roman Catholic, but
these statements were seized on as proving that on his deathbed
Pascal renounced Jansenism. Beurrier later admitted that he might
have misunderstood Pascal's references to his disagreement with
Arnauld and the other Jansenists. The priest construed the dispute
as meaning that Pascal had renounced their position on grace and
come over to agreement with the Pope. What Pascal probably
meant was that he quarreled with them because they did not go far
enough in resistance to the Pope. In any event we know that his
Jansenist friends visited him during his final illness, and if he really
changed his religious convictions completely at this time, it is hard
to account for his reconciliation with them. The simplest explanation is that Pascal died as he had lived, believing that Jansenism was

orthodox and that one could be loyal to the Pope while resisting him on a question of fact.

Instead of attempting to make any final appraisal of his life and work, it is enough for our present purpose to recapitulate the characteristics which make him a forerunner of existentialism. He was deeply conscious of the incongruity between man and nature, of the sharp contrast between subjective (i.e. knowledge of what it is to be a subject) and objective knowledge. Suspended between inescapable doubt and the need for certainty, he realized that no final solution could be reached by means of science or reason. The solution came to him not by getting rid of paradox but by embracing it. The form of the solution was not a system but an unrepeatable personal experience. Thus, for him, faith consists of intuition and decision; it is supra-rational and it presupposes freedom. Yet faith is not contra-rational, and freedom depends upon the divine determination of grace. All of these concerns come together in the reality of Jesus Christ. Not that He makes life fully comprehensible to the intellect; rather, He makes possible one's participation in its meaning through trust and love. All the oppositions—the greatness and misery of man, knowledge of God and estrangement from Him, original righteousness and Original Sin, doubt and certainty, pride and despair, self-love and self-hatred—are held together and resolved in the God-man. Unquestionably Pascal's position is logically circular, but faith is similarly circular, moving about its own center. His view of man and his view of God presuppose each other, and his view of Jesus Christ is the union of both. He writes about doctrine not from the outside but from the inside. Orthodoxy is important to him only in the sense that the Bible and the testimony of the Church enshrine historically the same truths which came to him in his direct encounter with the God of Fire.

Such, then, is Pascal the Christian existentialist. He embodies in himself the struggle between Christianity and secularism; he attacks rationalism; he undergoes intense suffering and inner conflict; he experiences a radical conversion; he comes into collision with the dominant theological orthodoxy of his time; he seeks to reach the skeptical, the sophisticated, and the world-weary; his greatest work consists of highly personal fragments instead of a philosophical system; he renounces the world in order to imitate the sufferings of Christ; he dies as he lived—sick, isolated, a strange mixture of pride and humility, of scientific acuteness and saintly devotion. Probably no sane man in this eminently sane twentieth century would take him as a model. Yet we cannot fail to see something of ourselves in his diagnosis; and Pascal never pretended that his words, very human words, could induce the remedy—'Certitude, certitude, feeling, joy, peace.'

NOTES

1. There is quite good evidence for supposing that 'The Discourse on Love' was actually written by Pascal, although the matter has been debated interminably. See e.g. Jean Mesnard, *Pascal: His Life and Work* (New York: Philosophical Library, 1952), pp. 53-6.

2. Emile Cailliet, in *Pascal: Genius in the Light of Scripture* (Philadelphia: Westminster, 1945), pp. 136f., finds no less than nine explicitly Biblical references in the Memorial. They are as follows: Exodus 3:6—'The God of Abraham, Isaac, and Jacob'; Matthew 22:32—a similar reference; John 20:17—'My God, and your God'; Ruth 1:16—'Thy God will be my God'; John 17:25—'O righteous Father . . .'; Jeremiah 2:13—'They have forsaken me, the fountain of living waters'; Matthew 27:46—'My God, my God why hast Thou forsaken me?'; John 17:3—'And this is life eternal, that they might know thee the only true God, and Jesus Christ, whom thou hast sent'; Psalm 119:16—'I will not forget thy word.'

3. *Pensées*, no. 552. Quotations used in this chapter are taken from the Modern Library edition of the *Pensées* and *Provincial Letters* (New York, 1941).

4. Bishop, *Pascal: The Life of Genius* (New York: Reynal and Hitchcock, 1936), p. 222.

5. *Pensées* and *Provincial Letters*, p. 379.

6. Ibid. p. 389.

7. Ibid. p. 393.

8. Ibid, p. 402.

9. Ibid. p. 403.

10. Ibid. p. 409.

11. Ibid. p. 417.

12. Ibid. p. 575.

13. On the matter of Pascal's fairness to the Jesuits, a great deal has been written pro and con. One of the clearest accounts is found in Mesnard, op. cit. pp. 97-101 (Editor's note).

14. *Pensées* and *Provincial Letters*, p. 597.

15. Ibid. pp. 599-601.

16. *Pensées*, no. 72.

17. *Pensées*, no. 1.

18. *Pensées*, no. 82.

19. *Pensées*, no. 99.

20. *Pensées*, no. 100.

21. *Pensées*, no. 347.

22. *Pensées*, no. 434.

23. *Pensées*, no. 416.

24. *Pensées*, no. 430.

25. *Pensées*, no. 536.

26. *Pensées*, no. 242.

27. Cf. *Pensées*, no. 555.

28. Cf. especially *Pensées*, no. 423.

29. *Provincial Letters*, pp. 612f.

30. *Pensées*, no. 792.

31. *Pensées*, no. 683.

KIERKEGAARD

KIERKEGAARD

was convinced that in so doing he had committed an unforgivable
sin. He believed that as a penalty a judgment of God was on the
death to be visited on his home. This dark foreboding was
children of whom seven were living. His prediction came true, how,
and when? Sören awaited his own end with acute dread. It could not
made with the sight of a new catastrophe. He became convinced that
he had the ill-omened... ... ... feeling... ... ...
consequences of ... in... ... ... while... ... ...
judging Sören, also one of his... own and... ... terrible ... mind
and from that... ... his... ... ... the other children. Kier-
by... ... ... our... ... ...
... ...

1. The Beginning of His Authorship

In any discussion of Christian existentialism, Sören Kierkegaard
is by all odds the most important figure. His influence extends not
only to theology but also to those writers whom we shall later discuss as representatives of non-Christian and atheistic forms of existentialism. Within one generation his works have leapt from obscurity to prominence. Outside Scandinavia, not much was known about
him in Europe until the beginning of this century, although he was
born in 1813 and died in 1855. Like Dostoievsky and Nietzsche he
diagnosed the sickness of modern man at a time when most people
could not believe him. And even though the events of the last fifty
years should enable us now to appreciate the acuteness of his analysis, he still arouses vigorous opposition in many quarters because he
seems to lead into irrationalism.

Kierkegaard's career was not at all obscure to the residents of
Copenhagen in the middle of the nineteenth century. He was recognized as a very great writer and was involved in controversies which
brought him painful notoriety. One of the foremost facts about him
is that he was subject to overpowering melancholy. By keeping a
voluminous journal and by writing his heart out in book after book,
he managed (more or less) to preserve his sanity. This melancholy
was deeply rooted in his family situation. His father had once gone
out on the Jutland heath, in a moment of loneliness and privation
during boyhood, had lifted his fists to heaven and cursed God. He

was convinced that in so doing he had committed an unforgivable sin. The father had also seduced a servant-girl shortly before the death of his first wife; then he married this girl, who bore him seven children of whom Sören was the last. He brooded over his offenses, and when, in later years, his second wife and three of his children died within the space of a few months, he became convinced that he had brought doom upon the whole family. As a reaction to his own sense of guilt, he subjected his children to a morbid religious training. Sören, who was sickly and sensitive, was terribly affected, and from the outset he felt different from other children. Later on he manifested an understanding of the doctrine of Original Sin which can hardly be paralleled in the nineteenth century, and the reason is not hard to find. He had a direct acquaintance with the way in which a father's guilt had influenced the lives of his children like an infectious disease.

Kierkegaard early learned how to conceal his melancholy and when he was a student at the University, spending a good deal of time at supper-parties and the theater, he was noted for his conversation, which was by turns gay or savage. One entry in his *Journal* shows how different his outward appearance was from what was going on inside: 'I have just come from a party of which I was the soul; witticism flowed from my mouth, all laughed and admired me, but I went away—and here there should be a dash as long as the radius of the earth's orbit ———————— and wanted to shoot myself.' [1] This inner division manifested itself not only in a sense of isolation but also in what came near to being a martyr complex. He looked back on his somber childhood as a sort of sacrifice. In manhood he felt compelled to break his engagement with Regina Olsen so that he could give his life to a higher cause. At the end of his career, when he launched an attack upon the Established Church, he expected to be arrested and persecuted. And from early childhood, the figure of Christ on the Cross haunted him as a reminder of the fact that the world slaughters love.

The immediate occasion for Kierkegaard's first book was his broken engagement.[2] He had become estranged from his father and drifted for a time away from his religious upbringing toward debauchery. When he fell in love, he felt it would be dishonest to marry Regina without telling her the truth about his father and himself, yet he was afraid that his twisted personality would destroy the girl. In a misguided effort to spare her feelings, he broke the engagement by pretending that he had been toying with her affections; then he found himself confronting a clear-cut alternative: *either* to turn backward into sensuality *or* to press forward, alone, toward spiritual integrity.

Hence the title of his book is *Either/Or*, and he calls the first alternative the aesthetic stage. His remarks about this stage must be read in light of the fact that he was deeply influenced by the literature and attitudes of nineteenth-century romanticism. Indeed, it is not even accurate to say that he 'passed through' the aesthetic stage, for he never completely eradicated its effects. He insisted that in Christianity the aesthetic is not so much destroyed as dethroned, and late in his career he wrote an essay to show that he had not lost touch with the theater and the arts. Nevertheless, personal experience convinced him that despair inevitably accompanies this stage. The young man in *Either/Or* can engage in social life, make shrewd psychological observations as a spectator, and touch brilliantly on one subject after another; but he is incapable of openness in human relations and has no sense of direction. What looks like perfect freedom turns out to be perfect bondage. A man does not so much choose evil as he simply drifts. His refusal to make decisions means that they are made for him. A defiant insistence on 'being oneself,' without restrictions, leaves one at the mercy of involuntary impulses because there is no formed self to guide them. It is in this condition of spiritual impotence that man falls into sin.

Kierkegaard discovered that aesthetic despair can be cured only by marching forward into what is temporarily a deeper level of despair. A man must abandon the spectator attitude. He must become honest enough to acknowledge his guilt. He must stop pretending that life is a trivial game. Then, and only then, can he begin to discover that true freedom involves spiritual dependence. Thus

65

at the very beginning of his authorship, the problem of the relations between grace and freedom takes a central position which it retains to the end. Kierkegaard consistently refused to separate the two terms. Freedom is perfect obedience to God, and providence (which he called 'Governance') educates a man by teaching him how to employ his spiritual gifts.

Even in Volume i of *Either/Or,* which is supposedly written by the aesthete 'A,' we find an anticipation of Kierkegaard's basic point of view concerning freedom. In an essay entitled 'The Ancient Tragical Motive as Reflected in the Modern,' a contrast is drawn between consciousness of racial solidarity and consciousness of individual responsibility. In Greek tragedy the element of guilt is ambiguous because the hero is partly subject to fate and partly the initiator of his own action. But the modern view really destroys the dimension of tragedy by regarding the hero as wholly responsible for his own innocence or guilt. In other words, on a 'Pelagian' view of free will where man attempts to be the Absolute, human life can be pathetic or comic, but never tragic. The fact that the modern age has lost the tragic dimension is closely related to its loss of the religious dimension. For religion combines a sense of individual responsibility, which goes beyond Pelagian moralism, with a sense of solidarity in sin and salvation which goes beyond Fate. At the end of the essay, 'A' imaginatively reformulates the predicament of Antigone in order to show how a theme can be at once modern and tragic. The story has to do with the psychological effects on the child of a guilty father. In 'A's' version everyone remains outwardly happy; only Antigone knows the truth, and she suffers anxiety (*Angst*). This is the category of modern tragedy that differs from 'sorrow' in ancient tragedy because it involves reflection. Antigone resolves to keep her pain a secret, and the family guilt, instead of being an external fact, is turned inward. Antigone is in love, but she cannot marry without telling the secret, and she cannot tell without betraying her father. The importuning of her lover increases her pain, but by giving him up she breaks the curse which would have been transmitted to succeeding generations. Here Kierkegaard is conveying a private message to Regina, for he even has 'A' put words into the mouth of Antigone's lover which Regina herself had used; and yet at the same time he is developing a 'general theory' of the freedom and bondage of the will. There could hardly be a better example of how the existential thinker seeks to arrive at an understanding of human life by relating everything to his own situation instead of abstracting from it.

2. *The Three Stages*

The three stages can be schematized in connection with this problem of freedom. The aesthetic, taken by itself, means an immediate continuity with nature and feeling before any moral distinctions are attempted. A man cannot succeed in remaining at this level, and he becomes demonic if he tries to, because a break with innocence must occur if he is to grow up morally. But he cannot remain at the ethical stage either; for, taken by itself, this implies that he is able to be self-sufficient. Thus it cruelly holds the individual responsible for things he literally cannot help, and at the same time treats man as though he were the master of his own destiny. Hence the third stage, the religious, alone holds out the possibility of a solution. For here, as the essay on tragedy has just indicated, man reaches the peace of continuity (community) on the other side of moral conflict, and he also reaches the fruition of personal responsibility within the context of collective guilt and salvation.

Let us look at these three stages in more detail. The aesthetic level leaves the meaning of life at the mercy of external events—at the mercy of fate and fortune. Since man thus has to seek for the answer outside himself, he cannot bear existence in the present; he turns toward an unreal past or an impossible future, or, in trying to escape from emptiness and boredom, he may plunge into feverish work and feverish amusements—which fail to solve the problem. A genuine remedy requires a union of the temporal and the eternal which might be characterized as 'finding everlasting significance in the present moment.' This is equivalent to deepened self-knowledge, because man himself is a union of the temporal and the eternal. Another way of putting the point is to say that the true conquest over time comes not by escaping from it but by being related to the Absolute *in the midst* of everyday existence. And the peril involved in holding aloof is that of literally destroying one's personality. I can suspend judgment to the point where I become incapable of making a decision. Detachment can lead to the kind of insanity which literally loses touch with existence. This situation calls for a decision, not between particular goods and evils but between accepting ethical status and excluding it.[3]

The real cause of despair is not something external, such as fate or fortune, but something internal, namely, a paralysis of the will. But how can a man make a decision if his will is paralyzed? Here we come upon a matter which was as mysterious to Kierkegaard as it was to Pascal. Neither responsibility nor determinism can be eliminated: the two are intertwined. My 'self' includes many factors which I did not create and do not will. Hence I cannot find freedom by trying to create myself *ex nihilo*. And yet I am not a machine; I already possess responsibility; I can enhance freedom only by a deepened awareness of influences which, in the first instance, I neither chose nor willed. I cannot change my past, but I can incorporate it transparently into my present self for which I take responsibility. That is why Christianity teaches that self-acceptance goes hand in hand with continual repentance. 'Self-acceptance' does not mean that I am perfectly all right just as I am. But it does mean that despite my real bondage to sin I have found forgiveness; because God accepts me, I am able to accept myself. Notice, therefore, how freedom and dependence are united. Freedom means inner honesty and openness. And dependence means that forgiveness is given to me; I cannot simply invent it.

Kierkegaard included intellectual skepticism and metaphysical speculation under the aesthetic stage because he saw them primarily as attempts to evade ethical decision. The alliance between skepticism and the spectator attitude is too obvious to call for special attention, but it explains why he sought the remedy for skepticism in a kind of commitment instead of in a kind of thinking. So far as metaphysical speculation is concerned, Kierkegaard regarded it as an attempt to solve the problems of life automatically, i.e. by logical necessity. Here he has in mind, of course, the system of Hegel, and his criticism of it is savage. In the face of tormenting conflicts, surging passions, ethical decisions, and the need for forgiveness, it is intolerable to be told by Hegel that the outer and inner worlds fit together into a total scheme which is wholly rational. We cannot cope with the agonies of life by adopting a system that blurs the difference between men and physical things by engulfing both in a single, all-embracing Necessity. This violates the very character of human history, for in so far as man acts ethically, his actions are not necessitated. And instead of triumphing over despair through a deepening of inward resources, the Hegelian system treats the individual as a mere item whose conflicts will vanish once he acquires a rational understanding of his place in the total scheme. It tries to remedy the agonies of the finite self by swallowing up the finite self.

So man confronts the *Either/Or*. But he cannot stand still on either the aesthetic or the ethical pathway. The former leads eventually into absolute depravity; and the latter leads eventually into absolute religiousness. That is why the first volume of Kierkegaard's book ends with 'The Diary of a Seducer,' while the second volume ends with a sermon.

But why can't the ethical provide a stopping point? Why isn't the highest goal of human life the attainment of that moral self-sufficiency whereby the individual makes his own discriminations between right and wrong? Kierkegaard's answer sets him against much recent philosophy in general and much recent existentialism in particular. He sees the ethical stage as manifesting in an acute form the conflict between universal demands and individual inwardness. He does not deny that objective thinking has a legitimate place here as it does in science and metaphysics. But in all these instances where objectivity gains the ascendancy, the universal takes precedence over the individual. In ethics this means that duty is fulfilled by

69

subordinating personal inclinations to the welfare of society. At its highest, this means a kind of resignation. But even the most exalted ethical heroism falls short of a religious relationship because it leaves the personal subordinate to the social and the legal. And whenever man believes that he can reach righteousness merely by fulfilling the letter of the law, then the ethical actually becomes an *obstacle* to faith. For faith involves a concrete individual in time standing face to face with the Eternal who reveals Himself as a Person in time. Another way of putting the point is to say that the ideal demands of ethics make us aware of our failures, but they do not give birth to a 'new life'; whereas faith begins with a reality— the reality of the 'new life'—instead of being based merely on ideals. Ethics, by deepening man's awareness of moral conflict, can prepare the way for salvation, but it cannot furnish salvation. 'O wretched man that I am! who shall deliver me from the body of this death?'

Here Kierkegaard stands in the tradition of St. Paul against Judaism and that of Luther against Roman Catholicism. And like these men he is careful to safeguard his thesis from antinomianism. In the story of Abraham and Isaac, which Kierkegaard retells in his book *Fear and Trembling*, the requirements of ethics and the requirements of faith conflict. Is Abraham a potential murderer, or is he being obedient to God? The question cannot be settled by pragmatic tests because *before* the result Abraham was either one or the other, and so far as externals go it is impossible to tell which. But Abraham does not simply reject the ethical. He is deeply conscious of family duty and he sincerely loves his son. Only a man who takes morality seriously has the right to pass beyond it.

The most remarkable thing about the man of faith is that after having renounced the finite and the temporal, he gets them back again. After breaking with the world, he is returned to the world. Hence outwardly he may be indistinguishable from his opposite, the philistine. He bears no exterior mark of religious superiority in his garb or manner. He may look like the neighborhood grocer. Yet this man has drained the cup of life's sadness; he knows that the wife, the family, the daily tasks he holds dear are not 'the answer.'

At the same time, they have for him the freshness of a new creation precisely because he has accepted their contingency. He knows that the meaning of life is not confined to worldly joys and sorrows. And it is only a man of faith who can thus combine absolutely the sublime and the pedestrian, the unconditional and the relative.

The Abraham parable, like the Antigone story mentioned above and like many of the stories in Kierkegaard's books, grows out of personal experience. He was thinking of his renunciation of Regina—though she might justifiably have been surprised to find herself in the role of Isaac, or, in the earlier instance, to find S. K. in the role of Antigone. He was convinced that if he had possessed sufficient faith, he might have gotten her back again. But he also had in mind the Christian story. Professor Bainton tells in his book, *Here I Stand*, how Luther's wife once said that she didn't believe the Abraham story because God would never treat a son like that, to which Luther replied: 'But Katie, He *did* treat His Son like that.' [4] The whole matter illustrates why Kierkegaard felt that a study of the Bible or of Christian doctrine does not amount to much until they have become vivid for the individual in terms of his own experience. And he writes his books, not in order to teach general definitions of Christianity, but so as to arouse the reader to ask 'How can I become a Christian?' Thus the transition from the ethical to the religious is made not by thinking but by what he called a 'leap.' Not until a man's attempts to solve life's problems by means of philosophical theory or ethical effort have come to a dead end is he really ready for this leap.

The themes which have just been discussed also underlie the cryptic and humorous little book, *Repetition*, which was published at almost the same time as *Fear and Trembling*. What *Repetition* really deals with, under the guise of trying to repeat externally an earlier experience, is the possibility of finding *inwardly* some eternally valid and constant meaning in life despite the continual change in which the self is involved. This, says Kierkegaard, is the 'interest' of metaphysics because metaphysics seeks the eternal; but it is at the same time the point at which metaphysics founders because as

71

soon as the actual changefulness and freedom of the existing subject are introduced, then the possibility of objective certainty disappears. Yet if some stable frame of reference cannot be found, the only thing to do is to let life go on like a stream. In other words, the trouble with metaphysics is that it cannot find a point of union between the Eternal and existence because it abstracts from existence; while the trouble with the aesthetic approach is that it also cannot find a point of union because it immerses itself in pure temporalism.

In *Repetition* it is suffering which drives the young man to seek a religious answer—an 'Archimedean point' above himself. Existence has become utterly meaningless to him. He asks: 'Who am I? How did I come into the world? Why was I not consulted? If I am compelled to take part in it, where is the director? If there is no director, where shall I make my complaint? Am I guilty or not?' [5] The last question illustrates the ambiguity of standing at the intersecting point of freedom and necessity. For the reason just mentioned, metaphysics cannot help him, and, as the pseudonymous author says, if he had turned to sensuality (the *terminus ad quem* of the aesthetic stage), he would have been lost. Instead, the young man identifies himself with Job, who rejects all attempts to understand his suffering by means of theory, rejects the conception of God as a tyrannical authority, and rejects the conception of providence which would explain away his personal tragedies in terms of a general plan. And in the end Job finds an answer, not in an idea but in the sufferer himself and in what he does with his suffering existence. As the young man says, 'Job does not cut a figure in a university chair and with reassuring gestures vouch for the truth of his thesis . . . He sits among the ashes and scrapes himself with a potsherd, and without interrupting this manual labor lets fall casual hints and remarks.' Job finds an answer in faith only when he gives up trying to understand, and lets his protest come out fully instead of suppressing it. Only so does he appropriate an answer which is genuinely *his*. What he gets then is a transformation of himself. After letting go of the world and of all the things his happiness, prosperity, and self-respect have rested upon, and so rising in freedom above dependence upon finite objects and results, Job gets everything back double. In order to understand Kierkegaard's point, of course, it is necessary to interpret the conclusion of the book of Job figuratively, not literally. What Job gets back is the significance of the relative, which has actually been heightened by coming into relationship with the Eternal through his personal encounter with God.

The young man in *Repetition*, like Abraham in *Fear and Trembling*, is an 'exception'; that is, he cannot find a solution to his problem so long as he remains within the universal patterns of the ethical, which in the case of the young man are typified by marriage. Yet in both instances passage beyond the ethical into religious faith is justified only because the ethical is first taken seriously. So far as faith itself is concerned, Kierkegaard confines himself in *Repetition* to the remark that to find the answer in suffering which links the individual to God is to anticipate the Christian concepts of atonement and rebirth.

3. Anxiety and Freedom

The closest Kierkegaard comes to a systematic statement of his view of man is in *The Concept of Dread* (*Angst*). Here he rejects the idea that individual sin could be necessitated by Adam's Fall. He takes the story in Genesis as symbolic of what happens in the experience of every man. Each person finds himself to be a mixture of bondage and responsibility. If we put the whole stress upon racial determinism, we fail to do justice to freedom, and if we put the whole stress upon individual free will, we fail to do justice to the fateful influence of social conditioning. Kierkegaard does not try to give a chronological explanation of how a person makes the transition from innocence to guilt. But he does try to show how anxiety accompanies freedom even *prior to* moral distinctions. What does he mean by freedom prior to moral distinctions? He means a condition of sheer possibility—the possibility of making something out of Nothing. Here man is like God because he is created in the image of God. Freedom means that we have a hand in making ourselves

73

what we are to become, but it also means that we can negate as well as affirm, we can destroy as well as construct. Freedom means that man can have kinship with Nothingness as well as with God.

This condition of indeterminate potentiality (which Berdyaev calls 'meonic' freedom because it derives from non-Being) is a condition of anxiety. Thus man's position is not only above the brutes; it is intrinsically more precarious, and we may sometimes try to run away from it so as to return to the irresponsible bliss of an animal condition. But we cannot really escape, and because of his freedom each man becomes aware of evil desire, sin, and guilt as springing from himself.[6] Thus from the beginning to the end of history, human nature is an ambiguous mixture of two factors: (1) the goodness of creation, which comes from God; and (2) the distortion caused by sin, which comes from man. Finitude, temporality, selfhood, and sexuality are not intrinsically evil; they are aspects of the goodness of creation. But we never encounter them in their unspoiled condition.

Several consequences follow from this outlook. For example, the cumulative sensuality of one's forbears can operate almost as though it were a necessitating power, but actually every individual is partly innocent and partly guilty. It is not his fault that sex comes into his experience as already spoiled by the wickedness of the race, but he *is* guilty in the sense that he personally originates attitudes which also spoil sex. Similarly, although selfhood is not evil, we never experience it except as already distorted by selfishness. Instead of saying 'sin is due to selfishness,' we should say 'selfishness springs from a person who is already sinful.'

Finally, sin spoils temporality. It is part of the meaning of freedom that man can transcend the temporal flux. Indeed, if we try to ignore the way man directs his life through memory and anticipation, what is left? Only the 'present,' which lies like an absurd geometrical point between movement and repose without occupying any time. It is an empty spot sandwiched in between past and future. Hence the only way we can do justice to human history is to define the Instant as the point where Eternity touches time. History is the setting in which man exercises freedom in seeking a right relationship with Eternity, and there is no way of describing man's 'present' without taking account of the fact that man transcends the present. The Instant, viewed as an atom of Eternity, may be called a finite attempt to fulfill time. Therefore Christianity has rightly diagnosed the problem of history when it seeks salvation, not by escape from temporality, in an Eternal meaning which, by entering history, transforms it. What all this signifies is that we could exist as purely temporal creatures, the way plants and animals do, only if we could succeed in killing the spirit. Temporality is not intrinsically evil, but once it has been distorted by sin, past evils become enslaving and the passage of time alone cannot alter them. The future can signify fulfillment only if there is hope of bringing into history something which is not naturally immanent in it. For sinful man, transitoriness becomes a curse, bearing all our earthly hopes toward annihilation; death becomes terrible instead of natural; and our human condition becomes something which we can neither tolerate nor escape.

4. Philosophy and Faith

This brings us to the center of Kierkegaard's work as found in the two books called the *Philosophical Fragments* and the *Concluding Unscientific Postscript*. Their main purpose is to show the difference between philosophical knowledge and Christian faith. The title of the former was chosen in conscious opposition to Hegel's idea of a system. Using Socrates as an example, Kierkegaard brings out the way in which philosophy must take for granted an unbroken affinity between the human mind and the ultimate truth. If, in accordance with the Socratic theory of reminiscence, the eternal Forms are always immanent in the soul, then no moment in time can have essential but only accidental significance. Because Socrates ironically confesses his own ignorance, he is vastly superior to those pretentious rationalists who think they can get a choke-hold on the Absolute by means of their systems. Yet even Socrates assumes that,

75

despite the limitations of the body, finitude, temporality, and 'opinion,' the soul is already connected with the divine. The truth may have to be evoked from a pupil by a teacher, but no teacher can establish the intrinsic relationship between soul and truth for another person. He can be, at most, the occasion for eliciting it or bringing it to light; and so Socrates refused to have disciples because he saw that no one could be absolutely dependent upon another man in the quest for wisdom.

On the other hand, Christianity takes for granted that the tie between man and eternal truth has been broken. Man finds himself unable to live *in* the truth. His chief difficulty is not intellectual, but lies in the area of the will, the heart. He cannot force himself to be sincere enough to see the full truth about himself. He is unable to reach that inner simplicity where his ideals and his actions form a perfect unity. Therefore Christianity affirms the decisive significance of time in a manner which Socrates (and Platonism) could never admit. For it, the way of salvation consists not in bringing to fruition something which man already possesses, but in being *re-created* so as to be able to be united with the truth instead of estranged from it.

If we ask how man fell into this condition of inner warfare, the answer is 'through his freedom.' And he remains in sin and error by continually forfeiting what would save him. But since all his efforts spring from an enslaved self, he cannot solve the problem by sheer effort. Nor will a presentation of the truth by a skillful teacher suffice, for *seeing* an ideal does not mean that we can live up to it. What is needed is a complete transformation of character, a regeneration of the individual from the ground up. But no human teacher can literally re-create a soul; only God can do this. Someone may protest that since man fell into difficulties through his own freedom, he can solve them by his own freedom. But this overlooks the decisive character of action and the binding power of the past. I can freely throw a stone across a pond, but I cannot freely make it come back to me. Similarly, I cannot undo the self I have formed. I cannot reach liberation by 'willing' because it is precisely the will that needs to be liberated. What I need is a new self by removal of the guilt of the old self, and only an atoning God can give me this new self. What God thus makes available is not merely an occasion so that once man receives regeneration he can then retain his grasp on the truth by his own power. The Moment is a point in time which has an essential, not just an accidental, relationship to union with God. Therefore Kierkegaard calls it the Fullness of Time.[7] Moreover, the conversion which takes place within man involves a transition as momentous as that from non-being to being. Therefore Kierkegaard calls it the New Birth. Since it involves the gift of a new self, it can happen only to the individual; conversion *en masse* is impossible. And what it means can be appreciated only by someone who has actually undergone it.

Man can be rescued only by a Saviour who reaches the human race where it is, in history. Yet since God does not need anything, what could prompt Him to take upon Himself the burden of human error and guilt in atonement? The only possible answer is: 'The love by which He moves Himself.' This is the eternal nature of God actualized in time. The purpose of revelation is to overcome the obstacles which prevent man from accepting what God offers—yet without obliterating the difference between God and man. And as such, revelation is aimed at the highest good of the individual, although it may not coincide with what man thinks will bring him happiness. Man would prefer a direct vision of God, but this, by ostensibly obliterating the difference between deity and humanity, would arouse illusions concerning the 'intrinsic divinity' in man. Actually man is always dependent upon God, but the problem is how to bring him to recognize and accept this dependence without overriding his freedom. The problem can be solved only if God, by coming to man in the midst of historical existence, offers a restoration of the loving relationship in such a way that the response of trust and gratitude can overpower the egocentricity of the will. God bridges the chasm by taking on the form of a servant, by becoming equal with the lowliest man.

One of the implications of this position is that a true notion of

77

divine omnipotence is to be sought at the point where God deals with human freedom instead of trying to think of it by generalizing from the nature of physical force. It takes more divine power to offer reconciliation than to sustain the heavens and the earth in cosmic orderliness, for reconciliation is offered continually, at the cost of suffering love, despite the fact that man, in his freedom, may reject the offer. If God remained aloof and unincarnate He might rule man by coercion, but that could never bring about a change of heart. Again, it might be assumed that revelation should simply take the form of a theophany, thus sparing God the necessity of incarnate suffering, but this is to go over to the Socratic view that man is already in a position to respond directly to the vision of God because the intrinsic connection between the human soul and the divine has never been broken. This is to fall into the error of Docetism.

Thus Christian faith and philosophical knowledge stand in sharp contrast with each other. The latter stakes its hopes on an intellectual mode of salvation which simply brings to light the goodness in man which is already there; hence it cannot fully acknowledge either the seriousness of our human predicament or the miraculous love whereby God takes the initiative in rescuing us. Furthermore, the central affirmation of Christian faith cannot be demonstrated. We *believe* that God became man in Christ, reconciling the world to Himself; we *believe* that the eternal entered time. But this kind of truth is very different from mathematics, science, or philosophy. For what we are talking about here is a personal relationship between God and man, where passionate trust in God's forgiveness and willingness to yield our hearts to Him are indispensable.

It follows that Christianity should not attach primary importance to proofs or doctrines. The most that ideas can do is point beyond themselves to this 'I-Thou' relationship. Proofs for the existence of God are futile except as they articulate what faith already grasps, and then of course they are not proofs. The evidences of order, intelligence, and purpose on which the cosmological and teleological proofs are based are ambiguous. The world has so much evil in it that there is no straight line of demonstration leading from it to

God. Moreover, if one is surveying 'the world,' then nothing may be excluded and there can never be a point where all the evidence is in. Hence the a posteriori proofs are inadequate because they cannot, of themselves, account for evil, and they could always be overthrown by new facts. On the other hand, the a priori (i.e. ontological) argument is also inadequate. It moves from the *idea* of God's perfection to the *idea* of His existence; but thinking, by itself, can never make the transition from ideas to actuality. In short, the ontological argument only moves from one concept to another; therefore it cannot be undermined by empirical evidence, but neither can it say anything about existence.

What philosophy should do, in such circumstances, is to admit its own limits, acknowledging that God cannot be reached by reason because of the absolute unlikeness between God and man, and that the attempt to equate Him with certain human values and experiences really abrogates belief in Him instead of making it intelligible. What usually happens, however, is that philosophy, forgetting its limits, produces an Absolute which transcends all finite relationships and contains all men in such a way that no man can be God in a special sense. Here God's otherness is circumvented by swallowing up the distinction between likeness and unlikeness in an identity of opposites. This might not be so bad were it not for the fact that the philosopher often claims to be able to work the Incarnation and the Trinity into his scheme, and thus to put Christian truth into proper perspective. Actually what he is propounding is utterly irreconcilable with Christianity. The living God whom we encounter in the 'I-Thou' relationship cannot be the philosophical Absolute, for in the latter all relationship disappears into unity.[8] Admittedly there is kinship between God and man in so far as man is created in the Image of God, but the difference, the estrangement, which arises through the abuse of freedom means that the main obstacle to knowledge of God is rooted in sin and cannot be removed by reason. Hence revelation takes the form not of supra-rational truths but of a personal act which restores broken fellowship and removes spiritual alienation. This personal act is the God-man in history.

Attempts to prove the deity of Christ, like attempts to prove the existence of God, are also futile. The God-man in history is beyond rational demonstration; He is the Paradox. Indeed, He is the Paradox in a twofold sense, for He discloses the absolute unlikeness in absolute likeness (God-manhood). He reveals to us both our sinful nature and our restored nature in such a way that we grasp what it means to be human, not through learning propositions but through our response, positive or negative, to His sacrificial love. The basic reason for rejecting Christianity is that one wants to be able to save himself by his own rational methods. A man does not want to have to accept salvation from God instead of on his own terms, especially when this involves seeing his sin clearly. Christianity denies that man has the security of an immanent and potentially adequate union with God in himself; yet philosophy can never admit this insecurity because to do so is to relinquish its totalitarian claims. Hence philosophy must always deal with Christianity in the form of trying to explain it; reason seeks to remove unpleasantness by pretending that the ultimate question concerning the meaning of life is within our control, when actually it is beyond our control. If we insist on trying to make the God-man directly intelligible, the utmost we can do is to *define* divinity in terms of our own ideas of what would best fulfill human nature. But to set up a definition does nothing to show that God-manhood has actually occurred in history.

Nevertheless, the deity of Christ is not completely concealed; it is *agape* expressed in human terms at the historical level. This genuinely human life is so different from the life of the natural man, however, that it stands above what is objectively valid for society. Christ cares nothing for wealth and power; He is free from anxiety because He has broken with the finite. Thus discipleship goes beyond rational understanding and the universal norms of ethics in precisely the manner in which, in the earlier works already surveyed, the religious stage is represented as going beyond the aesthetic and the ethical. Since security is reached only via the risk of faith, the disciples are likely to be humble men. The wise and erudite will prefer to take from Christ only what can be learned according to their methods of getting at the truth. But, as we have already seen, the disciple looks to Him for receiving a new self not for acquiring knowledge.

A word should be interjected at this point concerning Kierkegaard's method. Despite all that he says against rationalism and system-building, his approach to the problem we have been discussing is highly schematic. As we shall see more fully, his view of human nature as a synthesis of eternity and temporality, infinitude and finitude, freedom and necessity, coincides perfectly with his view of the God-man as a paradoxical union of these same antinomies. Hence his analysis of what man needs cannot be divorced from his conviction concerning what the atoning God offers in Christ. No doubt this is as it should be. It is a fact that Christian faith in God's forgiveness does not make sense unless one has already accepted in some measure (though this may be largely unconscious) a Christian understanding of sin and a Christian vision of what man is meant to be. This total view of life is of-a-piece, and Kierkegaard is right in thinking that it cannot be demonstrated either as a whole or by taking one segment at a time. But his attack on system-building should not blind us to the internal coherence which characterizes his point of view. There is a coincidence—for him momentous—between (a) Christ as the point in time where the Eternal offers salvation, and (b) faith as the point in time where man's relationship to God is decisively determined. If one protests that 'faith' can be directed toward God, conceived in non-Christian terms, or toward objects other than God, Kierkegaard's reply is that in such instances faith simply fails to fulfill its own nature. And if one asks what constitutes his criterion of fulfillment, the answer is bound to be discipleship to Christ. Hence the argument is indeed circular. But it is worth asking whether one does not always encounter such circularity where ultimate presuppositions are involved. For example, the dependability of reason cannot be demonstrated without in some sense taking it for granted before the demonstration begins.

There are two contrasting ways of attempting to prove the deity of Christ, and since both of them are still employed by theologians,

Kierkegaard's criticism of them anticipates contemporary Christo-logical disputes in a startlingly clairvoyant fashion. The first line of argument concentrates upon the historical facts. It is represented, roughly, by those who hold that by getting back to the historical Jesus we can rediscover the Gospel in its pristine purity—e.g. before the morbid distortions introduced by St. Paul, and the dogmatizing which led to the doctrine of the Trinity. Concerning this approach Kierkegaard declares that, at most, historical facts can show that Jesus claimed to be divine, but cannot possibly show that He actually was so. Moreover, although His human life was genuinely historical, it was not *merely* historical, and therefore anyone who tries to confine his approach to the historical events cannot be a disciple. Indeed, in one sense knowledge of the historical details is not decisive, inasmuch as a man could possess such knowledge without reaching faith. For example, two contemporaries of Jesus who witnessed the same incident in His ministry might agree on the empirical details, yet they could disagree completely concerning the significance of the happening because one believed in Him as Saviour while the other did not. For the same reason, the teaching of Christ is not, in one sense, decisive; for it is always possible to accept His ideas theoretically without being regenerated by Him.

The second line of argument concentrates upon what it calls the 'eternal truth' of Christianity, insisting that this is what is really important, rather than historical events about which we can never reach absolute certainty. An advocate of this position may affirm the historicity of Jesus and the grandeur of His deeds and teachings. But he will regard the essence of Christianity as a set of eternally true propositions to which Christ's relationship as teacher and revealer is (in the technical, not the derogatory, sense) accidental. Such an approach assumes that the way to make Christianity universally valid is to turn it into eternal essences which can be grasped rationally.

Against both positions Kierkegaard maintains that what Christ means cannot be apprehended through *knowledge* of either historical facts or philosophical truths. Faith is essentially related not to the teaching but to the Teacher, and He is neither (a) merely a historical human being nor (b) a universal truth. When the two are combined, as they are in Him, the result is the transformation of both. Reason is equipped to deal with universals and particulars, but not with this fusion which is the Eternal Truth *in* a historical person.[9] Therefore faith is directed toward a Paradox which remains baffling to reason, and issues in such contradictions as the belief that God was born and died, and the belief that a mortal man was raised again from the dead.

Before going further, however, we must ask one question concerning Kierkegaard's own position. It is easy to understand the sense in which he can be indifferent about the historical details; and modern critical scholarship would contend that it is impossible to get back behind the Gospel records, the oral tradition, the interpretations introduced by the early Church, to the bare happenings themselves. Indeed, the effort to arrive at an 'objective' picture of a man in abstraction from the reactions and interpretations of those who knew him is not only futile, the result would be bad as a piece of historical research even if it could be reached. For in historical writing, as contrasted with natural science, there is no virtue in describing bare facts; rather, the effort should be directed toward seeing facts in the context of the human reactions, beliefs, and interpretations which accompany them.

Nevertheless, affirmation of the historicity of the God-man is absolutely central to Kierkegaard's thesis. Therefore the question arises as to whether or not this affirmation is solely a matter of faith exclusive of historical knowledge. In a moment we shall examine what he has to say concerning the status of historical knowledge in general, and his claim that it can never reach more than high probability (approximation). His basic position is that since historical methods neither prove nor disprove the existence of the man Jesus, faith affirms in the face of what remains with an inescapable measure of uncertainty. But here the man of faith is no worse off than the atheist making his negative judgment concerning the religious meaning of the Gospel reports.

At the same time, it is important to remember that Kierkegaard does not suggest that faith can dictate what the answers (in terms of high probability) of historical research should be. Nevertheless, his position is not wholly satisfying, though it is hard to find a discussion of the problem in contemporary theology that is any more convincing. Does he mean to imply that since the ethical qualities of the human Jesus and the ideas contained in His teaching cannot in themselves produce faith in His deity, they are of no importance? Some phrases he uses sound as though this were the case; yet they must be put alongside the fact that the human figure—the form of a servant, the renunciation of power and prestige, freedom from guilt and anxiety—is, from Kierkegaard's standpoint, singularly *appropriate* for expressing the nature of God. Admittedly one cannot directly prove the deity of Christ by calling attention to the exalted character of His life and teachings. But neither can one hold (once again from Kierkegaard's standpoint) that the relationship between the nature of God and the particular qualities ascribed to the human life of Jesus is accidental. And if the historical manhood was an appropriate medium of revelation as, say, the life of a scoundrel or a despot never could be, then the historical details cannot really be a matter of indifference.

Because Kierkegaard insisted that faith is not a form of knowledge, many of his critics have leaped to the conclusion that it can only be a wholly subjective (in the bad sense) expression of what a man wishes or imagines to be true. On these terms, faith remains entirely within the confines of the individual's mind and will, and never has to meet the test of coming to terms with 'reality.' It should be clear from the foregoing, however, that Kierkegaard never believed that faith could be produced merely as an act of will, for he held that all willing reflects the bondage which shuts us off from God. Unless faith is related to God's *giving* of the condition that overcomes sin, then it is an illusion. Unquestionably, Kierkegaard believed that God is real and that He has revealed Himself in history in Jesus Christ, apart from what any individual may think, will, or believe. But he refused to refer to the reality of God and historical revelation as 'objective' because the latter word connoted for him demonstrable, conceptual knowledge, an abstraction from passionate commitment, personal decision, and the 'I-Thou' encounter. Indeed, although he believed that God was real apart from Sören Kierkegaard, he recognized that there was no way of *his* entering into relationship with God apart from Sören Kierkegaard's faith. And with such a recognition it is difficult to quarrel.

Thus far we have seen, concerning the Paradox, that both historical factors (ordinarily handled by perception) and eternal factors (ordinarily handled by conception as timeless truths) are involved, but neither can reach God. The former are confined to the empirico-historical; the latter are confined to essences. *Given* the God-man, what perception apprehends is not mere appearance; to regard it as such is Docetism. But without faith, what perception sees is just a man. Hence contemporaneity with Jesus offers no crucial advantages. Only by means of faith can anyone be directly related in time with the Eternal, and all men, whether they are contemporary with Jesus or live in a later century, must receive salvation directly from God Himself, not at second hand through some other human being.

5. History

Since virtually everything Kierkegaard says about the nature of faith presupposes the reality of human freedom, it is important for him to refute determinism.[10] He begins by asserting that the category of necessity is not applicable to becoming; it is applicable, rather, to propositions whose truth does not depend upon occurrences in the actual world (i.e. analytic propositions). The events of nature may *seem* to be formulable in necessary laws, but if these laws are built up by empirical generalization, then they are not really necessary but only highly probable. We can make successful predictions on the basis of them, and that gives rise to the illusion that the events in question happen necessarily. Nevertheless, if any proposition is necessarily true, what makes it so is a relationship between meanings, not a relationship between empirical existents. It follows that the category of necessity is not applicable to 'history' as a whole. In his use of this word, Kierkegaard wishes to take account of the fact that man not only undergoes change, like all events in nature, but can dispose himself toward process in such a way that his experience is made up not merely of happenings but of significant happenings. In a broad sense there can be a history of stars and rocks, but in the narrow, strict sense 'history' occurs only where human decision enters into the making and the meaning of events. Hegel made the colossal blunder of believing that the totality of the historical process could be grasped as a logically necessary system, when actually the two are irreconcilable. Necessary truths cannot apply to history; and history cannot be poured into the mould of a logically necessary system. Historical determinism may seem plausible because of the immutability of the past, but the undeniable fact that the past cannot be changed does not mean that the events in question took place necessarily *as they came into the present*. In a word, either all history is subject to complete necessitation or it is not; if one regards the past as logically necessitated, he must regard the future as also thus necessitated, and in that case there is no room for genuine freedom.

What are the implications of Kierkegaard's rejection of determinism for his view of historical knowledge? Since historical events cannot be grasped with logical necessity, all knowledge of the past and of the future contains an element of uncertainty. Most men easily understand this in connection with the future, but it is important to realize that establishment of rapport with past events as they really occurred also involves taking account of the fact that they were then unpredictable, surprising, and creative. Hence a capacity for wonder and imagination is indispensable in the historian. This condition is not fulfilled if the historian, in reaction against rationalism, swings to the opposite extreme of empiricism. Sense data alone cannot constitute a grasping of history because they merely present the flux of experience, missing that identity of the subject which is required if anything—especially man—is to remain 'the same' while undergoing change. In short, the means by which we apprehend the historical must have a structure analogous to the historical itself. Now faith possesses this character. The kind of certainty it reaches does not abolish the two forms of uncertainty which arise from the fact that (a) historical knowledge is not logically necessary, and (b) the events it grasps are contingent, i.e. not self-explanatory. At the opposite pole from faith stands doubt, and both are manifestations of freedom. So long as one remains within the sphere of the logically certain or of uninterpreted sense data, one can avoid doubt, but one will also fail to come to grips with history. One is able to grasp the meaning of historical events only by a free act, a decision which will be either positive or negative. In this sphere either faith or doubt is unavoidable. To ask for certainty in advance in these matters is like asking for certainty that one can swim before going into the water. Faith is directed toward something which has happened but did not have to happen, and in circumstances where it is impossible to demonstrate that it did happen.

If we apply these considerations not merely to the facts about, but to the *meaning* of the life of Jesus Christ, has Kierkegaard satisfactorily answered our earlier question? He seems to be suggesting that an adequate 'knowledge' of what took place in that life is to be reached, not by gathering factual information about it (which can be highly probable, but never certain), but only by a decision which brings my will into conformity with the significance of what He was and did. Undeniably there is a large measure of truth in this suggestion. Not only in religion, but in art, literature, politics, and many other fields, it is only the man who can enter into communion with the beliefs and values of a figure or an epoch in the past who can really recover the past. Yet this is not the whole story. If it is true that there are riches which are accessible only to the devotee, it is also true that limitations, defects, and perils are often visible only to one who can view the past with a measure of critical detachment. Moreover, even if we are willing to grant that the question of the deity of Christ must be dealt with by faith or doubt and cannot be settled by an appeal to rational demonstration or sense data, surely Kierkegaard has failed to make clear the relationship between faith and historical fact (as contrasted with the *meaning* of historical fact). He might reply that it is impossible to dissociate fact from meaning when dealing with historical questions. Nevertheless, he fails to meet squarely the kind of problem that would arise if the high probabilities of historical research went contrary to faith. For example, if it became highly probable, on the basis of newly discovered manuscripts, that Jesus never existed, or that He was a scoundrel, what would Kierkegaard's answer be? He might reply that the interpretation on which these new historical findings rest is itself riddled with negative attitudes toward Christianity, instead of being dispassionate; and such a reply would often have been pertinent in the past, for example in connection with the work of Strauss. But it does not wholly meet the situation now. Indeed, there probably is no Christological position which does not run the risk of falling into one extreme or the other; either it claims concerning the historical manhood a kind of certainty which does not attach to historical knowledge, or it turns the Incarnation into a principle, regarding the principle as what is essential, no matter what we may discover concerning the historical events whereby it has come down to us.

Furthermore, there is good reason to hold that Kierkegaard himself, at least tacitly, made a distinction between 'fact' and 'meaning' in his discussion of faith as the organ of historical knowledge. For he says that even the contemporary of Christ can grasp the historical only by means of faith, and this is nonsense unless what Kierkegaard has in mind is the revelatory meaning of the event, not merely what one can apprehend by means of sensory perception. The contemporary could be certain that Jesus existed, but he could not be certain, by logical or empirical means, of His deity. Kierkegaard goes on to suggest that the Gospel record stands, for us, in a position which corresponds to the sense data available to a contemporary. We can be sure that the Gospel presents a given picture, but like the contemporary, we also must go beyond the immediate evidence in order to reach faith, and in both cases faith is subject to the same sort of uncertainty. Once again, we need not deny a measure of truth in this suggestion. If followed through it might lead to a Christology which, like Paul Tillich's, puts the stress upon 'the picture of Jesus as the Christ' that we indubitably possess in the New Testament, rather than upon fruitless attempts to rediscover the historical Jesus. Nevertheless there is an ineradicable difference between the position of a contemporary and the position of a man in a later century. The contemporary only has one uncertainty to deal with, namely, the meaning of events. But men in later centuries have an additional uncertainty to confront in connection with the relationship of the Gospel record to the actual events. Faith is not irrelevant to this latter uncertainty, but it cannot deal with it alone, and Kierkegaard's discussion does tend to conceal that fact.

He sees clearly, however, that a man may assent to the general principle that the meaning of historical events is determined by faith and doubt, without assenting to the specific claim that God was incarnate in Christ. Indeed, he stresses the fact that Christian faith involves not only the uncertainty which attaches to any decision concerning an interpretation of historical events, but also the special risk of giving assent to something paradoxical. Therefore Christian faith is possible only if God 'repeats' the event in the sense of bridging the gulf between the believer's historical situation and eternity, just as in Christ the gulf between history and the Eternal was bridged.

6. The Church

One consequence of Kierkegaard's stress on faith as inward and individual is that he does less than justice to the Church, and at the end of his career he launched a vitriolic attack upon it. For him, to press forward beyond the universal demands of ethics, beyond the superficiality of the mob mind, beyond the conventional religiosity which offers a specious security and overlooks the necessity of risk and decision, meant ascending to a height of isolation where

89

the individual stands face to face with God as revealed in Christ. In his profound distrust of all mediatorial agencies except Christ Himself, he manifests the best in Protestantism. But in assuming that the establishment of an 'I-Thou' relationship with God requires a deep break with communal ties, he manifests the worst in Protestantism. In the *Fragments* his main reason for warning against the Church seems to be that its teachings can easily conceal the risky and paradoxical character of faith. He insists that no amount of 'believing what the Church has taught' is equivalent to personal faith. Appeals to the traditions and the continuity of an institution which has existed through many centuries cannot make the Paradox more probable or plausible. For one thing, the fact that millions of other men have believed does not spare me the necessity of making my own decision, because these millions might have been wrong. Even more important is the fact that the Church constantly tends to lose sight of the true character of New Testament Christianity by softening its demands, by making it reasonable, by adapting it to current assumptions. Thus to follow tradition *may* mean to move away from the Gospel toward some version of Christianity which has been domesticated within a given nation, period, or culture. Then it is easy to accept 'Christianity' without the slightest embarrassment as a matter of course. Specifically, to regard the Church as something that makes it possible for a child to be born into faith is to fall back to the Socratic level where there is no question of the need for a new birth because the only task required is to make explicit what is already latent.

Some might wish to claim that the historical uncertainties which arise in connection with the Bible are overcome by the Church because after all it exists in the *present*. This position takes for granted, however, that the Church today is in some sense apostolic, standing in continuity with the Church of the preceding centuries. Thus it, like the Bible, cannot really escape historical problems. In fact, it is impossible to prove that the Church's present belief is the same as that of the first disciples, and that it has maintained its identity through the centuries.

90

The main point is that it is a mistake to avoid the risk involved in faith by seeking objective assurances of any kind, whether by Church membership, baptism, or doctrinal orthodoxy. Doubts and temptations cannot be overcome by turning to any consideration outside oneself; if they are conquered, they must be conquered inwardly. Hence the most one man can do for another is to confess his own faith. This may provide the occasion for faith on the part of the other while leaving him free to make his own decision in solitude before God. If anyone is so foolish as to believe on the authority of another *man* (or group of men) instead of on the authority of God alone, then it does not matter much whether the other man is a saint or a Münchausen. Indeed, it would be incompatible with God's justice to put some men in a specially favored position, e.g. by contemporaneity with Christ or by being born into the Church. In the circumstances it is very difficult not to condemn infant baptism. What it ought to symbolize is that the child may become a Christian, just as when the child is born we know that he may become an adult. Christianity cannot be gained without personal appropriation and baptismal certificates will do no good on the day of Judgment. Faith is equally difficult and equally easy for all men; no man can supply the condition himself or receive it from another.

This passage, and others in Kierkegaard, sounds so extreme that it may be asked what he saw in the Church at all. Until near the end of his life, he regarded its existence as natural and justifiable; he participated in public worship and even preached occasionally. But his attitude was colored by the fact that, from his point of view, the most essential aspects of religious struggle and belief could not be communicated directly, and he was always suspicious of anything in which men could participate as a 'crowd' instead of as individuals. Above all, he warned against regarding anything other than God-in-Christ as capable of mediating salvation—whether it be the Pope, Biblicism, or orthodox doctrine; and he protested against any institutional security which might conceal the fact that churchmen remain existing persons in history, subject to fallibility, uncertainty, and the possibility of temporal defeat.

7. The Characteristics of Existential Thinking

Having seen the way in which Kierkegaard deals with specific issues, always relating them closely to his personal situation, we are now in a position to draw up a more precise statement concerning what he takes to be the nature of existential (he usually calls it 'subjective') thinking. As a matter of fact, he furnishes this statement for us in the *Postscript* where he discusses four theses attributable to Lessing.[11]

First, whereas objective thinking is concerned with producing results which can become public property, the subjective point of view concentrates upon the process of thinking, as it goes on uniquely in the individual, and omits the results. Therefore direct communication is appropriate for objective thinking, but subjective thinking requires indirect communication. Direct communication deals with those meanings which two or more men can share when everything unique in each is ignored. But in religious matters to try to make one's own truth another's, without allowing or requiring the other to go through the inward process involved in appropriating this kind of truth, may deprive the other of finding his own relationship to God. This explains why Kierkegaard refuses to offer demonstrations and answers, trying rather to arouse the reader to his own struggle by leaving the answer uncertain. Therefore it is ironical that, in our own day, the revival of interest in his writings has produced something like a Kierkegaard cult. He discerned the irony in advance when he wrote that if someone becomes convinced that no man ought to have disciples, and then stupidly asserts the principle *directly*, he will undoubtedly experience 'the peculiar good fortune of obtaining disciples to . . . disseminate this doctrine of not having any disciples.' [12] We should not conclude from Kierkegaard's remarks about indirect communication, however, that he fell into Sartre's mistake of holding that it is impossible to talk about 'human nature' because that involves a deterministic universal concept of 'man' which is irreconcilable with the fact that the free individual has to make himself what he becomes. Kierkegaard held that in the process of penetrating into his own inwardness, the individual is at the same time learning the truth about human nature as such. For example, he writes that whereas an objective approach enquires into 'the truth of Christianity,' a subjective approach asks, rather: 'How can I become a Christian?' He realizes that the latter question concerns only himself; yet he adds: 'If it is properly posed, it will concern everyone else in the same manner.' [13]

The second thesis has to do with the fact that the subject is involved in continual striving. We reach certainty in science and speculation by abstracting from the changing subject, but such certainty can never be final or all-inclusive because actually there is, of course, no such thing as knowledge apart from the knowing subject. The only fact that can be absolutely certain is one's own existence, and this fact cannot be absolutely certain for anyone else. This 'self' is both an infinite spirit and a temporal creature, and the possibility of death hangs over it at every moment. Hence no positive certainties can remove the basic uncertainty of life. But rather than face this fact, most people try to fix attention on what *is* controllable, dependable, and knowable. Thereby they achieve a certain pseudo-security by fitting in with the surrounding world and society as one object in a system of objects. This really means allowing human life to become spiritless; for our sense of the tragic and the comic rests on a recognition of the *incongruity* involved in being both an infinite spirit and a temporal creature. When one thinks of man's longing for the eternal, this incongruity is tragic; and when one thinks of how inadequate all external means are for expressing inwardness, the same incongruity can be comic. Man also tends to become spiritless, and to regard himself as a thing (object) instead of a person (subject), when he forgets his distinctive relationship to temporality. In order to strive, he must exist in time, and yet the aim of his striving is not a finite goal. One has to abstract from the way man actually deals with time in order to regard temporality as an external

93

continuum which flows along at an even pace. This physicist's conception of clock-time is only the schematic framework within which the living content of human experience falls. From the standpoint of that experience itself, man can transcend time and see how a Moment possesses infinite value and also how ten thousand years may be as a trifle. For man the stress falls on the meaning of events, not on their quantitative duration.[14]

The third thesis is that accidental historical truths can never serve as proofs for eternal truths of reason, and that the transition by which one bases an eternal truth upon historical testimony involves a leap. This has already been discussed. Kierkegaard mainly has in mind, of course, the fact that the central claims of Christianity are not 'direct' philosophical statements. But he is also defining existential thinking, as such, as opposed to any metaphysic which purports to arrive at a rational synthesis of the temporal and the eternal. For such a synthesis to be possible the conflict, the incongruity between the two orders would have to be resolvable by thought, and Kierkegaard has just tried to show why that is out of the question. The leap to which he refers, therefore, is not in the first instance a leap of thought, but a personal commitment. One takes the risk of believing that life is ultimately meaningful despite the fact that, because of the inescapable uncertainties which are epitomized in death, it may be, for all we can ever *know*, 'a tale told by an idiot.'

The fourth thesis is that the passionate search for truth is better than objective certainty, for we can reach such certainty only by abstracting from existence so as to deal with essences. This means that objective thinking cannot deal with the 'self' as it is; for the self is not pure ego-hood in general or pure reason; it is inseparable from passion, decision, and freedom. This also means that objective thinking cannot deal with history as it is, for history is not made up of the interplay of essences which can be grasped, *sub specie aeternitatis*, in a closed system. There is an absurd element in the givenness of existing things and processes such that their reality cannot be deduced from or wholly incorporated into rational principles. In short, history is *not* a logical system. And it is not a closed system, for the reason that it is still going on.

These four theses express a fundamental attitude which distinguishes existentialism from scientific philosophy—using 'scientific' in its broadest connotation (*Wissenschaft*). Every existentialist writer attempts, in his own fashion, to formulate the difference between the kind of truth which can be appropriated without personal commitment and the kind of truth which cannot. The first is best exemplified in those propositions of natural science, mathematics, and logic which are true regardless of who thinks them. Certain personal considerations, such as intelligence and devotion to scientific enterprise, may have a bearing upon the process of apprehension. But the true proposition itself is detachable from these considerations; once it is made publicly available it can be known by fools and knaves who could not possibly have discovered it. In some cases, at least, it is possible to illustrate the difference between a scientific and an existential approach to the *same* truth. Kierkegaard himself furnishes an example. It is possible for two men to agree on an objective definition of the essence of Christianity even though one is an atheist and the other a disciple. The crucial distinction arises from the fact that in scientific work it is desirable to reduce the personal equation to a minimum, whereas unless a man approaches religious questions with personal concern he cannot really know what they are about. The purpose of science is to uncover truths which are valid apart from the fact that each individual is different from every other. But Christian truth can exist only *in* men, and even if everyone gave intellectual assent to a set of doctrinal propositions, Christianity would not exist unless someone embodied in his life what these propositions refer to. Although Kierkegaard's statement is confined to the contrast between objective thinking and Christian faith, a more general contrast between scientific and existential attitudes could easily be developed from it.

In the first instance, science attempts to discover what is true (as a sort of *fait accompli*) in nature; on the basis of such discoveries applied science makes true in the external world events which would

95

not have occurred without the intervention of human intelligence. On the other hand, the existentialist is primarily interested in making true something inward. He already exists, and his main task is to become the true self which he in some sense potentially is. At this point the *Postscript* introduces a discussion of ethical decision which seems to contradict what was said earlier. In *Fear and Trembling* a sharp distinction is drawn between the universal demands of ethics and the decision of religious faith. Now Kierkegaard is concerned to show that decision plays a momentous role within the ethical stage itself. To be sure, in *Fear and Trembling* Kierkegaard agrees with Kant that duty is superior to the promptings of romantic impulse. Here the universal is higher than the individual. At the level of faith the individual is higher than the universal, so that what he called a 'teleological suspension of the ethical' is involved, but that is only because *God*, not personal feeling, takes precedence over the demands of society. (This is the meaning of Jesus' sayings about having to renounce family attachments for the sake of the Kingdom.) Hence Kierkegaard is sharply critical of Schleiermacher for confusing faith with feeling. Nevertheless, in this book the ethical was identified with the universal, whereas now, in the *Postscript*, Kierkegaard is about to contend that ethical decision is genuine only when it transcends the universal and becomes individual.

Once more, his attack is directed against the Hegelian system which proposes that personal judgments should be reached by studying world history. Actually, however, these two are incommensurable. Personal judgments have to do with good and evil; on the other hand world history has to do with what is great and influential, where accidental circumstances and collective forces play a determinative role. Hegel's position gives rise to the insidious temptation of judging the outside world. Actually, however, an individual ceases to be ethical when he starts judging his actions in terms of any sort of success or effectiveness other than intrinsic rightness itself.

The chief point Kierkegaard is trying to make is that it is perilous to equate fidelity to duty with what historical effectiveness demands, since then it is easy to claim that morality and expediency coincide. (As, for example, when one holds that what yields maximum economic profit is at the same time of maximum service to others, so that there is no conflict between selfishness and altruism.) Yet his statement is so one-sided that it sounds as though ethical self-development must be carried out in complete solitude without paying any attention to the social consequences of one's actions. What underlies this statement is Kierkegaard's conviction that although one can apprehend external things by means of thought, one can never grasp the ethical reality of another person in this manner. Ethical truth can only be reached via oneself, by one who has learned how to exist in himself. Since deceit is always possible on the part of other persons, no one can settle his own ethical questions by trying futilely to get at the inwardness whereby others deal with the same questions. Ethical sensitivity must be developed within the person first; then it can be applied to world history so as to differentiate between genuinely good men and merely famous or powerful men. This development of ethical sensitivity cannot take place if individual conduct is dictated by the operation of logical, cultural, or political laws. Here his remarks can be turned against Marx as well as Hegel. At most a study of historical laws (whether Hegelian or Marxian) can only show the effects of human action, and these give no infallible information about the moral quality of the motivation because a well-meant and an ill-meant deed can have similar effects. Kierkegaard also holds that Hegel's scheme turns into nonsense when one attempts to apply it in detail. For example, how can one deduce by logical necessity an explanation as to why Socrates was born exactly when he was, why his mother was a midwife, why he married Xantippe instead of someone else, and why he was condemned to death by just so many votes? Finally, the supposed objectivity of the system becomes a bit suspect when it 'has room for only one Chinese thinker, but not a single German *Privatdocent* is excluded, especially no Prussian.' [15] The best safe-

97

guard against imposing one's racial or national prejudices into the study of history is to recognize that historical knowledge can never be more than tentative. On the other hand the ethical, since it consists of individual decisions, has a content which is certain, not hypothetical.

Kierkegaard's argument is an expansion of the refutation of determinism which we have already examined. Its theological consequences also throw additional light on his critique of proofs for the existence of God. At one point he declares that reality can be a system only for God.[16] Man cannot apprehend reality as a whole because for him it involves a process that is still going on. God alone 'is in his eternity forever complete, and yet includes all existence within himself.'[17] It can legitimately be asked, as Richard Kroner has done, whether Kierkegaard forgets the restrictions placed upon thinking as a result of man's finitude and temporality when he makes such statements. But in any case it is clear that he wishes to differentiate his conception of divine sovereignty from the determinism which in his experience went hand in hand with rationalism. The exercise of God's sovereignty is to be looked for, not by trying to show that history as a whole is rationally ordered, but at that point where interplay takes place between human freedom and divine freedom. Since God alone understands the drama of history, man's proper role is that of an actor, not a spectator. Every man can strive to know himself in transparency before God, but he cannot know the plot of history; that is out of his hands, and the drama is not yet finished. In other words, the way to 'know' God is not to construct theistic arguments but to enter into the living struggle between His will and man's.

From this point of view, the problem of evil must be dealt with not by means of any speculative theodicy, but by taking on the task of becoming a person in the full sense. Unless this task is the highest purpose of human life, then the wastefulness of evolution poses an unanswerable problem. The race becomes a monster which uses individuals as means to its ends, and the purposes of history become like the movements of a shoal of herring. But if the task of becoming his true self is given to each man, then no individual is wasted. It may be added that although these reflections, and what Kierkegaard has said earlier about the abuse of human freedom, are relevant to the problem of evil so far as it concerns moral values, they say nothing about natural evil—including the suffering of animals. Kierkegaard seemed to assume throughout his life that if the fundamental evil of estrangement from God could be overcome, then the sufferings and tragedies which attend natural evil, though they can be intense and poignant, will never make life ultimately meaningless. Because of his general renunciation of cosmological and metaphysical interests, he makes no sustained attempt to examine the possible interrelationships between moral and natural evil. He is content to take suffering and transform it from being an obstacle to belief in God into being an indispensable pathway toward communion with God.

Thus Kierkegaard represents the task of entering into self-knowledge as consisting of problems which cannot be solved once and for all, so that the individual can then pass on to something else. In a manner which anticipates Marcel's distinction between a 'problem' and a 'mystery,' he holds that the appropriation of the simplest verities, which can be common to all men, learned and ignorant, demands a whole lifetime, and even that is never sufficient. For example, one never reaches the point, in self-knowledge, of so fathoming his own tendencies toward evil that the problem can be regarded as solved. With each new day a man faces further surprises and bafflements, and he is never safe from unexpected outbreaks of temptation and failure. Similarly, in the religious sphere, prayer seems to be something simple, but since it involves transparency and honesty in the relationship of man to God, the task of learning to pray is really endless, inasmuch as the task of entering into self-knowledge is an endless one. Finally, coming to terms with death seems to be simple. Anyone can see that he, like all other men, is mortal, and then turn his attention to the things he wants to accomplish. Yet really to come to terms with death requires taking account of the fact that its possibility attends every moment, and that therefore death must be overcome in every moment. One cannot meet this situation by learning arguments for immortality. The most they have ever proved is that some aspect of human nature (the soul or the intellect), *if* it is eternal, is immortal. But what we are really concerned about is not some aspect of human nature, but *this individual* man.[18] Concerning what lies on the other side of death, objective thinking can say nothing decisive: neither eternal life nor annihilation can be demonstrated. Hence when someone tries to prove immortality it is fair to suspect that he does not really believe in it. The only thing one can do, and this is part of the task of becoming subjective, is to enter into that relationship between ethical decision and the will of God which can be actualized now. The crucial question is whether I am expressing in this temporal existence anything which is at the same time my relationship to the Eternal.

Since our entire discussion of Kierkegaard has to violate what it is attempting to expound, turning what is highly personal into general propositions, and distilling the import of his indirect communication into direct statements, it is well to call attention to the passage which concludes his chapter on the task of becoming subjective. It is the passage in which Johannes Climacus, the pseudonymous author of the *Postscript,* describes how he became a writer.[19] One day he was sitting in a café smoking a cigar. For about a decade he had been a lackadaisical student, reading much, but spending most of his time in idling and thinking which came to nothing. As he was smoking it occurred to him that he was going to become an old man without really undertaking anything, while his contemporaries were becoming prominent by benefiting mankind with various mechanical inventions and metaphysical systems that make existence easy. The thought flashed into his mind that his contribution might be, with the same humanitarian intentions as the others, to make things harder. For at a banquet where everyone has overeaten, the man who fetches a vomitive may be the only one who sees what is really required.

100

NOTES

1. See Walter Lowrie, *Kierkegaard* (Oxford, 1938), p. 147.

2. Actually, a little book entitled 'From the Manuscripts of One Still Living,' and his master's thesis on irony, preceded this work, but these he never counted as part of his 'literature.'

3. The famous 'Midnight Hour' passage in *Either/Or*, ii, pp. 135f., shows that Kierkegaard knew at firsthand the peril of becoming like the demoniac, Legion, in the gospels, because amidst all the possibilities which he could follow out imaginatively and poetically, he could not find a unified, honest self. His use of pseudonyms reflects this fact; all of the pseudonyms are possibilities within himself which enable him to bring variegated and even conflicting tendencies into the open while still keeping them at a certain distance. If one objects that it is hardly 'existential' to adopt this method whereby the author is spared having to identify himself fully with anything he produces, the later Kierkegaard would agree. At the end of his career he came to view the pseudonyms as a demonic device, and abandoned them.

4. See Roland H. Bainton, *Here I Stand* (Abingdon-Cokesbury, 1950), p. 370.

5. *Repetition* (Princeton, 1946), p. 114.

6. As we shall observe, the relationship of freedom, anxiety, and Nothingness has become a major theme in contemporary existentialism.

7. He does so with entire awareness of the fact, of course, that under the guise of carrying through an experiment in thought he is 'inventing' what turns out to be New Testament Christianity.

8. A point, incidentally, which F. H. Bradley, the post-Hegelian idealist, also sees very clearly.

9. J. V. Langmead Casserly has based the main thesis of his book, *The Christian in Philosophy*, upon the claim that Christian revelation does justice to the nature of the personal and historical by uniting the universal and the particular in something which is neither, which Casserly calls 'the singular.' The chief contribution of Christianity to philosophy, he claims, is that it offers to discursive reason something which the latter cannot of itself produce.

10. The issue is rather complicated by the fact that Kierkegaard admits that determinism is, so to speak, half the truth concerning man, but he insists that, in a fashion not rationally explicable, man is both free and

determined. Hegel, on the contrary, whose historical determinism is opposed by Kierkegaard's polemic, claimed that he was making freedom intelligible, not undermining it metaphysically.

11. *Concluding Unscientific Postscript* (Princeton, 1941), pp. 61ff.

12. Ibid. p. 70.

13. Ibid. p. 20.

14. Much that Heidegger has to say about authentic and inauthentic existence, and about man's relationship to time, bears a strong resemblance to this passage.

15. Ibid. p. 134 n.

16. Ibid. p. 107.

17. Ibid. p. 108.

18. Kierkegaard not only refuses to try to demonstrate the existence of God or the deity of Christ, he also refuses to try to demonstrate the reality of the self. In this connection we may compare his criticism of Descartes with that of Pascal. Kierkegaard points out that the first word in the famous *cogito, ergo sum*, 'I am thinking,' already contains the assertion, 'I am'; hence it actually says more than the last word. 'What then does the *ergo* mean? There is no conclusion here, for the proposition is a tautology' (*Postscript*, p. 281). And if the 'I' in *cogito* is not a particular self but a purely conceptual *ego*, then the 'I' in *sum* is also purely conceptual; and one has merely asserted that thought exists, but has not proved that an individual person exists.

19. Ibid. pp. 164-5.

KIERKEGAARD

(CONTINUED)

KIERKEGAARD

(CONTINUED)

8. Kierkegaard's Irrationalism

In the light of the evidence now before us, we must examine the question as to the sense in which Kierkegaard may be called an irrationalist. The first point to nail down is that he never denies the appropriateness of objective thinking in mathematics, natural science, the study of historical *facts,* and metaphysical speculation. In all such instances, it undeniably establishes correlations between rationality in the structure of human thinking and rationality in the structure of the world. His protest arises only against those who claim that this is the whole story about either the self or the world, and that therefore objective thinking can be all-inclusive. He is quite willing to admit that anyone who has completely lost touch with the objective world is insane, but, he declares, it does not follow that the opposite extreme leads to pure sanity. On the contrary, 'the absence of inwardness is also madness,'[1] and one can say things that are objectively true and still be crazy. Once an inmate who escaped from an asylum, wanting to deceive people into thinking he was sane, decided that he would be careful to say something objectively true. He saw a ball lying on the ground and put it in his hip pocket; every time it struck him on his hinder parts as he walked, he said: 'Bang, the earth is round.' To be sure, the physician decided that the patient was not yet cured, but he did not assume that mental health could be judged solely by whether the patient uttered scientific truths. There are, in fact, two kinds of madness. One takes the familiar form of retreat into a private world of hallucinations where there is no contact through thinking and feeling with other persons and the external world. The second is not so easily recognized as insanity in our day because it is intimately connected with attitudes we thought were leading toward enlightenment and the triumph of critical intelligence. It is found in the sort of man who knows a great deal about natural science or psychology, and who can therefore manipulate physical processes or human beings with extraordinary expertness, but who himself has somehow become dehumanized. His habit of viewing the world as raw material for experiment, observation, and the dispassionate discovery of laws has made him insensitive to those dimensions of nature and man that can only be apprehended as the unique and mysterious *thisness* of each individual which awakens in us an answering response of feeling. This man has, like a chameleon, taken on the color of his view of the world. It is as though he had a card file, a calculating machine, a laboratory inside of him instead of a heart. And he is crazy.

Kierkegaard is considering not only the dehumanizing effects of scientific objectivity, but also the anonymity and conformity which produce the crowd. He writes as though he could foresee the fateful results in the twentieth century of a conjunction between technology and collectivism. The anonymous man, who needs to escape from the dreadful freedom of being an individual, seeks security by adaptation to the surrounding visible world, and thus fails to develop the inward strength which comes only through striving for faith in the face of irremediable uncertainty. In a worldly sense he can become quite successful. He follows the ideas of his class, his nation, his culture. Like a person unsure of the rules of etiquette, he simply waits to see what fork others will take. Nothing seems to be wrong with him, and yet he lives without ever having established his own relationship to the truth. Therefore such a man is a satire upon what it means to be human, for he is really a marionette. *Freedom dies at that point where man tries to bring his life into conformity with the visible instead of the invisible.*

Yet in his eagerness to stress the supreme importance of ethico-religious decision, Kierkegaard unfortunately asserts that by such decision 'the individual is in the truth even if he should happen to be thus related to what is not true.' [2] He even says, in effect, that our *concept* of God does not matter if the inward attitude we take toward whatever we worship is one of whole-hearted honesty and trust. Undeniably, honesty and faith have a certain value in themselves wherever they are present, but is it not both artificial and perilous to isolate this value from the total situation? Is it not indefensible for Kierkegaard to write as if the inward attitude can be sound even though worship is directed toward an illusion or an idol? The passionate commitments which we have witnessed in Nazism and Communism are enough to supply the answer. Nevertheless, we need to understand why he fell into this major mistake. He would not deny that the ideal solution is personal faith directed toward the real, living God. His point is, however, that an existing individual cannot be on both sides of this relationship at once; hence no man can see with finality how the two facts fit together. So far as the latter, the 'objective' side, goes, one cannot get beyond a postulate. Yet one is not really related with *God* except through passionate affirmation or denial in the face of uncertainty. Hence it is impossible to stop short at the postulate, as agnosticism does, weighing its relative probability. For to do this is actually to make a decision; it is to treat the question of God as though it were a theory, and this is to deny, by implication, that He is a living person. This part of Kierkegaard's argument is sound, but he draws an erroneous conclusion from it. It is one thing to show why an objective approach cannot be the sole method for dealing with religious questions, and why, in so far as it excludes passion and faith, it is intrinsically defective. Yet it is quite another thing to conclude, as he seems to do, that the objective approach is inapplicable to religious questions, and that it cannot be combined with passion and faith. Hence, while his negative warning against rationalism can certainly be accepted, Kierkegaard cannot be swallowed whole by anyone who sees the search for objective truth in any sphere (including the application of scientific findings and methods to the study of religion) as an integral part of his *passionately* affirmed ideal of Christian integrity.

Kierkegaard also ignores a further possibility—that of having demonstrable knowledge of God in some respects and having faith in Him in other respects, as this position is found, for example, in Thomism. As we have seen, he does not regard the arguments on which natural theology rests as philosophically conclusive, and he holds that its method—starting with the world and moving by inference and analogy away from faith—is intrinsically unsuited for entering into communion with God. The issue is a great dividing point in Christian theology. One group holds that there is no virtue in attempting to demonstrate the existence and unity of God, for such knowledge, even if we could attain it, is of little avail unless God is loving and forgiving; and all Christians agree that for the latter belief we are dependent upon His self-revelation in Christ instead of upon rational proof. Even such representatives of liberal Protestantism as Schleiermacher and Ritschl would fall within this group, along with Barth and Brunner, who have reacted violently against these nineteenth-century theologians in other respects, and also against each other. The second group would hold that it is fruitless to talk about God's love and forgiveness except on the basis of His existence, and that though a simple man can accept belief in His existence on faith, a philosophically trained mind has a right, and finds it possible, to demonstrate this existence. Thus God satisfies the intellect when man thinks aright as the heart is satisfied when man wills aright. The first position sets up a conflict between faith and reason representing an inner division within man himself, which it should be the business of Christianity to heal rather than to intensify or perpetuate. Kierkegaard's rejoinder to the second position has already been given. According to him, it attempts to attribute to existing man and his knowledge a condition of final victory over sin, striving, and finitude which will be possible (if at all) only in eternity. There alone could reality be for man, as for God, a system in which faith and reason coincide. But again Richard Kroner's question arises. How does Kierkegaard know this? If he really means what he repeatedly says about belief in God being objectively absurd, about faith in the Paradox standing in direct opposition to all human reason, and about revelation never being understandable even *after* the venture of faith, then it is difficult to see why he habitually refutes Hegel by pointing out contradictions. Although he can, by such means, show that Hegel was wrong in regarding his *Weltanschauung* as an internally coherent system, he cannot show that the *Weltanschauung* itself is false. Once absurdity, contradiction, and irrationality begin to be prized, how are we to differentiate between profound and ridiculous renderings of it?

Yet one point should be lifted out of Kierkegaard's indefensible irrationalism and preserved. Christianity exists not in doctrinal propositions, but in men. Christ was not a professor and the Apostles did not form a little study group for discussing problems in comparative religion. Moreover, the person who at least has passion in his atheism is much closer to God than anyone who toys with theism as a hypothesis. In other words, although Kierkegaard was wrong in holding that the person-to-Person relationship which stands at the center of Christian faith goes counter to thought, he was right in holding that it cannot be produced by thought. This comes out most clearly, perhaps, in connection with the forgiveness of sin. As he says, no one can really feel himself a sinner so long as he merely thinks about the matter, and no one can be relieved of guilt merely by accepting intellectually a doctrine to the effect that his sins are forgiven. So long as one confines himself to a philosophical approach, he never reaches the despair and joy without which sin and forgiveness have not even been encountered, let alone explained.

Furthermore, we should never forget that toward the end of the *Postscript* Kierkegaard re-emphasizes the fact that the Christian uses his understanding, like all other men, in connection with things that are in principle comprehensible. He can see the point of every objection against religious belief, and he should be able to state these objections as clearly as the atheist or the skeptic. He does not run away from the toilsome task of developing the intellect in connection with problems which the intellect is equipped to solve.

Where a matter calls for disciplined knowledge, he does not pretend to be able to deal with it by faith or by any other special sort of insight or intuition. Christianity is not 'wholesome fodder for simpletons because it cannot be thought.' [3] The core which cannot be thought is in a divine act which is incomprehensible to both the wise and the simple; therefore qualitatively all men are on the same footing, although quantitatively it may be especially difficult for clever pates to see why in this instance their cleverness provides no special advantage. The intellect can get rid of nonsense, and the Christian should be as eager to use it for this purpose as anyone else. But the Christian also uses his intellect to discern the limits of understanding; at that point he becomes aware of the incomprehensible, which is not nonsense. This he hangs onto by faith, resisting the attempt to claim that he can go beyond it and live by 'sight' as an incomparably clever metaphysician or seer. Hence, although as we have just seen, Kierkegaard makes some excessive remarks which obscure the true import of his position, his main thesis is not that faith conflicts with reason as such, but rather with reason which has forgotten its own proper limits. Doubtless he was wrong in assuming that to philosophize is, almost necessarily, to forget those limits, and yet the history of metaphysics provides copious support for his assumption.

9. *Protestantism and Monasticism*

Since the main stress in the foregoing discussion of existential thinking has fallen upon the ethical, it is necessary to examine once more the leap from the ethical to the religious. The former is interested solely in one's own reality, whereas the latter is infinitely interested 'in a reality which is not one's own.' [4] Many people are able to plan and sacrifice for the sake of achieving finite goals, but it is rare to find an individual in whose life all finite satisfactions are subordinate to the absolute end, for eternal happiness cannot be included in a list as one good among others. It is a misunderstanding when some earnest gentleman asks to have eternal life explained to him briefly and clearly while he shaves. No explanation has the slightest relevance. His own life is the answer to the question at issue, and the earnest gentleman alone can know whether his life has an absolute *telos* for which he is willing to sacrifice any and all finite goods. To be interested in being Christian 'in so far as professional ambition and family responsibilities will permit' is to try to serve two masters.

Does faith lead, then, necessarily to some form of monasticism? Kierkegaard had to confront this question squarely because a complete renunciation of the world indicates an affirmative answer. He admits that, as compared with a self-satisfied Protestantism which has compromised with the world, monasticism is incomparably superior. He is incensed by sermons that begin by talking about the contrast between virtue and pleasure but gradually make virtue so common sense and profitable that the two become indistinguishable except that one remains a bit more prudent than the other. The real contrast turns out to be between a wise, long-range way of getting advantages for oneself, and an impulsive, short-sighted way. Monasticism is mistaken, not because it protests against this complacent attempt to combine worldly success with Christianity, but because it thinks that inwardness can be achieved by getting rid of the external world. No arrangement can completely remove finite ends, and whether a man lives in the world or in the cloister, he cannot avoid the task involved in sustaining an absolute relationship to the absolute *telos* while remaining in the midst of finitude, temporality, and the temptations of egocentricity and of the body. A man can achieve inwardness while continuing to participate in the ordinary events of life. Thus Kierkegaard must be regarded as attempting to recall Protestantism to its basic principle. It presupposes that all men can live in accordance with that ethical and spiritual responsibility which places no intermediate authorities between the individual and God; it presupposes that all tasks, not merely the ministry or the priesthood, would be seen in the light of divine vocation. But he was also issuing a sharp warning—which was to become devastating—against the perils of abuse which attend the very strength

111

of this Protestant principle. Monasticism at least acknowledges that the attempt to live in both kingdoms at once involves a real problem; it has to be rejected, not for this reason, but because it claims 'merit' for seeming to express what every man owes God (namely, complete fidelity) and because its concept of holiness blurs the absolute distinction between God and man.

But Protestantism must realize that it can become superior to monasticism only by taking seriously the Gospel of voluntary suffering. People want to be thought courageous for facing up to life when the only risks they take are connected with the pursuit of selfish ambitions. Wholly calloused people like to be regarded as bearing their sorrows nobly when their only sorrows are connected with not getting what they want. Then such courage and sorrow are labeled 'Christian.' Consequently one often trembles for himself in church, not because the parson is too severe but because he is far too polite. He ascribes virtues to his hearers in a way which makes any honest man embarrassed.

Nevertheless, a man of common sense will always want to know how he can be sure in advance that the sacrifice which Christianity demands is worth the price. The answer is that anything which can be guaranteed in advance cannot be striven for in an absolute venture. The only 'advantage' Christianity has to offer, a trustful relationship to God, cannot be defined apart from the mode of acquisition. On the surface Christianity seems to make everything easy. By means of the Gospel and God's grace the individual gets salvation without having to do anything himself. But actually self-knowledge, which leads to an awareness of sin, that is, of one's inability to save himself and of one's need for grace, is the precondition without which belief in Christ makes no sense. And this precondition is the hardest thing in the world to meet, for it involves a shattering of man's attempt to be self-sufficient. Even the acceptance of orthodox doctrine, if it omits this precondition with its personal agony and struggle, becomes mere assent to a set of static certainties which closes the door to any saving awakening.

Hence Christianity is paradox. Revelation is signalized by mystery, faith by uncertainty, the ease of accepting God's grace by its difficulty, and religious happiness by suffering. But Christian suffering must be sharply distinguished from external misfortune; for no matter how 'well off' the man of faith may be, he shares in the suffering which all men confront, not because he seeks it but simply because he realizes that he is implicated in it. Therefore when a sermon tries to meet the problem of evil by telling an individual that there are others who are worse off, or that by surviving he will win through to some kind of external success, it is really a piece of sentimental poetry which is helping the hearer to avoid becoming religious. And such discourses are never convincing because the favors of fortune are not, in fact, uniformly bestowed on deserving persons. Instead, the sermon should presuppose that all men are sufferers. Therefore all men need religious faith, for it alone *can* give relief from frustration and anguish by helping a person to realize that there is something worse than earthly tragedy: estrangement from God. Either the clergyman has something to offer that is quite beyond the joys and despairs of finitude, or he is 'a spiritual-secular slobberer in full canonicals.' [5] It is also a complete distortion when someone says that after many failures he finally tried religion, and ever since his business has flourished, his married life has become congenial, and so forth.

The inescapability of religious suffering is connected with the fact that temporal life is a riddle which man cannot answer. He cannot find joy either by immersing himself in temporality or by running away from it. He cannot find serenity by concealing the ultimate uncertainty behind such certainties as the world can offer. Those who try to run away only delude themselves into thinking they have reached bliss without suffering. Perhaps the most serious temptation of all is confronted at that point where a sincere man, having found God in some high moment, thereafter claims possession of Him and ceases to venture lest he risk losing the treasure.

Nevertheless, dependence on God does not involve utter deprecation of what man can do. We have a right to confidence in our capacity to accomplish finite things. It is only when finite accom-

113

plishments are deified, when what man can do is regarded as providing the only values 'really worth while,' that religion should enter with a little jest—so long as one remembers that it is the reality of God, not the believer's own perspicuity, which makes this humanism ludicrous. Protestantism rests on the principle that it is possible to relate all human accomplishments, continually and invisibly, to God. Admittedly this is so strenuous that it is like asking a singer to hit high C at any moment and hold it indefinitely without the slightest outward sign of effort. If it is impossible, then monasticism may be the only honest alternative.

10. Guilt

Kierkegaard admits that instead of going forward to conclusive results, his method leads backward. The existential thinker starts with the task of relating himself absolutely to the absolute *telos;* this requires an inward break with the world; and when one realizes the extent to which he has failed he is aware of being essentially in a condition of guilt. Thus he is farther away from reaching the goal than he was when he started. Yet if each step leads him deeper into a recognition of what it means to exist, then that is, in a sense, progress as compared with the sort of philosophizing which contemplates beautiful goals and then assumes that a man can be off instantaneously, like Icarus, soaring up toward them.

If man's condition is essentially one of guilt, it might seem that he is forever excluded from being related to eternal happiness. Yet if God comes into touch with human life, He reaches man as he actually is, i.e. guilty. As a matter of fact, a man who is remote from his own guilt is also remote from God, because he is remote from himself. Guilt presupposes responsibility, of course, because if existence is intrinsically and necessarily evil (i.e. if creation *is* 'the Fall') then the blame can be thrown on God and man is guiltless. But if man were thus innocent, it could never occur to him to renounce the notion of guilt, as applied to himself, for he would have no consciousness of it to renounce. We can claim quite rightly, in connection with particular instances, that we are innocent, but no one is wholly innocent in the sense of having no guilt-consciousness whatever.

It is only in contrast to eternal happiness that one can apprehend what it means to be in this *condition* of guilt. The moral judgments of society, which are always relative, fail to reach the core of the problem because what is involved is the individual's relationship to God, not how he is to be rated in comparison with his fellow citizens when judged by legal or social standards. And since the condition is an abiding characteristic of human existence, it is childish to think that on a certain day one falls into guilt, then a week goes by when one is innocent, and then something goes wrong again. It is also childish to think in terms of making a fresh start or of deriving comfort from the fact that others are just as bad. If responsibility and guilt characterize all human existence, then consciousness of them must be maintained steadily, not turned on and off in accordance with shifting circumstances. Yet most people have feelings of guilt only in special moments, just as they can only recognize danger when it is right on top of them. In such moments they make holy vows which are promptly forgotten as soon as the peril has passed.

Religion has to do, primarily, with man's basic condition. Its standpoint is relevant to those standards of law, custom, and morality whereby the world judges men to be relatively good and evil, but it should never be equated with them. If what inwardness grasps concerning essential guilt is lacking, one might as well go over to the illusion that bad men and good men alike cannot help being the way they are. Then forgiveness becomes meaningless because responsibility has become meaningless. Perhaps the greatest contrast between religious and civil notions of guilt comes out in the fact that while specific infractions can be dealt with by specific punishments or amendments, the man of faith knows that nothing he can do, in as much as he is temporal, can remove the blockage which stands between him and eternal happiness. He who applies the absolute standard to himself will not be able to live in the blissful

115

confidence that if he keeps the Commandments and is never put in jail, he is a splendid fellow almost too good for this world. Since most people today have lost touch with religious self-understanding, however, 'one often . . . encounters men who are full grown . . . who . . . would undeniably be regarded as promising children if it were the custom for every man to become two hundred and fifty years old.' [6] For they think they can pay for their guilt simply by taking a licking. Even worse, there are many today who think they can deal with the problem by pointing out the continuity between men and animals, or by calling attention to social statistics which show the prevalence of a given practice. But if the individual is higher than the species, and if ethical judgments concerning what groups do come back, finally, to personal conscience, then the attempt to remove guilt by running hither and yon among relative concepts is like trying to prevent a boat from sinking by running from one deck to another.

11. Despair

Early in his career as an author, Kierkegaard drew his reflections about man into something approximating a systematic account in *The Concept of Dread*. Toward the end of his career he does the same thing again in *Sickness unto Death*. The latter book anticipates many of the principles of depth-psychology, but it works them out in direct connection with an interpretation of their theological significance. In it Kierkegaard asserts once again that the main trouble comes from within man not from external fate or fortune. Hence the sickness unto death, despair, has nothing to do with physical illness and mortality, over which Christianity stands triumphant; its locus is the spirit, the self.

We shall concentrate on Kierkegaard's schematic discussion of the self for the sake of the light it throws on the preceding material. The self, he declares, is a synthesis of the infinite and the finite, the eternal and the temporal, freedom and necessity. Because man is not self-sufficient, and because he can achieve true selfhood only

116

by being related aright to God, he falls into despair in connection with his estrangement from God. This takes two basic forms: (a) despair at not willing to be oneself, and (b) despair at willing to be oneself. A third form, despair at not being conscious of having a self, falls below the reflective level and, for our purposes, can be ignored.

Man in despair usually regards himself as a victim of external circumstances, but when he recognizes that the trouble is internal, he only intensifies his predicament if he tries to cure himself. For it is only one whose proper destiny is fellowship with God who could fall into a disease which is intrinsically spiritual. This, then, is Kierkegaard's formulation of the grandeur and the misery of man which we have already met with in Pascal. The same possibilities which mark his superiority over the beasts go hand in hand with the possibility of falling into a condition which, when actualized, may lead to utter meaninglessness and perdition. Unlike a physical illness, despair does not simply run its course once it is contracted; on the contrary, it is being contracted in every instant, for it is related to the eternal in man. Instead of literally killing a person it involves the torment of not being able to die. It manifests man's linkage to eternity in a negative way in that he can consume himself indefinitely without getting rid of the self.

Since the point will call for further discussion in another chapter, we need to be clear that Kierkegaard is here developing a doctrine of human nature. He is not putting forward a statement which is limited to autobiography, for he insists that despair is universal and that we should not be deceived by those persons who declare that they are untouched by it. The most complacent people are those who are least aware of their own difficulties, and their health and security are merely fictitious. When disaster comes along and plunges them into despondency, we are not to assume that everything has really been serene up to that moment; what happens is that a despair which has been present all along, despite the individual's unconsciousness of it, has come to the surface. Such a catastrophe may be salutary if it leads to a cure, but it is perilous if one

117

does not even want to be cured. One who without affectation acknowledges that he is in despair is a step nearer being cured than one who is unconscious of it.

After this preliminary statement of the problem, Kierkegaard carries forward his analysis in accordance with the following scheme: 1. Despair viewed in terms of the factors in the synthesis of selfhood, (a) finitude/infinitude, (b) possibility/necessity. 2. Despair viewed under the aspect of consciousness, (a) unconscious, (b) conscious. Under the last category, conscious despair, appear the two fundamental forms of 'not willing to be oneself,' and 'willing to be oneself' which we shall call, for the sake of brevity, 'weakness' and 'defiance.'

1. (a) Since the self is a synthesis of finitude and infinitude, despair arises when either factor gets out of equilibrium. The despair of 'infinitude' manifests itself in fantasy. Here the role of imagination is fundamental, and it can affect every aspect of experience. Fantastic feeling takes the form of abstract sentimentality about mankind in general and heedlessness toward individuals. Fantastic knowledge involves endless expansion of erudition as an escape. Fantastic willing attaches itself to lofty purposes and resolution which have become detached from the fulfillment of specific conditions in daily tasks. Hence the fantastic individual is isolated from both the real world and the real self. Moreover a genuine relationship with God is impossible for him because God destroys our illusions of being infinite and denies us the fantasies after which we yearn. It goes without saying that a man can be fantastic in these ways and still conduct his life so that he appears to himself and others to be quite normal and happy. The despair of 'finitude' manifests itself in narrow-mindedness and spiritual meanness. A man becomes a dead-level conformist; he loses his individuality in fear of conventions; he represses the impulsive side of his nature instead of using and channeling it. Yet the resulting despair often goes unnoticed because the person is successfully adjusted to the conventions of his group and is wise in the ways of the world. Worldliness is made up of successful men who are not themselves.

118

(b) The despair of 'possibility' arises when one has become detached from the inescapable limitations of life. Here the individual constantly toys with imagined possibilities, but he never matures because he fails to discover which are attainable for him and which are not. Sometimes he yearns for something grandiose he could never accomplish; sometimes he is paralyzed by fear of dreadful possibilities. The despair of 'necessity' issues in fatalism or in philistinism. Fatalism means mute submission and spiritual suffocation. On the other hand, the philistine lives in a trivial province bounded by ordinary possibilities and is therefore spiritless. He cannot cope with reality because it transcends his parrot-wisdom and platitudes. Thinking that he has mastered life, he is impotent before possibilities higher than those he has envisioned. The only real remedy for despair of necessity comes at the point where, so far as human resources are concerned, the individual is completely enslaved. Then the question is whether he can have faith in God, for Whom all things are possible. This faith involves acceptance of one's own destruction—i.e. death to the enslaved self; but instead of being destroyed, the person receives divine help—perhaps by withdrawal of the terror which has enslaved him, perhaps by having to face the terror fully for the first time.

2. (a) 'Unconscious' despair can occur because most men do not regard facing the truth as the highest good. Instead, they want to keep their illusions. When a man is really unhappy but imagines he is happy, he regards anyone who shatters his illusions as a spiteful enemy. Some men deceive themselves by judging everything in terms of sensuous categories—the agreeable and the disagreeable. (Incidentally, this might well be applied to those Freudians who attach an exaggerated explanatory importance to the pleasure-pain principle.) There are others, i.e. philosophers, who deceive themselves by erecting a vast metaphysical system which embraces the whole of reality but has nothing to do with life; then the thinker has to cling to his illusions for the sake of retaining the system. In a sense, ignorance may be bliss; but in another sense, one who is unconscious of his despair is in the worst predicament of all because

119

he is farthest from achieving 'spirit.' Admittedly a distinction between unconscious and conscious despair is an oversimplification, however, for there are many levels of partial clarity and obscurity. For example, a man may know that he is in despair and yet be mystified concerning its cause. If there is such a thing as complete clarity, i.e. full conscious awareness of one's total motivation, then despair disappears as it is reached.

(b) We now come to Kierkegaard's discussion of 'weakness' and 'defiance' which is, in many ways, the heart of the book. The despair of weakness (not willing to be oneself) can take the form of enslavement to outward circumstances. If a man sees himself as just one temporal thing among others, all his wishes, enjoyments, and aspirations have to be 'this-worldly.' But this leaves him at the mercy of external happenings, and prevents him from learning anything through suffering because he is only interested in getting it over with as soon as possible instead of becoming a self through it. It is easy for such a man to wish to be someone else because he thinks that things can be remedied by altering circumstances; therefore if he had so-and-so's wisdom, wealth, or wife, everything would be all right. If reflection intervenes and the individual begins to realize that his troubles originate within himself, he then feels that he is the passive victim of his own defects. Since this seems to be an even more irremediable bondage than slavery to outward circumstances, persons of the 'weak' type tend to run away from reflection as much as possible. As they become older they dismiss despair as a youthful phase which they have now fortunately outgrown, when really youth was the period in which they might have started forward on the long struggle toward self-discovery; in veering away from it and settling down they have regressed to something far more childish. They have become the sort of grown men and women who have as many illusions as children, except that theirs are more encrusted and rigid. To assume that despair is peculiar to youth is to assume that faith, wisdom, and spiritual depth come as a matter of course, like second teeth and a beard. But actually one never enters more deeply

120

into self-understanding merely by becoming older, though it is very easy to run away from it, losing one's capacity for passion and imagination amidst the mediocrity and somberness of middle age.

The despair of weakness can also be found, however, in men who truly thirst after eternity but who have given up hope of ever finding it. Just because this despair is more agonizing and intense, salvation may be nearer, for the wound of reflection has gone too deep to be covered up by evasion. Yet the peril of this form of weakness is that it produces an introverted personality. Such a man has contempt for those who cannot exercise self-control, and he takes pride in his own suppression. Because he wants to be alone and strong, he finds it laughable that the only use our society can make of solitude is as a punishment for criminals. Yet this introversion must be understood as an armor of pride which covers an underlying weakness and hopelessness, and to remain in this condition indefinitely is intolerable. A man must be driven out from behind such armor in order to reach faith. The trouble is, he may turn to vice, suicide, or insanity instead.

In the other form of conscious despair, 'defiance,' man tries to overcome finiteness and necessity on his own power. By sheer assertion of will he wants to make himself free or perfect. No matter what form this self-assertion takes—and it may lead to exertions which look like religious heroism of the highest order—it is atheistic in practice because here a man proposes to create himself according to his own specifications. The *active* form of defiance lacks seriousness; inasmuch as the individual has no judge over him, he is irresponsible, and there is no firmness in his character; at any instant he can destroy everything he has posited and revolt absolutely. Hence all his magnificent feats of will power are built on sand. The *passive* form is one in which the individual is unwilling to hope that his distress is remediable. He accepts temporal suffering, as it were, eternally. Therefore he hates life but he determines to be himself in spite of it. He wills defiantly to be himself with his torment, without any hope of salvation. And it is false to assume that

121

such a person will gladly accept help from God or from another man. He wants help, but on his own terms. He does not like the humiliation of having to accept it unconditionally. He clutches his torment because it gives him the right to be resentful, and he is enraged at the thought of a salvation which might remove this.

On the basis of his psychological analysis of despair, Kierkegaard moves forward into theological interpretation. He holds that the greatness of human spirituality must be seen in light of the fact that God is both the criterion of selfhood and its goal whether men are aware of this or not. The pagan and the natural man have only human standards; hence they are in a sense unconscious of their sin. One wonders in passing how Kierkegaard formed his ideas about pagan and non-Christian cultures, in view of the fact that they prevailingly judge human good and evil in the light of their own conceptions of God. Christianity deepens one's awareness of sin, and therefore it may deepen one's actual sinning because it is so severe that one rebels against it. Yet in offering a deeper apprehension of the problem it at the same time opens the way to a cure.

Kierkegaard always writes about anxiety, guilt, despair, and sin as basic conditions—in contrast to particular, outwardly expressed instances of these same categories. What can be psychologically analyzed as despair *is*, from the theological standpoint, sin; for sin can be defined as despair at not willing to be oneself or at willing to be oneself *before God*. This definition may seem to ignore specific sins, such as theft, murder, adultery, and so on. But Kierkegaard's point is that these spring from despair, and that even if one succeeds in avoiding them, one's whole life may still be mired in sin, for God knows secret wishes and thoughts, not merely overt acts. Therefore the opposite of sin is not 'virtue' but faith. The latter word must not be understood as assent to doctrine; rather, it is the condition which man enters into when, in willing to be himself, he is at the same time transparent before and grounded in God.

People are offended at Christianity because its goal would make man something so extraordinary that we are not able to get it into our heads. Hence it is silly to try to promulgate Christianity by removing the offense. We do not like to admit that the most deep-seated evil is due not to ignorance but to the defiant will. We do not like to admit that if there is salvation for man it comes from beyond himself, and in a form which must be humbly believed by yielding the whole self. Of course we all *know* what the Christian view of sin is, but that is very different from appropriating it—just as a man can say words which show that he has a good conceptual understanding of sacrifice, mercy, and generosity, but when he acts it is obvious that he has not appropriated what he knows. Christianity takes seriously the fact that the evil will perverts the intelligence, whereas the philosopher always needs to overlook this fact. Therefore it stubbornly holds out for a change of the whole man. So long as we are in sin, i.e. estranged from God, all our talk about it is at bottom an excuse, a nervous attempt to justify ourselves without having to be changed. When we confront God's self-revelation which discloses the depths of our condition, and when we realize that so far as our own resources go, sin is insurmountable, the sole alternative is between believing and being offended. But if only a genuine Christian, who is rare, is fully aware of sin, then is not sin in the strict sense also rare? Yes, Kierkegaard is willing to admit that the lives of most men are too spiritless, and their despair too superficial, to be called sinful. Men are subject to fate, pathos, tragedy, without ever realizing what underlies their true condition.

Surely it is an indictment of what passes for Christianity in our age that authentic consciousness of sin is so rare. For most people the daily condition of being in sin is so seldom noticed that it has come to be regarded as normal. Only strikingly bad deeds are counted as new sins, and the rest of the time they assume that everything is going moderately well. Yet it is remaining in the state of sin which is decisive; any particular offense is merely a manifestation of the state. We must think here in terms of a consistent condition of the whole character, and man will always tend to integrate himself around one of the alternatives just mentioned, believing or being offended, having faith in God or faith in human self-sufficiency. In so far as a man enters into Christian faith, he brings to every specific temptation a total, formed character structure which would be impaired if he succumbed. But the other sort of integration is also possible. The slogan 'Man for Himself' [7] can stand for a total orientation which would be threatened if the individual weakened for so much as a moment and gave in to the 'temptation' of depending on a divine source of creation and redemption. In such circumstances obdurate refusal to have anything to do with the theological dimension and with such categories as 'sin' and 'grace' must be understood as a man's last attempt to hold himself together.

On the other hand, however, merely to assert that the Christian understanding of man is profound while the humanistic interpretation is superficial provides no guarantee whatever that one's life fulfills what one is talking about. It is possible to take a Pelagian approach toward consciousness of sin as toward anything else. Then a man feels that if he can only *force* himself to admit his own sinfulness and to follow a path of vicarious suffering, he will be a Christian. Actually, however, this is the opposite of faith, for it depends upon man's accomplishments instead of God's grace. Moreover, much ostensible penitence is bogus; it is a covert way of asserting one's virtue rather than an expression of genuine contrition. Self-castigation and calling oneself a miserable sinner may be a way of maintaining the illusion that, after all, one has a deeply sensitive conscience. Hence to become so preoccupied with sinfulness that one can 'never forgive himself' is unchristian; for God forgives, and real penitents will pray for that forgiveness.

Face to face with Christ, the despairing person either from weakness dare not believe, or from defiance will not believe, in forgiveness. Thus the presence of Christ converts the two fundamental forms of despair into their opposites; for before Him the defiant man wills not to be the self he really is, i.e. a sinner, and wants to dispense with forgiveness, while the weak man despairingly wills to be the sinner he is in such a way that there is no forgiveness. The

124

encounter with God as man's goal and measure therefore brings to expression the deepest estrangement as well as the deepest nearness. Thus we cannot take for granted that penetrating existentially into what Christianity is all about will lead to glad acceptance of God's love; it can also lead to the most extreme form of sin, that of being offended at this love.[8]

It is of course impossible to penetrate into what Christianity is all about so long as the meaning of Christ is explained as reflecting a general principle of God-manhood, such that all men are in some sense 'divine.' This principle can be grasped without making any leap of faith, and it offends nobody. But it cannot be the Gospel's message of forgiveness; for in that message God grants and man needs; there can be no coalescence between divinity and humanity at this point. The misunderstanding which turns the Incarnation into a general principle can only occur where men have forgotten that the individual is higher than the race, and hence come to think of themselves in collective terms—Humanity, or the State—which can then be identified with God. Undeniably Christian belief in the God-man has played a part in the confusion which leads people to believe that man is God. It is as though the confusion were God's fault for coming into human history instead of maintaining His aloofness. But Christian faith can always fight against deifying humanity or the state so long as it remembers that sin pertains to the individual. Concepts, of course, can only deal with 'man' and, as we have seen already, there can be no seriousness about sin so long as it is merely thought about. But before God in Christ only individual men exist, and every individual exists as a sinner. Not even forgiveness destroys the infinite qualitative difference between what it is to be God and what it is to be a man. And not even Christ can remove the possibility that some men will be so offended at Him that His work of mercy turns out to mean the exact opposite, extremest misery, for them. Though He offers what we can never by our freedom bring about, He offers it to our freedom. What He forever is—the self-revelation of God in history—cannot become the truth 'for me' apart from my decision.

125

12. The End of Kierkegaard's Career

During the closing years of his life, Kierkegaard developed the same ideas in an increasingly strident manner. As we now examine his last writings, leading up to and including his attack on Christendom, it will become obvious that this attack was implicit in his point of view from the outset, and that it was clearly foreshadowed in quite early utterances.

The book called *Training in Christianity* begins with a meditation upon the words: 'Come hither, all ye that labor and are heavy laden, and I will give you rest.' This is the invitation of a spiritual physician who takes the initiative in seeking out needy persons. He is willing to share the lot of the lonely man, the wage slave, the sick, the dying, and the desperate. Christ speaks to them in language free from condemnation, offering the peace and forgiveness which all men need. But then Kierkegaard inserts a *Halt!* Instead of pressing forward to accept His invitation, humanity flees in the opposite direction. What is the trouble? The difficulty is that instead of relieving one of poverty and persecution, fidelity to Christ will deepen a man's suffering. The kind of help He offers is not what we expect, and the cure seems to be worse than the disease. From a prudential point of view, the invitation is not at all attractive. No wonder that fashionable men, wearing silk gowns in handsomely carved pulpits, try to tone down the Gospel a bit so as to make it more appealing to their congregations.

In order to drive home his thesis that there is absolute opposition between Christ's mission and all ordinary human standards, Kierkegaard draws an imaginary picture of how His contemporaries judged Jesus. The wise and prudent men are willing to grant that He is an extraordinary person, though of course His claim to be the Messiah seems to them to be somewhat exaggerated. The main trouble is that He is so unbelievably naïve about human nature. Instead of consolidating His position among influential people, He goes about serving the uncultured herd. He makes no provision for

His own future; and although He momentarily enjoys popularity, He is just fool enough to stick by His principles instead of shifting ground when opposition begins to arise. From the standpoint of the wise and prudent it is too bad that some of His sayings can't be edited a bit so as to make them practical, for they obviously contain a certain ethical insight; but it is equally obvious that the Good and the True cannot be effectively pursued by renouncing everything except trouble and hardship. After all, an ethic must be ruled out of court if it imposes too high a standard upon mankind.

A clergyman admires Christ's honesty, but fears His revolutionary intention of starting a new society with fishermen and artisans. After all, progress comes by gradual evolution under the guidance of well-educated leaders, not by destruction of the established order. In the clergyman's opinion, Jesus should present His credentials properly to an ecclesiastical assembly and win a majority vote before claiming to be the Messiah. And so it goes. A philosopher criticizes Christ because He offers only aphoristic utterances instead of a metaphysical system. A statesman regards Him as dangerous, but rests content in the assurance that He will bring about His own downfall because of His failure to build up a strong party on the basis of a definite political program. A solid citizen forbids his son to join Christ's disciples because all of the really 'sound' men—including Pastor Green, who is such a good mixer at the club—will have nothing to do with Him. A mocker finds Him priceless, since if one man can be divine, then any man can be; in fact, the mocker intends to assert tomorrow that *he* is divine, and Christ can't contradict him without undermining His own claim.

Of course, everything turns out as these sensible people foresaw. Christ comes to a bad end. He loses His popular following, falls into conflict with political and ecclesiastical authority, and gets crucified. This is the utmost that secular history can say about Him. Now ask yourself whether you want to accept His help or to run rapidly in the opposite direction. Ask also whether any of us today are really different from those who crucified Him because He exposed the hypocrisy of their claims to virtue. People run away from

127

Him in every age because, instead of removing inconveniences, He brings up the most inconvenient matter of all. Really believing, as He does, that sin is man's ruin, the only help He has to offer is that of divine forgiveness. In fact, Christianity is so demanding that no one will think of accepting it unless he is deeply conscious of his own spiritual misery and enslavement; only then is it possible for him to discern that the Gospel is really gentle and gracious in comparison with his present condition.

The chief objections to accepting the deity of Christ are not intellectual but spring from the fact that we cannot stand to confront the fusion of divine and human goodness He embodies. Accordingly, people who become offended at Him attack one side or the other of this fusion. The first group say that it is blasphemous for a *man* to take upon himself the role of Saviourhood. They resent the exalted claims He makes in being able to forgive sins, cast out demons, and offer His flesh and blood for the redemption of the race. A person can join the Church today, however, without even noticing this possibility of offense. Instead he spends his time puzzling over the dogmas of theological professors without whose help Christianity came into the world, but who are helping to smuggle it out of the world.

The second group of people follow an opposite line of attack. They resent the idea that God, if and when He enters human history, should come as a lowly man, a carpenter's son. Even the disciples could not accept the fact that Christ must suffer, and they deserted Him at the crucial moment. Nevertheless the decisive mark of Christianity is voluntary suffering, and the Church drifts into paganism whenever it confuses Christian suffering with ordinary adversities which do not befall people voluntarily at all. This is like confusing 'selling all that one has, and giving to the poor' with losing one's shirt on the stock exchange. Men can come to terms with natural misfortune in one way or another, but they cannot understand the acceptance of suffering which could be avoided merely by softening the spiritual requirements a bit. When our comprehension is thus brought to a halt, going forward into Christianity involves not a new kind of thinking but a new kind of willing. Lest this statement be misunderstood, Kierkegaard does not conceive of the 'willing' as something which the individual does on his own power. The 'new kind of willing' is man's response to God's grace. It is the 'new creature' who does the 'new willing.' Of course sensible men will not accept suffering unless they see something to be gained by it; and since the only gain Christianity offers is fellowship with God, those who understand gain exclusively in terms of worldly advantage are repelled. Indeed, the criticism that Christianity makes harsh demands of men is far more defensible than the silly apologetics which invite a man to come to church so that he can increase his personal charm, his income, and his circle of influential acquaintances.

Christ's whole life shows that there is no way to reach the triumph which Christianity promises except by sacrifices which grow in proportion with the loftiness of the aim. And since we must either follow Him or reject Him—we cannot gaze at His life as detached spectators—the Gospel puts a pressure upon us that seems cruel. Yet actually it is the world that is cruel. Christian self-sacrifice can always be avoided by playing the game according to the harsh rules of the world, i.e. through the simple expedient of quenching love. Therefore, woe to the church which triumphs in this world; for then it is the world that triumphs. We adjust Christ to suit our own convenience instead of letting our lives be judged by His own. We abolish God and direct our energies toward purely temporal goals. We start down a very broad-minded, humanistic road which is so much in line with modern culture that anyone can easily travel it without altering his life at all. The only trouble is, it leads to hell. Look at the kind of world we live in, and then ask whether it was mere stubbornness which prompted Christ to try to overcome it. Suppose that instead of resisting it, He had adjusted Himself to it— by forgetting the love of God and what man was meant to be.

Kierkegaard assumes that most people will refuse to follow Christ when they grasp what is really involved. But he insists that the question remains for each individual: 'Will *you* follow Him?' When

Christianity began, men took it so seriously that they were enabled to do great and wonderful things; therefore Satan had to change his tactics. He got the Church to imagine that it could domesticate itself within the culture of the age. Then millions flocked to it, and it grew—like a man with dropsy. Now the Church can retain its popularity only by telling people what they want to hear, instead of telling them the truth. Preachers begin to 'defend' the Gospel, and in that moment Satan wins. Congregations are flattered and listen tolerantly when someone begs them please to have a good opinion of Christ; on this condition they pretend to accept Him. As a result it is so safe to be called a Christian today that one can affirm his willingness to die, if need be, for the Gospel, without the slightest danger of being put to the test. Indeed, since discipleship has been abolished and mere admirers of Jesus have been accorded the first rank, there has been a promotion all down the line; at the bottom this has created a class of Christians so comical that they might well be exhibited for money in a sideshow; they are the free-thinkers who have tried to undermine everything essential to Christianity, but who nevertheless resent being forbidden to call themselves 'Christian' so long as the name vaguely connotes kindliness and decency. Thus anti-Christians have now become merely broadminded Christians. Some of them even occupy pulpits. In that case they take the prestige of the ministry, the good reputation, the salary, and the manse—and leave Christ to do the suffering.

In *For Self-Examination* and *Judge for Yourselves!* (the latter was not published until more than twenty years after Kierkegaard's death) Kierkegaard pursues the same themes, but he takes account of the fact that what he is saying can easily be misconstrued as a revival of the doctrine of salvation by works. His main aim, of course, is to show that justification by faith must be understood in terms of a conversion of the whole man which inevitably expresses itself in the transformation of his pattern of life. Whether the Danish Lutheranism of his time was worse than other centers of Protestantism is beside the point. Kierkegaard saw, or at least thought he saw, it betraying the true meaning of justification by faith in two ways: first, by trying to combine it with, or even subordinate it to, a metaphysical interpretation; second, by counting the Church as having already reached a state of grace so that it need only quietly meditate on its good fortune instead of engaging strenuously, in fear and trembling, in the struggle to appropriate what 'following Christ' really implies. Yet it can hardly be denied that Kierkegaard has shifted his ground. Up through the *Postscript,* and even beyond, his thesis is that the presence of faith cannot be judged by outward expression; its renunciation of the world is wholly inward. In his late writings, where he abandons the pseudonyms and indirect communication, Kierkegaard writes as though faith cannot be genuine unless a man follows the Pattern, not only inwardly but also outwardly, i.e. in his works.

In order to try to demonstrate the authentically Protestant character of this later position, Kierkegaard (in *For Self-Examination*) enters into an amusing imaginary conversation with Luther. When Kierkegaard protests that he has faith, Luther replies that no protest is needed if a man has it, while none avails if he does not have it. What Luther wants to know about is the sacrifice made for the Gospel, and when Kierkegaard reiterates that he *must* have faith, since he has described it in more than a dozen books, Luther declares: 'I believe this fellow is mad.' To describe faith only proves that a man has literary gifts, and to shed tears in the process only proves that he is a good actor.

In the conclusion to *Works of Love* Kierkegaard suggests that the best way to test one's faith is to look into the Gospel as a mirror. If a man approaches it with irresoluteness, what he gets back from it is—his own irresoluteness. If a man approaches God with a hard heart, what he gets back seems harsh and severe because it reflects his own hard-heartedness, while if anyone approaches God with loving humility, what he gets back is gracious and enriching. That is why forgiveness on our part is a condition of our being forgiven. How can a man believe that God's forgiveness is real if his own life is an argument against there being such a thing as forgiveness? Conversely, to accuse another man is to accuse oneself. Once

131

a thief stole a hundred-dollar bill and went to a fellow-criminal to get it changed. The latter took the bill into the next room, and when he came back greeted the thief as though he had never seen him before. The thief was so enraged that he took the matter to court, but the first question the impartial judge asked was: 'How did you obtain the hundred dollars?' No man who is aware of God's presence can regard himself as in a strong position for making accusations. He will realize that, once strictness gets started, God can always, so to speak, overbid him. Thus the Gospel is not only a mirror, it is also an Echo which intensifies our voices and takes away all pretensions to merit. If we shout 'I demand *justice!*,' the Echo from heaven will reply, '*I* demand justice!' Who is bold enough to think that he can pass this test? But if we fall on our knees and cry out 'Grace!,' the answer comes back, 'Grace.'

Among other things, Kierkegaard was concerned lest a pedantic approach to the Bible be allowed to soften the impact of its truth. The Bible is a very dangerous book: give it a finger and it will take your whole hand. Yet since it is passed around freely, even to impressionable young people, a way has evidently been found for reducing its power. One efficient device is to weight the conflicting opinions of commentators. Presto! Judgment is suspended, and one can rest in the pleasant assumption that he would certainly follow the Bible's bidding if only he could arrive at a clear exegetical interpretation. No wonder most people ignore the Bible as an antiquated document while the rest read it learnedly—as an antiquated document. The remedy is to look at one's image in the mirror of passages which are quite clear. 'Give all thy goods to feed the poor' and 'Turn the other cheek' are about as hard to understand as 'It's a nice day.' Now it is natural to beg for compassion from God in the face of such difficult requirements, but it is evasive to insert variant interpretations between oneself and the Word, like a boy putting napkins in his pants before a thrashing. Another method for softening the impact of the Bible, of course, is that which tries to turn it into a collection of objective truths. This method keeps its teachings at a safe distance and regards applying them to oneself as morbid and introspective. In order to illustrate the difference (once more) between objective and existential thinking, Kierkegaard retells the story of David and Nathan. David has rationalized his marriage to Bathsheba. He tries to tell himself that it was Uriah's own foolhardiness that got him killed. He tries to tell himself that it is a kingly act on his part to marry the widow of a fallen soldier. After hearing Nathan's story about the ewe lamb (ii Samuel: 11, 12) David remembers his own reputation as a poet and makes some cultivated remarks about the artistry of its presentation. But then Nathan says: 'Thou art the man.' Immediately David's attitude toward the story leaps from being objective to being existential. He already knew at some deep level how guilty he was, but he could evade the knowledge so long as he could maintain a detached, dispassionate attitude. The word 'Thou' applies to him individually; it makes him see himself in the mirror.

In order to be clear about Kierkegaard's intention, we must add that he recognizes the value of Biblical criticism in its proper sphere, just as he has already recognized the value of objective thinking with a similar restriction. We must also remember that he intended his attack to be for the purification, not the destruction, of the Church, and his diatribes, as will become more apparent in a moment, could only have been produced by an intensely religious man. He hoped, quite naïvely, that by means of such arguments as we have just surveyed he would be able to force Bishop Mynster of the Established Church to admit that it was offering a cheap and easy substitute for Christianity, instead of the real article. That would have satisfied Kierkegaard (so he says). But when these books went largely unheeded, he decided that he would have to use dynamite to blast the Church into some sort of honesty. As a result he launched the pamphleteering attack which caused such a horrified sensation in Copenhagen and ended with his death. He fell paralyzed in the street, after writing the last pamphlet, and died a few weeks later.

As our examination of his thought draws to a close with examples taken from this attack, we must remember that his tone is strident and his charges excessive because he regards himself as a lone individual fighting against the whole weight of ecclesiastical and public indifference. It is only fair to add, however, that Kierkegaard both hated and clung to Christianity throughout his life. He discerned the peril of regarding himself as a better Christian than others, and fell into the peril. He contemptuously spurned public recognition, and yearned for it. Ex post facto he interpreted all of his terrible experiences—his 'crazy upbringing,' the broken engagement, the ridicule directed at him by the *Corsair*—as a training in self-offering which had prepared him all along for entering into faith, and it was intolerable for him to think that anyone could reach Christian beatitude cheaply and complacently. Furthermore, it is noteworthy that those who come in for the largest measure of his scorn—bishops, professors, parsons, married men—are precisely those who have enjoyed the 'normal' blessings of accomplishment, recognition, and family life which were within the reach of his gifts—in some ways he *was* the greatest teacher and preacher in Denmark—but were forbidden to him by his peculiar development. Hence two judgments can and must be pronounced upon Kierkegaard which he would have disliked most. He remained so isolated that he was really incapable of love in either the Christian (Agape) or the secular (Eros) sense. And despite the magnificence of his endowments and his literature, his life was pathetic. But no one has a right to make these judgments without first subjecting himself to the sort of self-scrutiny which a sympathetic study of his writings makes unavoidable. And then one who judges him will realize that he is like a thief standing beside a fellow criminal. The important thing is to take him at his word when he says that he does not want to have disciples. Then the defects of his life and thought need not obscure the faith to which he sought to point.

Let us now take a glimpse at the *Attack upon 'Christendom.'* Those who want to contend that Christianity is essentially unhealthy can cite this book as providing ample confirmation, while those who insist that Christianity need not be so unbalanced will find themselves in a camp which Kierkegaard regarded as timid and hypocritical. Let the reader find his own gloves for picking up this hot poker. Kierkegaard was goaded into launching the attack when Professor Martensen, who succeeded Mynster as bishop, delivered a eulogy in which he declared the latter had been a witness to the truth. Kierkegaard withheld his protest for several months, but finally declared that Mynster's preaching omitted the decisive element in Christianity (voluntary renunciation of the world and of self), while the Bishop himself had enjoyed all the comforts and eminence of a brilliant career. It is as ridiculous to call him a 'witness' as to call a woman a 'virgin' when she is surrounded by her numerous troop of children. Nevertheless, Martensen was adamant and preached a Christmas sermon on the text, 'Ye shall be my witnesses' (Acts 1:18). So Kierkegaard picked up the phrase about 'a diversity of gifts' and elaborated upon it. Where Mynster was so gifted at concealing the weaknesses of the Established Church, Martensen is equally gifted in laying them bare. Where Mynster was gifted at yielding shrewdly, Martensen is gifted at trying to bluff it out. Where Mynster was gifted at maintaining the Established Church, maybe Providence has selected a successor who is gifted at killing it. Kierkegaard advised the clergy to ask the new bishop to go easy, since there is not one of them who is not comical when viewed as a witness. As it happened, Martensen's sermon was delivered on the day after Christmas, when the martyrdom of Stephen is commemorated, and he said that the word 'witness' 'rings on this day with a peculiar sound.' Kierkegaard agreed that this is true since either the clergy makes Stephen ridiculous or vice versa.

In the face of ensuing silence, Kierkegaard increased the pressure. He insisted that the complete crew of bishops, deans, priests, congregations, and expensively equipped buildings give rise to a dangerous optical illusion—the illusion that Christianity exists. When the individual thinks of himself, he admits that he is not a Christian; when he thinks of ten neighbors, he *knows* that they aren't; but when the statistics run into hundreds of thousands, the mind becomes confused. In order to cut through the confusion of his age, Luther had to set forth ninety-five theses, but Kierkegaard needs only one:

Christianity does not exist in Denmark. He declares, 'Quite simply, I want honesty.' We claim that in our ordinary self-interested pursuits we are trying to be Christian; this is like claiming that in taking a comfortable trip to London a man is trying to reach the moon since in order to get there he must leave town, and obviously he *has* left town. Besides, no one ever reached the moon so anyone who leaves town can be counted as making the effort. If people will frankly rebel against Christianity Kierkegaard declares that, strangely enough, he is with them; for a frank rebellion can only be made by recognizing what Christianity requires. As it is, however, he cannot tolerate a situation where a well-groomed favorite of the fashionable world mounts the pulpit in a magnificent cathedral, sees before him a congregation of prosperous people, takes as his text: 'God hath elected the base things of the world, and the things that are despised'—and nobody laughs!

Therefore he launches into a bill of particulars in his indictment. What has become of preaching? It has become a form of escapist poetry which transforms something solemn and fearful into a pleasant and perhaps amusing discourse. What has become of the sacraments? So far as baptism is concerned, you must picture a young man who is an agnostic, but who feels constrained to join the Church after he gets married and has a child. He comes forward with another young man who is also an agnostic (the godfather); they stand together at the baptismal font and promise to look after the baby's Christian nurture. So far as the Lord's Supper is concerned, you must picture a business man who knows that everybody has to be hard-headed in order to make a decent profit, but who also knows that unless he is a member of the Church, people may doubt his respectability. Therefore two or three times a year he puts on his best clothes and goes to communion in order to commemorate the suffering and death of Christ.

What has become of theological training? The candidate starts out to seek first the Kingdom of God. But he soon discovers that the first thing he needs to seek is a parish and a salary. Eventually he gets them, but then he discovers that the salary is inadequate because he has now acquired something else—a wife. Everyone expects him to preach about seeking first the Kingdom of God, but nobody expects him to live that way. What has become of Christian education? The parents cannot teach the child that he has been born into a world of sin; childhood is not equipped to comprehend anything so serious. Consequently, parents and teachers babble foolishly about what a beautiful world it is and how God is a great help even though, unfortunately, He cannot be expected to fulfill quite every wish. The child either grows up and repeats this babble, or he comes to a point where he painfully recognizes that his teachers were liars.

What has become of the ministry? There is not one honest minister. They all try to combine being successful professional men with being disciples of Christ, though the combination is impossible. They ought to wear stripes, like convicts, to symbolize their double allegiance. Many parsons have entered the profession because where the general standard of performance is so mediocre, it is easy to reach a position of eminence with a minimum of effort. If a man is bothered by his hypocrisy, all he has to do is go to his wife; she will point out that as long as they have each other, nothing else matters, and besides, as she adds, all the other parsons have the same misgivings. Thus, by disregarding the impractical methods of Jesus, the minister can become the head of a thriving commercial organization which is peddling a phony product. But Christ has given the judgment on all this. If He walked into a church today He would call it not a place of robbers, exactly, but a place of business. No doubt it is shocking to envisage Him with a whip in His hand, using severe language, but this is only because we have made Him into such an insipid, sentimental figure.

So runs Kierkegaard's indictment. But the fact that he published his sermon on 'The Unchangeableness of God' immediately after this outrageous invective shows that he was anxious to have his protest understood as springing from within the Church, not as delivered from the outside. No matter what we think of its content, the motive of his deed stands for the fact that Protestantism can never regard its own ranks as immune to the need for reformation. Occasionally Kierkegaard warns skeptics and mockers against taking comfort in his remarks, even though they would give anything to be able to do what he is doing. Irreligion has no power against sham religion; only religious seriousness—'laughter administered in fear and trembling' [9]—can wield the whip that is needed.

13. Conclusion

Our survey should have made some of Kierkegaard's strengths and weaknesses obvious. He was aware of spiritual disintegration going on beneath the surface of Western civilization at a time when nineteenth-century belief in progress and in the goodness of human nature was in full flower. He anticipated such phenomena as depersonalization and collectivism, depth-psychology, and the Theology of Crisis. He was a poet and a prophet of unquestionable gifts whose great attraction for many men in our day is that he puts into words, with uncanny penetration, their deepest secrets and fears.

But Kierkegaard's own inner ambiguity should make us alert to certain dangers. He was able to formulate several important factors connected with the wholeness of personality only by reaction against his own sickness. This is not to his discredit. But it should be remembered that the man who could diagnose spiritual disease and prescribe the remedy with such acuteness spent most of his life in a desperate struggle with psychosis. Psychosis throws a great deal of light on normal men, and there are schizophrenics whose momentary insights are staggeringly clairvoyant. Having broken with our culture, they can sometimes see it as it really is. Nevertheless, the fact remains that Kierkegaard's illuminating remarks about openness and self-acceptance were written by a man in whom shut-upness and self-hatred continued to the end of his days. The final period, when he thought he had come through to clarity, seems to be the very point at which his desire for martyrdom, his feeling that he alone was right and everyone else wrong, got the upper hand. He was a more appealing figure when, as Johannes Climacus, he confessed with humor that he could describe faith without claiming to have reached it, than he was when he was hurling savage epithets at a dead Mynster and a distinguished Martensen. Furthermore, the intensity of his devotion to an exacting version of Christianity must be seen in connection with his underlying hatred of his upbringing, his sufferings, his destiny; and his rejection of philosophy must be understood in connection with the fact that no available intellectual means were powerful enough to conquer his own skeptical, nihilistic tendencies. In a *Journal* entry for 17 October 1835 he points out how Christianity makes unreasonable demands upon people instead of trying to accommodate itself to human nature; how it requires a radical break with the normal pursuits of worldly existence; how it insists upon a desperate leap of faith instead of constructing a systematic world view. He pictures the genuine Christian as condemning temporal life and as preoccupied with eternal punishment; and he contrasts this Christian with the talented scholars and scientists who have carried forward human progress. For these reasons Kierkegaard at the age of twenty-two was on the verge of rejecting Christianity. Notice that his view of Christianity remains substantially unchanged, even though he turns from rejection toward faith. May not apostasy have lurked in the background of his consciousness to the very end, held at bay by his struggle for faith, while expressing itself obliquely through pseudonyms and at last through an attack on Christendom?

Although for the dominant side of Kierkegaard's personality it was self-evident that existential thinking and Christian faith go hand in hand, what about the submerged side, the side which was 'offended' at faith? In his descriptions real atheism and skepticism—as contrasted with rejection of theistic hypotheses and toying with doubt as a methodological device—are as existential as faith. But Kierkegaard was so preoccupied with demolishing objective thinking that he paid little attention to what would happen if an existentialist were to break away from Christian moorings and pass through the three stages into some *other* form of faith. For Kierkegaard, belief in God set limits to the scope of philosophy, but it also set limits to his own irrationalism, anti-moralism, and revulsion against

139

conventional Christianity. Suppose these limits were removed, what then? Sartre is one answer.

Kierkegaard's influence is most salutary when it is used almost exclusively as a corrective. It is treacherous to try to build a positive view of life or of the Christian faith on the basis of what he furnished. For, in the first place, his attack on philosophy was so predominantly directed against Hegel that it failed to pay sufficient attention to other philosophical possibilities. To be sure, he anticipates several of the defects of naturalism, pragmatism, and even logical positivism, and most of his polemic against humanism, if it is valid at all, is perhaps more devastating in the twentieth century than it was in the nineteenth because the events of the last fifty years have made secular humanism so unstable and implausible. But by closing the door on any possible concordat between Christianity and metaphysics, Kierkegaard overlooked what has become one of the most promising developments within the existentialism of our day—a metaphysics that can do justice to such categories as anxiety, guilt, decision, and mystery without falling into either idealistic or realistic forms of objectivism. A metaphysics which could deal with 'men of flesh and bone' (the phrase is Unamuno's) and with history as drama might revitalize the question about man's relationship to Being, thus rescuing the philosophy of our day from being merely an extension of the scientist's laboratory or a playground for logicians obsessed by semantics. If that were to occur, then a possibility for *rapprochement* between philosophy and Christianity would open up what Kierkegaard failed to discern, for then metaphysics and faith would once again be dealing with the same problems—one might even say the same realities—instead of forever passing each other like bishops on a chess board.

In the second place, Kierkegaard failed to attach as much weight to the problem of community as to the problem of the single individual. Yet if Christianity is true at all, its solution to the peril of 'the crowd' must at the same time be the solution to the peril of isolation. Admittedly Kierkegaard *talked* about both problems, and he represented the 'I-Thou' encounter with God as putting an end to man's estrangement from his neighbor as well as his estrangement from himself. He held that at the level of faith men enter into the only authentic equality, that of being human in the solidarity of guilt and as recipients of God's offer of salvation. Such equality ineradicably underlies, and in the light of eternity abrogates, all the relative degrees of talent, virtue, power, wealth, and wisdom which place barriers between people. Still, no one can read *Works of Love* without suspecting that 'the neighbor,' for all its concreteness as a noun, was an abstraction for Kierkegaard's feeling. And no one can read the pathetic reminder in his last pamphlet that he counted himself as belonging to the plain people, even though they found him ridiculous, without realizing that Kierkegaard (as he there admits) was heterogeneous from first to last. There are as many explanations for why he turned away from marriage as there are pages in *Stages on Life's Way*, but one of them, certainly, was that he could not enter into inter-personal relationships fully and naturally. He was cursed by shut-upness and even when he finally broke through into direct communication, it took the form of a relentless explosion which left him more alone than ever. He could not allow himself to have a wife, a professorship, a pastorate; so long as he was using pseudonyms seriously, he could not even let himself have his own thoughts. Hence, although much that he writes about the Church must be taken to heart by anyone who cares about its vitality, we must remember that the conditions he specifies for spirituality are laid down by a man who never knew much at firsthand about the meaning of fellowship, either religious or secular.

This leads directly to the third point. For all the brilliance of Kierkegaard's remarks about history, they are impossibly one-sided. No matter to what degree personal decision may be operative in historical events, it always occurs in the context of movements which must be viewed in the light of biological, cultural, and other considerations. Kierkegaard does not deny these considerations, but he deprecates them by associating them with Hegel's determinism.

Whereas he strikes an astute and delicate balance in his discussion of the interplay between determinism and freedom in the life of the individual (cf. *The Concept of Dread*), he fails to strike a similar balance in dealing with the question of the historical conditioning of groups and masses. He stressed only one side of that commerce between the individual and the past without which an approach to history is impossible. I cannot make my evaluation of an age, a people, or an event perspicacious solely by coming to terms with what it means for me to exist—though admittedly these same evaluations will be sterile if I have not done so. Any 'decision' on my part about the meaning of historical data must be related to qualities which were really there, and even if I, or my whole epoch, is oblivious to them, they remain there to be ignored or recaptured. Hence the objective as well as the subjective side must be taken into account. For what any individual is, becomes, or decides to be takes place in a continuum which links the present to the past objectively as well as subjectively, and the objective aspect of the linkage is not merely physical or factual but includes meanings as well.

Having made these negative comments, I must add the hope that they will give little comfort to the derisive detractors of Kierkegaard who have merely been nauseated by him instead of discovering his efficacy as a self-styled vomitive. These detractors include a multifarious assortment of people: rationalists, disciples of John Dewey, provers of God and immortality, pro-Freudians, anti-Freudians, Fundamentalists, the Pope, Boston personalists, behaviorists, Buchmanites, socialists, and capitalists. There are also those who have refuted him without reading him; those who have read him but are annoyed because they cannot understand him; and those who, having read and understood him, are enraged by what Jaspers refers to as 'the thorn he stuck in our consciences.'

But there will also be others who rightly find in Kierkegaard a most redoubtable 'knight-errant of faith,' for whom his stringent and sometimes intemperate words come as a drastic self-revelation in the light of God's disclosure of Himself, and we may be sure that this is just as Kierkegaard intended it to be.

142

NOTES

1. *Concluding Unscientific Postscript,* p. 174.
2. Ibid. p. 178.
3. Ibid. p. 495.
4. Ibid. p. 288.
5. Ibid. p. 395 n.
6. Ibid. p. 490.
7. The slogan is deliberately taken over from the title of Erich Fromm's book because Kierkegaard's critique of humanism is patently applicable to Fromm's position there expressed.
8. The whole subsequent development of existentialism has tended to verify this statement, leading to either intense religious commitment or intense atheism.
9. *Attack upon Christendom* (Princeton, 1944), p. 219.

CHAPTER IV

HEIDEGGER

HEIDEGGER

1. Heidegger and Existentialism

The next thinker we shall discuss disclaims being an existentialist, and although he esteems Kierkegaard highly as a religious writer, he makes it clear that, in his opinion, a philosophy which rightly discerns its own task will not be deterred by Kierkegaard's strictures. Heidegger's main aim is to construct an ontology on the basis of which it will be possible to understand both the achievements and the failures of the history of Western metaphysics. He is a very systematic writer who invents his own technical terminology. To be sure, many philosophers have found it necessary to coin new words and meanings in order to express what they have discovered; one need think only of Aristotle and Whitehead. But Heidegger uses the peculiar structure of the German language, including elaborate puns, to further the inner meaning of his argument. Consequently translation is often well-nigh impossible. Sometimes the development of major concepts is also based upon a special use of the root meanings of Greek and Latin words. When all these characteristics are taken into account, his style and method may seem to be as remote as Hegel's from anything existential. Why include such a philosopher in our discussion at all? Admittedly it has become customary to mention him in the same breath with Kierkegaard, Sartre, and others, but is the custom fair either to Heidegger or to the reader?

One answer is that Heidegger has had a tremendous influence

upon the existentialists we shall examine in subsequent chapters. Sartre's conception of Nothingness reflects this influence quite directly, and all the others have found it necessary to take Heidegger's contribution into account no matter how much they may disagree with him. And if we were to examine contemporary Protestant theology in the thought of such writers as Brunner, Bultmann, and Tillich, we would find the same thing to be true.

A more important answer, however, is that Heidegger's system embodies some of the considerations which we took into account at the end of our discussion of Kierkegaard. He is one example of what can happen when existential and metaphysical concerns are fused instead of placed in opposition. Despite the fact that he seeks to transcend both concerns, and apart from what we may think about the success or failure of his particular effort, he is groping in the direction which I regard as one of the most promising in contemporary thought. If, as some writers claim, certain aspects of his *Weltanschauung* can be combined with Christian faith, then the point of view which achieves such a synthesis will be a new departure in modern philosophy and theology. On the other hand, if the main import of his contribution is intrinsically irreconcilable with Christian belief, then the profundity of his thought makes it, in the long run, a much more serious challenge than many of the philosophical tendencies which are now regarded as major threats by Christian apologists.

Martin Heidegger was born in 1889. Although he gave up his original intention of entering the Roman Catholic priesthood, he wrote his dissertation on Duns Scotus. The influence of theological categories on his thinking is largely indirect but traceable down to his present position. Among the great philosophers those on whom he has written most extensively are Plato and Kant, and among recent thinkers those who have influenced him most decisively are Nietzsche and Edmund Husserl, his own teacher. Heidegger was a professor at Marburg when he published the first volume of his *magnum opus* entitled *Being and Time*. The sequel has never appeared, thus opening up possibilities for misunderstanding his real intention.[1] In 1928 he succeeded Husserl at Freiburg where he continued to teach until the end of the Second World War. Because of the fact that he supported the Nazis when they came into power, though he later became somewhat disillusioned, he was forbidden to teach for a time after Germany was taken over by the Allies. In recent years, however, he has returned to writing, and his influence today upon students of philosophy in Germany is probably greater than it was before Hitler came into power.

One of the distinguishing marks of his personality has always been his solitude, and to an outsider it remains a puzzle how anyone who stresses the independence of the individual as Heidegger does could ever have looked with the slightest degree of favor upon Nazism. A conjectural explanation would need to take account of several things. First, his sense of closeness to the soil, especially his native Swabian land. Second, the influence of Nietzsche, which prompted him to feel that Western civilization had become spiritually bankrupt and that a radical transvaluation of values was needed. Third, a mystical tendency which had nowhere to go except to associate itself with his feelings about the homeland. Fourth, a stress upon resoluteness and courage which could easily be channeled in the direction of political decision and martial virtues. But these remain mere conjectures, and the qualities to which they call attention have continued to characterize his thinking since the Nazi debacle as well as before it.

2. Being and Time

In what follows I have not hesitated to abandon Heidegger's technical terminology wherever it makes difficult or impossible an exposition of his meaning in English. Of course a certain amount of distortion is the price paid for lucidity, but since my main purpose is to provide a sketch which will give some notion of his teaching to a person who has not read his works, I have striven for lucidity first and accuracy second. There is little virtue in an 'introduction' which can only become intelligible by reading the German text.

149

The one regrettable, but inescapable, difficulty is that those who are not familiar with the German are unable to protect themselves against the distortions I have felt compelled to introduce.

Heidegger's main desire is to construct an ontology, but unlike classical metaphysics, which approached ontology via cosmology, Heidegger's starting point is man. Here we encounter the first distortion. I have said 'man,' but his word is *Dasein* ('being there'), which has a special connotation in view of its connection with *Sein* ('Being'). Heidegger is interested in man not for the sake of giving a psychological or cultural account, but in man as a peculiar instance of being; even if man is the only instance of *Dasein*—i.e. of 'being there' in this peculiar way—Heidegger's main concern is with the relationship between this instance of Being and the structure of Being, not with man alone. Yet because he has not completed *Being and Time* those who initially regarded that volume as a contribution to philosophical anthropology are scarcely to be blamed.

He begins by distinguishing man from things. Things fall into two classes for Heidegger: either they are simply present (*Verhanden*), or they are seen from the standpoint of their utilizability (*Zuhanden*). In any case, one can obtain firsthand knowledge of what it means to be a man only through one's own existence. Things are grasped by means of objective, general concepts where, for purposes of thought, any particular under a given class may be replaced by any other. But human nature can be grasped directly only as an individual subject. There are aspects of human nature, of course, which can be studied by the sciences and formulated by means of objective concepts. Yet Heidegger stresses the great difference between grasping human existence internally and looking at man externally. The most important feature of being an individual subject is that a man is personally concerned about his own existence, and can come to terms with what he is only by coming to terms with his possibilities. Because a man can make decisions with reference to these possibilities, he can either gain or lose his true self. Against those approaches which merely note in a prosaic way that among the various things which do in fact exist in the world, man is one,

Heidegger insists that man is not a thing in the world. Man is 'Being' in the world; and this is not something to be taken for granted. Indeed, the peculiar characteristics of what it means to be a man tell us something of crucial importance about the structure of Being itself, something we can never learn by means of the natural sciences or cosmology.

Once this point is granted, we realize that any conception of the world that abstracts from man's concern and from the other distinctive characteristics of human existence is bound to be superficial. We must take into account the fact that the individual organizes his conception of the world in the light of how he finds himself placed in it. Consequently Heidegger begins his analysis of the external world with utensils, i.e. with things as they are encountered and disposed of in daily life, instead of with the phenomena of nature as described by science. Thus he begins with the fact that man is primarily concerned with external things as they affect his interests and needs. Even the theoretical pursuits of natural science are, after all, carried on by men who remain within the correlation between concern for their own existence and concern for how the external world affects that existence. Hence it is wrong to claim that an approach which abstracts from this correlation can give an adequate account of man and the world.

Similarly, Heidegger approaches the problem of the self not by trying to talk about an 'I' abstracted from the external world and the human community, but by talking about everyday experience. At this average, anonymous level, the individual lives mainly in terms of 'what one does' or 'what one does not do.' The German word is *Man*, and Heidegger's concept of *das Man* might be roughly translated as 'the anonymous one.' He is largely merged in conventional mass reactions. This is what Heidegger calls the unauthentic existence, and the individual reaches true selfhood only by rising out of it, though naturally he can never completely separate himself from it. Yet even at the unauthentic level, if it were not for the kind of light which human consciousness sheds, 'things' would be neither knowable nor unknowable. That is why, as we have just seen, an account which leaves the subject aside is always a severely limited enterprise; it cannot possibly produce an ontology because it is the human subject who incorporates *knowing* into the structure of Being.

Ideally, one might say that a man should grasp the whole of reality and then reach self-understanding by viewing his own place within the total scheme. Actually, however, it is impossible to philosophize in this way. Man begins by finding himself thrown into existence; he must orientate himself as best he can, and any approximations he may make toward attaining a view of the whole are profoundly affected by this starting point. Man comes into awareness of himself and his surroundings as one left to his own devices and thrown onto his own responsibility. Therefore his attention is directed toward those things, persons, and qualities in himself which can serve his concerns or threaten his existence. His understanding attaches significance to these things—other persons and qualities in himself—in terms of how they may serve the dominant aims thus developed. In so far as the individual moves toward a unified philosophy, he does so not by means of science but by seeing how external and internal factors can be significantly connected with his own potentialities. His search for a unified world view involves interpreting natural laws in the light of human possibilities that they may be made to serve.

To sum up: Man is passively thrown into existence, but after finding himself in the world he can begin to take the initiative in discovering the meaning of his own existence and in disposing of his potentialities accordingly. Therefore he confronts a major decision. Either he can try to interpret himself as one thing among others in the world, subordinating selfhood to thinghood, or he can project his possibilities in such a way that they become that for the sake of which he exists as man. This is the decision between unauthentic and authentic understanding, and it has to be made continually because it is always possible to retrogress.

At the unauthentic level thinking and talking move in the realm of commonplace and uncriticized interpretations; much of man's intellectual energy is given over to mere curiosity, where the new attracts for the sake of its novelty and where what goes by the name of thinking is really a distracted attempt to avoid restlessness. Man is then entirely preoccupied with his everyday concerns; he is lost in externalized anonymity; his joys and sorrows are completely at the mercy of the way things happen. Everything may seem to be completely in order because everyone else seems to be living in the same way. But actually this condition is Heidegger's equivalent for bondage—Original Sin. For in such a condition man is alienated from his authentic possibilities. He may not be enslaved to anything else, but he is enslaved to his own superficial, bogus self. He is continually falling away, not from something he once possessed in the past, but from that true self which is latent in him and which he might be realizing.

Heidegger's discussion of anxiety throws light on this whole matter. Like Kierkegaard and Freud, he distinguishes between 'anxiety' and 'fear.' Fear is directed toward some definite object whereas anxiety is not. Because man is free, he can run away from his possibilities in order to remain at the level of an externalized existence. But his running away is accompanied by anxiety. *What* he is running away from cannot be specified as an object; yet he feels that this 'something' is of a threatening nature. The possibilities of his true self threaten to displace the adjustments whereby he has tried to make room for himself as an item in the world. And this is a real threat, for if these possibilities are followed up man enters into what it means to be an isolated individual. Notice, however, that anxiety has both destructive and constructive aspects, depending on how it is used. It is like a flame which surrounds the portal of freedom. If one is driven away by the flame, he falls still deeper into self-estrangement because he is unable to pass through the door of freedom into the realization of his true self. But if he can face and absorb anxiety, it will be like a flame which drives him through the door. The fact remains that once he crosses the threshold, man is cut off from that commonplace kind of existence where the pattern of his life was determined by the everyday world.

153

The fundamental characteristic of human existence which Heidegger calls 'care' (*Sorge*) reflects this total situation. Man finds that his being is in advance of itself, i.e. he finds himself already existing before he has found out what it means to exist. He is already concerned about the world and the human community before he has discovered the proper relationship of these factors to his own possibilities. Hence Heidegger's analysis of the human situation is crucially connected with his interpretation of temporality. Death is the end whereby a man's existence becomes complete, and man's capacity to anticipate death, to see it as the context within which every moment falls, is the basis for any attempt to grasp his existence as a whole. (The word 'whole' should be understood as connoting an inner, organic unity, not an aggregate.) Heidegger is not talking about death in general; he is talking about the individual anticipating his own death. Here, supremely, the difference between what it means to be a man and what it means to be a thing is underscored. For the purposes of objective thinking, one particular thing is replaceable by another of the same order. So far as external functions of the community are concerned, it may be true that one man is replaceable by another. Where death is concerned, however, no one can take my place; I have to do my own dying. Heidegger wants to give an ontological exposition of the way human existence deals with itself as moving toward death because he regards such an exposition as more fundamental than anything biology, medicine, psychology, ethnology, theology, or philosophical theodicy can say about the same topic. Death is that unique potentiality of *Dasein*— i.e. of 'being there' as man is—which involves *being no more*. And when the individual takes this potentiality upon himself he enters fully into the meaning of isolation, for death cuts off all relations to the world and to other human beings. Moreover, there is no possibility of escaping the anxiety connected with running forward to the thought of death. One can try to treat such anxiety as an occasional, morbid mood, but the effort works only so long as one remains at the unauthentic level. One runs away from the thought of death by becoming completely preoccupied with the world of one's care; tries to treat it exclusively as an external event, like any other event in nature; talks about the fact that 'people die' without identifying the 'people' with 'I.' Hence one runs away from the kind of courage which alone can allow the full dread of death to arise and can stand face to face with it; by superficial attempts to reach tranquillity man estranges himself from his own innermost, absolute potentiality, and in the very effort to run away, he betrays the fact that he is essentially concerned about death.

The authentic attitude toward death, on the other hand, enables a man to see his existence as 'thrown into being toward its own end.' It means freedom for death in the sense that all human potentialities are discerned as accompanied by this one extreme potentiality, the impossibility of existence. Here, as we have seen, the individual enters into complete isolation because none of his concerns for the world or for other people can solve his problem; and since death cannot be overcome, it teaches him that the extreme potentiality of existence is that of renunciation. He sees all his other possibilities in their stark finitude and also understands other human lives as finite wholes which come to an end. He enters into the certainty of death, not as an inevitable external happening, but as something whose inward significance is more certain than anything encountered in the world of objects. The indefiniteness of the moment of its occurrence becomes for him not the occasion for an indefinite postponement of having to face it, but rather the occasion for a continual confrontation with Nothingness.

The contrast between unauthenticity and authenticity may be described in connection with other human characteristics. At the unauthentic level, conscience simply means listening to other people so as to be able to fit in with what 'one' does. But the authentic call of conscience comes from the potentiality of the true self. This call is not based upon what the individual is reputed to be or what he has achieved or what he stands for in the community. It does not offer information about events. There is no sounding of a voice; indeed, conscience speaks only through silence. It goes against one's expectations and wishes in so far as one is immersed in everyday cares. And yet it comes from the self. Efforts to attribute conscience to something outside the self treat it as though it were like our relations to objects—whether the outside source be regarded as God by the theologian or as physiological stimuli by the biologist. Nevertheless the source seems strange because this voice of conscience seeks to turn the individual away from everyday existence; it tells him that the things which men ordinarily regard as normal and acceptable are inadequate because they fall short of his becoming a full, independent self.

Hence the call of conscience makes man aware of guilt. Basically guilt is connected with a deficiency, a lack of something which the individual might become, and all particular feelings of guilt as associated with particular faults or evil deeds must be understood as presupposing this condition of being guilty. The authentic way of dealing with guilt, therefore, does not try to run away from it. Rather, it involves accepting the guilt of not yet having realized what one might become; it regards this as the starting point of human existence; upon this foundation the individual is to project himself into his own potentialities. He can choose himself only by accepting his guilt, for this is the same thing as being willing to listen to the call of conscience which is coming from the authentic self.

Willingness to listen to conscience is also connected with openness—a readiness for the kind of anxiety which accompanies the discovery of what authentic existence requires. Heidegger speaks of this willingness toward conscience, guilt, openness, and anxiety as a *resolve* to become one's own true self even though one must remain in the world. On such resolve is based genuine human fellowship, where one isolated individual truly understands another. This is contrasted with the superficial gregariousness which often passes for having social relations. Resolve so changes the individual that instead of regarding himself as surrounded by circumstances and chance events which provide general conditions and opportunities, he now sees himself as in a situation which is something to be mastered. Similarly, resolve transforms action from being mainly a series of external, practical activities into being primarily a development of inner resources which can be stronger than mere happenings. Heidegger rejects, however, all attempts to ground conscience, guilt, and resolve in a permanent self which transcends the world. He regards substance theories of the self as erroneous because the kind of sameness and permanence they talk about characterizes objects instead of persons. There is no self that transcends man in the midst of his care. Personal identity is not something given; it is something that has to be won through the resolve which leads to isolation and independence while remaining in the midst of the world. Therefore selfhood is to be understood not by abstracting from care, but in terms of existence in and through care. Similarly, it is to be understood not by abstracting from temporality, but by discerning how temporality provides the basis for its structural wholeness. Man's capacity for running forward toward authentic existence by way of resolve is the foundation of authentic existence itself.

This brings us to the point where we must pay special attention to Heidegger's discussion of time and temporality. According to his teaching, man can become a true self only because he can tie the modes of temporality together. Where ordinary conceptions of the future regard it merely as something not yet real, Heidegger interprets it in terms of man's running forward in thought toward his own potentialities of Being. Where ordinary conceptions of the past regard it merely as something which has happened, Heidegger interprets it in terms of taking upon oneself the being-guilty into which one has been thrown. Man can move forward toward his true self only by moving backward so as to incorporate his own past at the same time. Conversely, any segment of the past can be understood only in the light of inner potentialities that it was driving toward or running away from.

Finally, where ordinary conceptions of the present regard it as consisting of the objects that exist in the 'now,' Heidegger interprets it in terms of the resolve which 'renders present,' and actively takes upon itself as a situation to be mastered, whatever it encounter.

Thus resolve, which is essentially directed toward the future, so incorporates the past as to render the present a concrete situation to be dealt with by inner resources. Heidegger even writes as though the future elicits the past so as to engender the present, and he also writes as though the inward structure of temporality produces the continuum of 'time' which we conceive as flowing evenly outside us and apart from us. Man always exists in the present, but the significance of the moment depends on whether it is moving out of the fallenness into which the individual was born toward the authenticity which is possible.

Although man can never stand outside temporality, temporality stands outside itself by producing what Heidegger calls the three 'ecstasies' (*ekstasis:* literally, 'standing out') of past, present, and future. Therefore to regard human consciousness as simply immersed in flux is to miss the essential character of temporality itself. For it is a structural whole, not a flat plane where the moment runs along a line. Each 'ecstasy' implies the other two, and the fact that human existence in care can be a structural whole is based upon this unity of temporality as a structural whole. The unauthentic standpoint misses this because it regards the future merely as something that will happen, looks upon the past as over and done with, and fails to infuse the present with resolve. On the other hand, the authentic standpoint does not leave any of these three ecstasies to mere happening. Hence it is at the opposite pole from an interpretation which detaches events from what they mean in terms of the human significance of filled time. The bearing of a thing upon human interest, and perhaps even the actual position of the thing, may become matters of indifference for pure theory.

For example, the physicist in dealing with time may concentrate on formulas which entirely leave aside the concerns of existing individuals, and his interest in the future may have to do exclusively with whether objects will or will not conform to what his formulas anticipate. Thus science deals with selected, abstract aspects of the world of objects, but we should never take what it can tell us about the objective processes which may characterize physical things as an excuse for forgetting the way in which men deal with time. As soon as questions of significance are raised, the temporal world must be seen as the setting in which man runs forward toward his own possibilities, incorporates his own past, and fills the present with resolve. The care of human existence in the world provides a framework within which scientific findings can be set, but the reverse is impossible; scientific findings cannot provide the framework for understanding the meaning of human existence.

The fully human way to approach the problem of temporality is in terms of historicity. Man as a being in history finds the meaning of his own existence only by taking account of the history of the race. Thus he is implicated in a process different from that which characterizes the changes undergone by objects. The former involves decision; the latter involves only succession. In terms of this usage a mountain, stone, or tree does not have a 'history' in the strict sense. Decision discerns the potentialities of authentic existence which a man can accept out of the heritage he receives. Decision enables him to accept the past in entering upon his destiny instead of having it laid upon him as an unalterable weight. Decision frees man for continuing whatever in his heritage he regards worth repeating. At the authentic level this does not mean blind and automatic conservatism; it means, rather, the establishment of a present kinship with whatever in the past history of a culture has been genuinely original. Thus the appropriation of tradition and the repetition of it in the present, are orientated forward toward the fulfillment of possibilities.

From such a perspective the significance of natural things and events, and the significance of things men have made and used, is seen in light of the fact that the inner core of history is individual existence. The unauthentic approach reverses this order and tries to see the individual as an item in the world-historical process. Therefore it is incapable of taking a firm stand, it is oblivious to genuine potentialities, and it merely 'takes note' of what has happened instead of entering into the human decisions by which events originally happened. An 'objective' approach to history cannot come into real touch with what it is supposedly studying. Only by decision can the individual prepare for an understanding of world history and of his position in it. The only authority a free person will acknowledge in connection with tradition derives from those potentialities which are worth repeating. The facts which a historian studies are meaningless unless they can be related to his personal decisions and to the decisions of the men in the past who produced those monuments, documents, and other materials which he has to interpret. All this must be taken into account if the historian is to study the past in such a way that its implications for the future can be understood. The selection of what is to be studied and interpreted requires an existential choice on his part.

None of this means that he falls into subjectivism in the bad sense. He does not ignore or tamper with factual data. But if his aim is to come into touch with history as it really happened—a goal which is missed entirely if he tries to model his discipline on the way natural sciences deal with objects. It is served only in so far as he can ground his studies in a sound ontology. Once again, from the perspective of the way man deals with history in terms of meaning, it is possible to organize the factual data which a historian must study; but the reverse is quite impossible—to imprison individual, human existence within the framework of a succession of factual data.

Before leaving our discussion of *Being and Time* to examine some of Heidegger's later writings, let us take account of certain points of similarity and difference between him and Kierkegaard. These can be noted without raising questions about whether, in any given instance, the one thinker was consciously following or departing from the other. Some of the similarities are so obvious that a bare listing of them is sufficient. Heidegger's contrast between authenticity and unauthenticity is roughly parallel to Kierkegaard's stress upon the individual as over against the crowd. Both writers insist that a world view in which science, conscience (ethics), and history are to be seen in proper perspective must take its point of departure from personal concern and from what it means to be a self. Both discern that anxiety is linked with freedom, that guilt is to be conceived primarily as a condition (instead of being confined to specific acts), that death hangs over every moment and must be confronted in terms of what it means to the individual. Both see the achievement of true selfhood as involving a renunciation of the world of everyday cares; and man's central problem is diagnosed not as a lack of knowledge but as a lack of resolve. Finally, both insist that historical knowledge must be construed in the light of decision on the part of the historian and on the part of the men of the past whom he is studying.

So far as differences are concerned, the most notable one, on the surface, is that Heidegger is attempting to construct a philosophical system, whereas Kierkegaard was attempting to avoid one. Accordingly, the former wants to get beyond personal experiences which vary with the temperament of the individual. He wants to provide for the inescapability of passionate inwardness, but he hopes to incorporate it into an ontological structure. Whereas Kierkegaard felt that the aesthetic stage, science, speculation, and ethics could only find their proper place in subordination to faith, Heidegger holds that the true interrelationship between subjectivity on the one hand and science and the unauthentic level on the other can be seen only in the light of a structure which includes and transcends both. But the contrast between the two thinkers in these respects is easily exaggerated. We should not attach too much importance to the fact that Heidegger aims at an ontology while Kierkegaard renounces speculation. For the latter's polemic was directed against a type of metaphysics which purports to transcend temporality and human decision, whereas Heidegger places these at the center of his system. Furthermore, although Kierkegaard denied that faith can be regarded as subordinate to any human form of knowledge, he certainly held that both faith and knowledge, so far as their manward side is concerned, are transcended by God. And since Heidegger has refrained from giving positive information about Being-itself which would enable us, *à la* Hegel, to see how each particular level and process fits into the all-embracing whole, he can hardly be accused

161

of offering those 'results' of which Kierkegaard was so profoundly suspicious. Then if we remember Kierkegaard's remark about reality being a system for God, there is a certain similarity about the manner in which both writers point to the ground of Being, while both remain so impressed by its strangeness that they refrain from making direct statements that presuppose its intelligibility.

The most impressive differences arise at another point, however. Heidegger says nothing about faith, about eternity, about a religious stage which is superior to conscience and metaphysics. His 'new sort of willing' is a resolve whereby man answers the call of conscience which comes from himself. For Kierkegaard the 'new sort of willing' is in the first instance a gift of God, and ethico-religious decision is a response to this gift. Furthermore, where Heidegger speaks of getting thrown into existence and of becoming aware of the fact that one is in a condition of guilt, the only term which stands in contrast to what he is describing is 'the possibility of authenticity.' From Kierkegaard's standpoint, on the other hand, coming into existence is due to divine creativity, and the condition of guilt must be set in contrast with an essential goodness which man has lost through his freedom. Since Kierkegaard never represents 'original righteousness' and 'Original Sin' as providing an account of the *temporal* genesis of human life and sin, they must be understood as *Urgeschichte,* i.e. as presuppositions which lie behind the interpretation of history and cannot be derived from historical existence itself. If now we look forward instead of backward, a comparable contrast between the two writers emerges. For Heidegger the meaning of human life is bound up with temporal possibilities. Death is the absolute one which gives structural wholeness to individual existence. On the other hand, Kierkegaard always views the temporal possibilities of human life, which end in death, in light of the possibility of a God-man relationship which is not naturally immanent in temporality. At this level guilt is not merely accepted but overcome; sin is not merely acknowledged, but forgiven. Man becomes what he was created to be, he recovers that true self which he has lost, his freedom is fulfilled by grace, and while suffering in time he is related to eternal beatitude. Hence all human possibilities are to be judged in the light of the presence of God; temporal past and future are to be interpreted in the light of supra-historical categories which have a decisive bearing upon the origin and destiny of man as 'spirit.' But these categories are not the products of speculation. They are gratuitous unless the Eternal has actually entered time in the God-man, and we delude ourselves if we think that we can so transcend historical existence as to weave time and eternity into an intelligible system.

Despite the similarities mentioned above, therefore, these two writers breathe strikingly different atmospheres. Heidegger is cut adrift from Christian moorings. Although he stresses the fact that man can transcend 'time,' he sees the totality of human existence, including knowledge, as contained in the structure of 'temporality.' There is no room in *Being and Time* for anything like Kierkegaard's conception of eternity or for his view of man as a joining of time and eternity.

The issue which arises here is of the utmost importance. One of the charges Christian thinkers hurl at their opponents is that a secular philosophy cannot do justice to the self-transcending character of human existence in its awareness of finitude, guilt, freedom, and destiny, and frequently this charge is thoroughly justifiable. But Heidegger succeeds in taking all these points into account (whether he does justice to them is another question) without introducing anything remotely resembling the Christian conception of God and without making room for Christian belief in eternal life.

Oscar Cullmann's book *Christ and Time* raises misgivings in connection with the same problem from a different angle. He insists that the contrast between eternity and time is philosophical and unbiblical. Accordingly he temporalizes the supra-historical categories which have to do with ultimate origin and destiny by speaking of three 'ages': (a) before Creation, (b) our stream of history, (c) after the Parousia. What Cullmann's book unwittingly shows is that if his exegesis is right, then the New Testament must be supplemented by theologians who are able to set forth a valid contrast between time and eternity, for the notion of temporality becomes meaningless when one tries to apply it to the first and third ages mentioned above. Cullmann writes as though it were possible for us to deal with these problems like men of the first century instead of men of the twentieth. For example, he asks us to accept without explanation the idea that salvation occurs in a *temporal* resurrection; moreover, we are not to fall into body-soul dualism, even though we must accept the Pauline teaching that the interim between the death of our corruptible bodies and the taking on of our spiritual bodies will be spent by the believer 'with Christ.' Finally, Cullmann criticizes Kierkegaard on the ground that his conception of contemporaneity with Christ transfers faith back into the time of the Incarnation instead of moving forward to the third age. This leads him to declare that Kierkegaard undervalues the peculiar significance of the present for redemptive history. These criticisms are utterly mistaken. Admittedly it was only on the basis of an interpretation of 'the Eternal entering history,' which Cullmann does not like, that Kierkegaard was able to develop his idea of contemporaneity with Christ. But this teaching affirms, instead of denying, that the Risen Christ is accessible to men in the present, and Kierkegaard's discussions of redemption explicitly deal with it as pointing forward. Instead of undervaluing the present for redemptive history, Kierkegaard's teaching concerning 'the Moment' stresses it as strongly as possible.

The main reason for introducing Cullmann at this point is that Heidegger's system makes one acutely aware of what can happen in a world view which is confined to temporality even though it stresses the fact that man can transcend flux. As far as I can see, though on this point he is so brief as to be cryptic, Cullmann's 'Biblical' view leaves God in about the same relationship to temporality as Heidegger's view leaves man; and it is hard to imagine a worse fate for God.

3. *The Essence of Truth*

Heidegger's essay on 'The Essence of Truth' [3] can best be regarded as an extension of his distinction between authentic and unauthentic. He begins with the ordinary conception of truth which defines it as arising when percept corresponds with object, and he suggests that the strongest form of this theory occurred in medieval theology. So long as it was believed that the human mind and external things were created by God, it was possible to argue that in so far as both reflect the mind of God they can come into conformity with each other. The unity of the divine creative plan provides the basis for the possibility of knowledge. Recent philosophy, having abandoned this theological ground, holds that no supernatural explanation is needed; the possibility of conformity between thoughts and things should not surprise us in view of the fact that human reason has developed through interaction with the world. But Heidegger points out that recent philosophy has failed to produce an ontology which shows how man and his knowing fit into the structure of Being. Taking for granted that truth consists in conformity between thought and thing, it also assumes that the opposite of truth is simply the nonconformity of a statement, proposition, or idea with the thing to which it refers.

He challenges these recent assumptions by resurrecting some very old questions. Since there is a great difference between thought and thing (e.g. the object is material and spatial, as the proposition is not), how can something completely unlike the object 'conform' to it? If we say that perception or thinking *re-present* the thing in consciousness, we must assume that somehow the object 'comes across the open' into our consciousness while nevertheless remaining just where it is and just as it is. But this accessibility, this openness of the object, cannot be created by the thinking mind or by any act of representation. Consciousness can receive an object that is accessible, but cannot make it accessible.

Therefore Heidegger insists that we need an account of Being

165

which will incorporate the fact that existing things can remain what they are and at the same time be open for cognition.[3] Our ontology will need to make clear how human reason submits to a directive which enjoins it to express what-is just as it is. It will take account of the fact that the real criterion for judging between more and less adequate representations of the object is the openness of the object itself. From the standpoint of such an ontology, the practice of attributing truth exclusively to 'propositions as formulated by minds' is wrong. Truth cannot arise in the mind unless it has already been initiated by the object. Bringing our thinking into conformity with what the object makes accessible is not an automatic process. To accept as a binding criterion what the object makes accessible is a *free* act, and the difference between right and wrong thinking is grounded in freedom. Heidegger's intention at this point is easily misunderstood, however. He is not trying to suggest that volition has anything to do with making a statement true. The kind of freedom he is talking about is not subject to the caprice of man; it is, rather, grounded in the structure of Being. Freedom reveals itself as the acceptance of what-is as it is. This means participating in its openness. Truth comes about not by a correspondence between two utterly disparate factors. Rather, it comes about through the free participation of man in the revelatory 'coming across the open' of the object. Greek thought suggests this at the point where it makes 'the unconcealed' and 'the true' cognate terms. Just as the object can be known only if it opens itself, so the mind can know the object only because freedom enables man to 'ex-pose' (*aus-setzen*) himself, to 'stand out of' (*ex-sistere*) himself, in the act of participation. Freedom and truth coincide where an 'ex-position' of man into the revealed nature of what-is occurs. Hence freedom does not mean the random ability to do and think whatever we please. It means self-transcending acceptance of participation in the revelation of what-is-as-such.

Freedom is thus the unfathomed and essential basis on which man is able to exist. But by 'exist' Heidegger does not mean simply 'continue to survive'; nor does he mean 'finding moral and religious

166

meaning for life' as does Kierkegaard. Rather, he means man's ability to face and to accept the nature of Being-itself. For Heidegger the ability to raise the ontological question and to stand by the onto-logical answer is the core of what makes man human. Man becomes a historical being, i.e. a deciding, resolving being, at that moment when the first thinker asks: 'What is what-is?' This is a question about what-is as a whole, and as an unfolding presence.

One of the most difficult points to make clear is Heidegger's dis-tinction between *Sein* and *Seiende*, for which there are no exact English equivalents. His translators have adopted the device of dis-tinguishing between 'Being' and 'what-is,' and I have followed this usage. The main difficulty is not simply linguistic, however. Heideg-ger wishes to make his readers aware of the difference between Be-ing and every particular instance of what-is, but his intention goes further; he also wishes to distinguish between Being and the totality of that which is. One of his theses is that past metaphysics has not been justified in taking some particular aspect of what-is (e.g. mind or matter) as the clue to what-is as a whole. A second thesis is that by posing the problem about what-is as a whole, metaphysics enters its proper territory, but this only provides the setting and not the answer. Since traditional metaphysics has failed to move beyond this setting, Heidegger in one sense wants to transcend metaphysics, but really his intention is simply to reform and correct the meta-physical enterprise by grounding it in fundamental ontology. Hei-degger's remarks about 'mystery' in this and the succeeding essay must be understood in the light of his assumption that what-is as a whole points beyond itself to Being. And his remarks about human freedom reflect his conviction that man, *Dasein*, has the unique possibility and vocation of being aware of his relationship and the relationship of all things to Being, even though man remains in the midst of what-is.

Instead of saying that man possesses freedom as a property, Heidegger holds that the converse is true. The self-transcending structure of *Dasein* possesses man in such a manner that it confers upon him that relationship with Being which is the distinctive char-

167

acteristic of his history. As we saw at the beginning of this chapter, Heidegger treats *Dasein* as fundamental and human nature as something which participates in it, even though it may be the case that men are the only instances of *Dasein*.

Thus far Heidegger has been seeking to throw into focus the objective side of the problem of truth. Rather than saying that truth is the mark of some correct proposition formulated by a human mind, he asks, 'How does what-is so disclose itself as to invite statements, ideas, and thought which faithfully accept it?' He does not ignore the subjective side, but he insists that our view of the role of man is incomplete if it stops short with truth-and-error as they arise in connection with perceiving or thinking, and thus neglects the ontological position of freedom. A further clarification of his view requires that we make another sharp distinction. By 'what-is in totality' he does not mean the world viewed as an aggregate of objects. This essay has already been referred to as an extension of his distinction between authentic and unauthentic; it is now time to bring out the fact that for him natural science is one example of unauthentic understanding, while his own ontology seems to him an example of authentic understanding. His point can be expressed by saying that wherever natural science has extended the attitude of technical control toward what-is, it has diminished or eclipsed the kind of approach which could be alert to the way whereby what-is opens or reveals itself to us.

The notion that the scientist humbly waits for things to tell him what to think needs to be debunked. To be sure, he submits to certain selected aspects of what reality makes accessible to him, but for the sake of his own purposes of power and control. He submits in order to be able to predict and to arrive at general formulas. The scientist is not really interested in the whole of any individual object for the sake of knowing the whole of what-is in the same manner. Hence Heidegger suggests that if one approaches reality with scientific purposes in mind it may become impossible to approach it with a readiness to be attuned to *whatever* is revealed. It is where what-is remains mysterious, rather than where science has mastered it, that

the metaphysician finds his starting point. And the endless prolifera-
tion of standardized scientific findings, accompanied by the assumption that everything can be known in this way, constitute serious
contemporary obstacles to metaphysical thinking. For these attitudes are indifferent or hostile to the revelatory character of what-is
on which the very possibility of metaphysical truth depends.

Whenever what-is as a whole does succeed in manifesting itself,
and we find ourselves caught up in attunement with it, the event
cuts across the field of our everyday calculations and activities as
something incalculable and incomprehensible. We realize that we
are not dealing simply with items in nature and history. The totality
with which we are now confronted contains all these items, but it
remains something indeterminable, and so long as we fix our attention on particularities, no matter how wide our scope, the totality
remains concealed behind them. This kind of failure to gain access
to the truth must be sharply distinguished from specific instances
of error or ignorance. Just as he has already dealt with guilt as a
condition from which specific instances issue, he now deals with
being in untruth as a condition from which specific instances issue.
Say that we have knowledge of 50 per cent of the items and processes in the world and remain ignorant of 50 per cent. The latter
are unknown, but our failure to apprehend them is not of the same
order as our failure to be attuned to the revelatory character of
what-is as a whole. The latter estrangement from truth cannot be
remedied by increasing our store of knowledge from 50 to 100 per
cent. In fact, the expansion of scientific knowledge may even increase our estrangement by leading to indifference toward the metaphysical problem.

What is it, then, that underlies a participation in essential truth?
Heidegger's answer is: 'Mystery.' Not an isolated mystery concerning this or that, but the single fact that absolute mystery pervades
the whole of human existence. Man finds himself already in the condition of estrangement from essential truth when he sets about the
business of examining his own bits of specific knowledge and ignorance, and one way of leaving the mystery of this estrangement

169

unexplored is to become fully preoccupied with gathering truths about objects. Furthermore man in this fallen condition uses his freedom continually to forget the mystery. He resolves to become interested in things he can hope to change by means of practical activity instead of in revelation of that which is indeterminable. To be sure, man encounters enigmas even in the sphere of practical activity, but he always has some hope of making them unimportant by subordinating them to accomplishments which bring events within his control.

Mystery is not abolished by being ignored. It leaves man to rely on his own resources; abandoned thus, humanity builds its 'world' out of whatever intentions and needs happen to be most suitable and immediate, and rounds out the picture of reality by means of projects, plans, and hopes. Yet the more man takes himself to be the measure of all things, the more he becomes estranged from the ground of truth and regards it as inessential. This turning away from mystery toward the manageable, Heidegger calls 'erring,' and it has marked similarities with what Kierkegaard termed 'existing in untruth.' Here a man can live in error even though he makes no mistakes in scientific findings or logical judgments. Such error is not something outside man, like a ditch he falls into occasionally; it is the basic condition which characterizes all his plans, aims, restlessness, and attempts at self-understanding. Intellectual mistakes are simply the most superficial form of error. The basic error is estrangement from the ground of what-is and hence estrangement from oneself. But there is a potentiality in man which can be evoked if he can face this basic kind of erring and enter into its implications, instead of ignoring or denying it. This is the potentiality of *not allowing* himself to be led astray. This is authentic resolve, which can be evoked only by so catching oneself in the basic condition of error and estrangement as to be directed toward the mystery of human existence.

Where authentic resolve is present, the everyday miseries and needs of men become relatively trivial as compared with their ultimate misery and need. The latter stem from the fact that Being

170

contains the negation of what-is—Nothingness. Hence freedom, which is grounded in Being, is at the same time grounded in Nothingness.[4] Participation in the essence of truth means that human freedom is attuned to the inclusion of Nothingness within the ground of freedom. It is therefore not surprising that when the ontological question presented itself to the Greek mind, a philosophy arose among the Sophists which was an attempt to escape from this question by means of giving dominion to common sense. The Sophists tried to cover up the ultimately problematical character of human existence by entertaining only those questions which can be answered by regarding man as the measure. Ever since, true philosophy has had to manifest a twofold character. First, it has been gentle because it has recognized why life and thinking pervasively remain at the unauthentic level, and the metaphysician himself, although he hopes to rise above this level, knows that he must start there. In the second place, however, true philosophy has been difficult because by authentic resolve it has striven to catch 'existing in untruth' in order to force it to yield the secret it conceals.

Philosophy can acknowledge no outside authority. It cannot receive support from natural science or from theology. It is only by philosophizing—i.e. by living in the courage which faces the metaphysical question—that the eternal laws of truth can be maintained. This is not an enterprise whereby pure reason apprehends eternal essence. On the contrary, metaphysics is a historical act of the whole man, and only by penetrating into the structure of this situation can we see what it means to say that Being includes knowing. Not that we take human nature as the clue to the nature of reality in some theistic or personalistic fashion. On the contrary, man comes to understand himself as possessed by a freedom which is grounded in Being and Nothingness.

In connection with earlier remarks about guilt and conscience we have witnessed the manner in which Heidegger takes categories congenial to Christian theology and uses them in a non-theological way. 'The Essence of Truth' brings the same point to mind with reference to what the theologian would call 'revelation,' 'the tran-

171

scendence of God,' and 'the noetic effects of sin.' Concerning the first, we should note Heidegger's emphasis upon the correlation between (a) what comes to us and (b) man's freedom. This correlation provides the context within which particular instances of correspondence between thought and object become possible; therefore the correlation itself cannot be grasped as an 'object' by a 'thought.' So long as we recall Heidegger's desire to hold aloof from theology, we have no right to claim more than a similarity of structure. But such similarity is discernible when the theologian holds that revelation is actualized only where there is fusion between (a) what comes to man from God and (b) his free response. Heidegger speaks of facing the question of the meaning of Being, whereas the theologian speaks of confronting the self-revelation of God; but both the metaphysical act and the religious act involve decision on the part of the whole man in history, and a major obstacle is to be found not in the way he employs his intellect, but in the way he employs his freedom.

So far as the second expression ('the transcendence of God') is concerned, Heidegger's emphasis on mystery may at first sight seem to place him completely at odds with Christianity. Much that he says about mystery can be understood as an emphatic warning not only against regarding man as the measure, but also against that anthropomorphism upon which belief in a personal God rests. In his 'Letter on Humanism' (p. 76) he writes: 'Being—this is not God nor the ground of the world. Being is farther than all that is and yet it is nearer to man than any one being, be this a rock, an animal, a work of art, a machine, be it an angel or God. Being is what is nearest. But the proximity itself remains farthest from man.' Nevertheless, this same stress upon the mysteriousness and strangeness of Being links Heidegger to the *via negativa* which presupposes the coincidence of Being and Nothing, and which has always acted as a corrective in Christian theology against the perils of anthropomorphism.

No major Christian theologian, in speaking of God as personal, has ever so ignored the otherness of God as to forget that language is at best symbolical or analogical. Some modern theology has unwittingly fallen into the danger of making man the measure by trying to define God by means of some man-world correlation manifest in reason, or feeling, or 'values,' while secular humanism deliberately bases its case on this correlation and leaves God out. Both Heidegger and Barth can be understood as reactions against this pattern of thinking, even though their reactions take very different forms. In Heidegger it is 'Being' which cannot be grasped; in Barth it is the transcendent God. Nevertheless both would claim that what they are referring to puts man's titanism in an embarrassing position. From both perspectives, the attitude of the positivist who wants to confine his attention to verifiable knowledge and manipulatable phenomena rests on a covert form of dogmatism. His kind of certainty looks promising only so long as one turns a blind eye to what it leaves out. From Heidegger's standpoint, it leaves out ontology; from a Christian standpoint, it leaves out God. In both instances, the particular meanings which can be established by science and action fall within a context that may turn out to be meaningless, because the question about 'the meaning of Being'—or, in the case of Christianity, the reality of God—has not been faced. Perhaps the question is unanswerable, but it is escapist to pretend that there is no problem.

Here what Heidegger regards as the essential task of philosophy and what Barth regards as the essential task of theology confront a common foe. The foe is the whole structure and mood of modern civilization which prompts us to believe that the only worthwhile questions and answers about the meaning of human existence are to be found within the man-world correlation. Perhaps it is wrong to assume that one must be able to appreciate the metaphysical question before he can appreciate the theological answer.[5] But at least it cannot be denied that Heidegger's approach to metaphysics creates a situation in which fruitful interplay between philosophy and theology can once again occur, no matter how fierce the struggle between them may turn out to be.

The third expression, 'the noetic effects of sin,' has already been dealt with by implication. Here again, the measure of correspondence between Heidegger and Christian theology should not be exaggerated. The point of similarity to be noticed is that in both instances all human thinking proceeds from a condition which is already one of estrangement from the ground of Being; in so far as man rises out of the condition, he does so not primarily by exercising his intellectual capacities, but by entering with his whole self into a freedom which is related to the transcendent Ground. In Christian theology more is said about the effects of moral evil in corrupting the intelligence than one can find anywhere in Heidegger. Indeed, he does not regard his distinction between authentic and unauthentic as reflecting moral categories and moral judgments, in the ordinary sense, at all. Nevertheless both approaches define 'living in Untruth' in terms of estrangement from the ground of Being and from oneself, and both assume that to rise above such untruth requires a renunciation of the everyday world and its conceptions of joy and sorrow.

4. What Is Metaphysics?

We now turn to consider Heidegger's important essay on 'What Is Metaphysics?' [6] At the outset he lays down two principles. First, every metaphysical question covers the whole range of metaphysical problems. Second, the metaphysical question can only be put in such a way that the questioner is directly involved by his very questioning. In other words, all philosophical problems finally come back to the question mentioned in the preceding essay about the nature of what-is, and this is a question where the meaning of human existence is directly implicated.

If the first definition is true, it means that only metaphysics can provide a unified and inclusive view of the world, and Heidegger is concerned to defend such a thesis against the sort of scientism which would ignore or deprecate metaphysics. For example, he points out the dangers involved in trying to unify knowledge by making all disciplines conform to a mathematical model. Each discipline, he contends, should be allowed to find the kind of strictness appropriate to it, i.e. the kind that will enable it to study its data without distorting them. When one attempts to impose upon history the kind of exactitude appropriate in the physical sciences, one makes it impossible for the historian to deal with events as they really happened. Then if we remember that the pre-scientific and extra-scientific activities of man must be included in our purview, it becomes obvious that the sciences by themselves cannot furnish a unified *Weltanschauung*. Metaphysics can do so because it studies what-is, to which each science and all those human activities which fall outside the scope of science are related.

The positivistic scientist may protest that he does study what-is and nothing else. The scientist, Heidegger grants, pursues one legitimate way of studying what-is, but he makes an extra-scientific assertion whenever he adds: 'That's all there is, there isn't any more.' As a scientist, he has no right to declare that nothing outside his methods is knowable, real, or worth bothering about. As soon as he addresses himself to the problem of whether anything does lie beyond the scope of his methods, he encounters a problem that cannot be dealt with scientifically. The scientist may insist, however, that any attempt to deal with the 'nothing' that lies outside the scope of science is silly, for it is compelled to treat 'nothing' as though it were something. Heidegger admits that logical thought does turn 'nothing' into a 'something.' This is the end of the matter if we assume that anything reason is unable to comprehend cannot be investigated. On the basis of this assumption, the logical activity of negating (e.g. A is not B) explains how the concept 'Nothing' arises. 'Nothing' is simply a summary term for everything that reason has rejected as not real, not thinkable, etc. But, says Heidegger, we at least have the right to ask whether the reverse may not be the case. May not the logical activity of negating be dependent upon 'Nothing' as prior? If so, then reason itself is somehow dependent upon 'Nothing' because what reason asserts is inseparable from its activity of negating. Clearly reason itself cannot decide the issue as to whether it is or is not dependent upon 'Nothing' as prior. Therefore our inquiry into this issue cannot be created by logical activity. What can transcend logical activity? Heidegger answers, 'encounter.' The answer, if there is one, must be *given* to us instead of created by our minds.

How can we possibly go about trying to arrange for an 'encounter with Nothingness'? (This is the title of Helmut Kuhn's book on existentialism.) Heidegger takes his clue from ordinary language. If one asks for an off-hand definition of 'Nothing,' someone might reply: 'Nothing is the opposite of everything that is.' Notice, however, what this definition implies. It suggests that only by first encountering everything that is and then having it succumb to negation could we hope to encounter Nothingness. Therefore our pathway necessarily takes us into metaphysics with its incessant question: 'What is what-is?' But how can a man, a finite being, render 'what-is in its totality' accessible? At a pinch we can think of it as an idea, and then we can imagine it vanishing, but to imagine the obliteration of an idea is very different from imagining the obliteration of what it stands for. Actually we cannot comprehend 'what-is in its totality'; but we can and do find ourselves in the midst of it all the time, and it stands as a reminder that everything finite is contained in this unknowable whole. In moments when we are not preoccupied with external things or with ourselves, a sense for this wholeness may come over us. One example is boredom. Not boredom with a particular book or play or form of work, but finding oneself drifting in the abyss of existence as in a mute fog which draws everything into a queer kind of indifference. The sense of wholeness here comes out in the fact that *everything* is meaningless, pointless, tasteless, colorless. 'What-is in totality' is like a bottomless sea into which all distinctions vanish. But at the opposite extreme we can get a similar sense for this wholeness in the joy we feel in the being—not just the personality, but the being—of someone we love. Then everything is wonderful, meaningful, and positive. Both complete emptiness and complete fullness can characterize our encounter with the 'object' of metaphysics.

The fundamental way in which we become attuned to the Nothingness attending what-is is anxiety. We must remember the earlier distinction between fear and anxiety. The latter is not directed toward something definite; it permeates soul and body; everything withdraws from us, turns against us, and threatens us. There is 'nothing' to hold onto. While everything positive slips away, the only thing that remains and overwhelms us is 'Nothing.' We also slip away from ourselves so that what remains is not a definite 'I,' but a pure 'being-there' (*Dasein*). All of our attempts to say 'yes' to life are powerless in the presence of this kind of anxiety. Indeed, much of our striving to put forward positive interpretations and attitudes merely testifies, obliquely, to the abiding presence of Nothing, which we dread. Our thought systems and our practical activities are attempts to run away from this encounter. The proper way to express what happens when anxiety reveals Nothingness is to say, not that 'what-is in its totality' has been annihilated (this is impossible), but that it has become untenable. This 'making of what-is repulsive' is not annihilation, but nihilation (not *Vernichtung*, but *Nichtung*).

Freedom is grounded in this fusion of what-is and Nothing. Man does not simply rest in existence as one item among the totality of beings. Only because *Dasein* can be projected from the start into Nothing can man so transcend himself as to be self-related. Instead of simply being what he is, man—though he already exists—has to become what he is capable of becoming. One mark of this freedom is the fact that man can ask why there is something instead of nothing. Another mark is that the 'possibility' freedom involves is rooted in Nothing as well as Being. If what-is were simply a datum, and we were simply data, there would be no freedom. Freedom means the possibility of falling away from what-is as well as the possibility of turning toward it. Some may object that if anxiety is connected with freedom, then we should experience it as a continual condition. Heidegger, like Kierkegaard, replies that anxiety may be infrequent as a conscious phenomenon because in one way or another we become preoccupied with external things and activities, thus turning aside from the encounter with Nothingness. But in so doing we thrust ourselves into an anonymous, distracted existence which eloquently testifies to anxiety as a constant possibility even though we manage to prevent it from registering very frequently in consciousness.

Let us return, however, to a consideration of the role of logic. If Heidegger is right, then the 'object' of metaphysics destroys the sovereignty of reason in philosophy. What he calls 'nihilation' is more fundamental than the logical activity of negating, and the latter is only a superficial mode of the former. Conflict between people, the violence of loathing, the pain of refusal, and the bitterness of renunciation are far more powerful forms of nihilating than is the logical act of denial. Their testimony to the pervasiveness of anxiety may be repressed by various methods, but anxiety certainly cannot be removed and conquered by any means at the disposal of intellectual activity. It is only the courageous man who can register, instead of repressing, the deepest awareness of anxiety, and who can at the same time cope with it by other than intellectual or activistic means.

Metaphysics involves a resolute inquiry in which the very meaning of the inquirer's existence is at stake. It looks beyond things as an aggregate to see them in a total perspective. But there is no way of encountering what is beyond this aggregate without at the same time encountering Nothingness. For if every metaphysical question covers the whole range of metaphysics, then the question about Nothing pervades the whole of Being. Classical metaphysics tried to deal with this problem by saying that from nothing comes nothing (*ex nihilo nihil fit*). Christian doctrine, on the other hand, denies this proposition and makes 'Nothing' the essence of all 'beings' apart from God; it declares that from nothing comes *created* being. Both approaches suggest that the problem of Being and the problem of Nothing must be dealt with as a single theme, and Hegel seems to mean this when he declares that pure Being and pure Nothing are one and the same. But the analysis should be carried through to the point where it becomes clear what the inseparability of Being and Nothing really implies. Heidegger concludes that *Being-itself is finite in essence*. And because man (*Dasein*) can transcend himself as projected into Nothing, he can see the essential finitude of Being.

178

Against the Christian doctrine of *creatio ex nihilo,* therefore, Heidegger declares that every being, in so far as it is a being, is made out of nothing (*ex nihilo omne ens qua ens fit*). The Christian is willing to say that all created being comes from nothing because he has God to exempt from the *'nihil.'* But what does Heidegger's own position mean? It may be interpreted in an atheistic sense as meaning that theism implies belief in God as a being higher than man whereas in fact there is no such being. It may also be interpreted as meaning that since Being can only be deployed through finite instances, the contrast between *Seiendes* and *Sein* is identical with the contrast between 'what-is' and 'nothing.' Certainly it must not be taken, however, as implying that Being-itself is identical with the finite world. The whole finite world is contingent, and there is no being (God) which transcends it. But unless Heidegger retains his conviction that Being-itself, which is conjoined with Nothing, transcends it, the whole fabric of his ontology falls to pieces. Concerning this puzzling passage we shall have more to say at the end of this chapter, but no remarks (of mine, at least) can make it anything more than puzzling.

At least it is clear why, from Heidegger's standpoint, natural science cannot tell us about the essential nature of man. This essential nature is the capacity of *Dasein* to go beyond what-is in such a manner that Nothing is revealed as the ground of freedom. Only so can the strangeness of what-is force itself upon us and awaken our wonder. Only because of wonder does the 'Why?' spring to our lips. And only because the 'Why?' is possible can man fulfill his nature. In this sense metaphysics is the essence of human existence, and no scientific discipline can hope to rival its seriousness. In comparison science does not seek the ultimate truth for its own sake; it objectivizes everything it touches, turns it into something calculable, and ignores mystery. Someone might retort that this is far better than to end in Heidegger's nihilism. His reply is to call attention to the fact that every serious attempt to specify Being has to take account of the fact that it is not an object; Being-itself can be denoted only by saying 'not that' in contrasting it with every existing

179

thing. Thus it is right to say that Being never and nowhere exists. What is that which is completely other than what exists? One can answer 'Being,' and one can answer 'Nothing.' Anxiety, which attunes us to this Being-Nothing is ambiguous in the sense that it has both positive and negative aspects. To be ready for this anxiety is the same thing as being able to say 'Yes' to ultimate truth. Religious awe displays a similar ambiguity mixed with both aspiration and dread. Unless man has the courage to encounter Nothingness, he cannot enter into his own essential nature as one capable of asking the metaphysical question.

Finally, Heidegger defends himself against those who dislike his acknowledgment of the limits of reason. He replies by saying that what remains forever closed to logic is always closer to man than anything he can arrange by means of rational formulas. What is this? It is the linkage between his own nature and the truth of Being. Since this relationship between man and ultimate truth can be entered into only by means of freedom, it must be maintained through freedom. That is why man will commit himself to the preservation of this kind of truth no matter what may happen to himself or to anything in existence. This willingness is a kind of sacrificial, thankful response to what has given man his stature, and it requires renunciation of the world. In this metaphysical thinking, which is both act and sacrifice, man dedicates whatever he can make of himself to the preservation of the dignity of Being. Thus it stands above all calculations as to what is expedient or inexpedient, all desires to find an answer to the meaning of life in terms of everyday purposes, all attempts to produce results. Metaphysics is akin to poetry in that the metaphysician seeks to let his words be fashioned by Being while the poet seeks to name the Holy. The thinker and the poet 'dwell near to one another on mountains farthest apart.' [7]

Our examination of 'What Is Metaphysics?' has taken account of the explanatory postscript which was added some years after Heidegger had delivered the essay as his inaugural lecture at Freiburg. Though the lecture repeats certain points discussed earlier in this chapter, important confirmation has been provided for one of the suggestions growing out of the essay 'The Essence of Truth.' Heidegger stands in the tradition of negative mysticism. His remarks about Being and Nothing are strikingly similar to that coincidence between 'the positive divine' and 'the negative divine' which W. T. Stace has recently discussed in his *Time and Eternity*. But Heidegger seems to break with this tradition when he concludes that Being-itself is finite in essence, just as he breaks with Christianity in *Being and Time* by refusing to make room for 'eternity' as transcending the structural whole of temporality.

5. God Is Dead

The last writing we shall examine in this chapter is an essay taken from Heidegger's *Holzwege*. The book is too long to be surveyed as a whole, and I have elected to discuss the essay on 'Nietzsche's Saying: "God is Dead." ' There are two reasons for this. In the first place, although a separate chapter on Nietzsche lies beyond the scope of this volume, Heidegger's treatment will do something to remedy the deficiency. In the second place, many of the same problems we have just dealt with appear here in a new and illuminating context.

Heidegger takes Nietzsche's saying as a symbol for the destiny of Western man, and he construes it as meaning that the whole concept of an intelligible world, transcending the sensible world, has lost its power. Thus the expression 'God is dead' applies not only to Christian belief but to the total tradition of Western metaphysics. Before going further, it is necessary to quote extensively from the relevant passage in Nietzsche's book, *Joyful Wisdom:* [8]

'Have you ever heard of the madman who on a bright morning lighted a lantern and ran to the market-place calling out unceasingly: "I seek God!"— As there were many people standing about who did not believe in God, he caused a great deal of amusement. Why! Is he lost? said one. Has he strayed away like a child? said another. Or does he keep himself hidden? Is he afraid of us? Has he taken a sea-voyage? Has he emigrated?— the people cried out laughingly . . . The insane man jumped into their midst and transfixed them with his glances. "Where is God gone?" he called out. "I mean to tell you! *We have killed him*—you and I! We are all his murderers! But how have we done it? How were we able to drink up the sea? Who gave us the sponge to wipe away the whole horizon? What did we do when we loosened this earth from its sun? Whither does it now move? Whither do we move? Away from all suns? Do we not dash on unceasingly? Backwards, sideways, foreward, in all directions? Is there still an above and below? Do we not stray, as through infinite nothingness? Does not empty space breathe upon us? Has it not become colder? Does not night come on continually, darker and darker? Shall we not have to light lanterns in the morning? Do we not hear the noise of the grave-diggers who are burying God? . . . God is dead! God remains dead! And we have killed! How shall we console ourselves? . . . The holiest and the mightiest that the world has hitherto possessed, has bled to death under our knife,—who will wipe the blood from us? With what water could we cleanse ourselves? . . . Is not the magnitude of this deed too great for us? Shall we not ourselves have to become Gods, merely to seem worthy of it? There never was a greater event, —and on account of it, all who are born after us belong to a higher history than any . . . hitherto!"— Here the madman was silent and looked again at his hearers; they also were silent and looked at him in surprise. At last he threw his lantern on the ground, so that it broke in pieces and was extinguished. "I come too early," he then said, "I am not yet at the right time. This prodigious event is still on its way,—it has not yet reached men's ears. Lightning and thunder need time, the light of the stars needs time, deeds need time, even after they are done, to be seen and heard. This deed is as yet further from them than the furthest star,—*and yet they have done it!*" It is further stated that the madman made his way into different churches on the same day, and there intoned his *Requiem aeternam deo.* When led out and called to account, he always gave the reply: "What are these churches now, if they are not the tombs and monuments of God?"'

The death of God leads to nihilism, but Heidegger insists that nihilism is not the invention of a few philosophers in recent times. On the contrary, it expresses a whole spiritual movement which has come to the surface in power politics and catastrophe. *Beneath* the surface lies man's awareness of the strangeness, the sinister character, of Being-itself. The intellectual rejection of belief in God is merely a consequence, not a cause, of the fundamental revolution which has been taking place.

Nietzsche believed that the old norms of transcendent goodness, truth, and beauty were dead, and that it was necessary for modern man to say 'No' to them. But he regarded this destruction as a transitional phase in the preparation of a new stage of history. In it man will himself take over the task of creating value which will be defined in terms of what preserves and enhances life amidst the struggle for survival. This is what Nietzsche called 'the transvaluation of all values,' and in the new ethic, as he conceived it, there would be no fixed norms. Our aims will reflect the endless striving and dynamism of life; they will disclose the facts that life never stands still and that when it stops expanding it has already begun to decay. He holds that this 'will to power' runs through all existence, and that man enters into his proper dignity at the point where he becomes conscious of this principle and bases his existence upon it rather than upon God or eternal ideals.

But what Nietzsche meant by 'the will to power' is grossly misunderstood if it is associated merely with unbridled selfishness and cruelty. It is a principle whereby man consciously orders the available possibilities of his environment, and to reach this sort of mastery one must be disciplined, must first of all master himself and his own capacities. Furthermore, the primary means by which new possibilities are to be envisioned is *art*, by which Nietzsche meant to include not merely poetry, painting, and music, but the whole range of man's capacity to participate in creativity from biological

183

reproduction to the development of great institutions. Most important of all, the idea of 'will to power' must be understood as a *philosophical* doctrine. Nietzsche says, in effect, that we apprehend reality only through ourselves as wills. Therefore we must understand our systems of knowledge and ethics as reflecting this. We have no knowledge that is really separable from the way in which we evaluate, and there are no ethical standards separable from the way in which *we* justify and condemn. Consequently we are free to discern that what is 'right' satisfies the will and enhances power. Here Heidegger adds that Nietzsche has succeeded in describing the principle which actually governs human affairs in our age whether we choose to admit it or not.

God had to die before man could pass into this higher dimension where he realizes that he, man, determines and establishes values. On the other side of the transition stands the Superman. But Nietzsche is not talking about a political conqueror; he is talking about a new kind of humanity fit to take over mastery of the earth. The point is not that man usurps God's place. God's place is already empty. Rather, man now realizes that since there is nothing transcendent to fall back upon, he must no longer be dependent; he must take upon himself the task of self-realization and self-affirmation. But the madman's remarks about the loss of all sense of direction, the cutting loose of the earth from the sun, the drifting through infinite nothingness, show that Nietzsche was well aware of the perils and the poignancy of the situation.

Heidegger makes it clear that, in his opinion, Nietzsche dodged the ultimate issue. Even if what he says about nature and man is correct, Nietzsche never faced the difference between human existence and Being. But Heidegger is lenient because, as he sees it, no one else has solved the problem which arises at this point. Thinking must operate by means of its own structures, and no one can stand outside these structures to see whether or not they are in harmony with Being. Therefore the goal of metaphysics always transcends man's grasp, and yet all attempts to avoid metaphysics really presuppose this problem instead of obliterating it. If Nietzsche is right that the Christian and Platonic systems of the past are dead, then we must face the issue today in a new way. Nietzsche dodged the issue by trying to center his vision of reality in man-as-valuer instead of in Being. Yet his work should warn us that the most fatal blow against God takes the form of trying to equate him with our human ways of valuing.

Agnosticism and atheism are innocuous compared with the damage which theology suffered in the nineteenth century when it attempted to construe the ground of Being in terms of the so-called moral argument for theism and Ritschl's interpretation of value judgments. For this line of approach means that God is no longer thought of, in the first instance, as Being. It condemns theology to following a route which also evades the metaphysical question. And yet this murderous blow against the integrity of theology was struck by theologians themselves. That is one of the reasons why religious perspectives today are as inadequate as the prevailing political, economic, sociological, and scientific interpretations for explaining what has happened to man, inwardly, in our era.

The plain fact is that man stands face to face with Nothingness, and in order to enter into the implications of this fact, we must remember what the madman said. He called out unceasingly: 'I seek God.' He was crazy because he had turned away from the ideals which men had previously believed in. The madman knows that they have become empty. But notice that he has nothing in common with the complacent scoffers who stand around making jokes. These men no longer seek God. They are heedless of what they have lost, and they are blind to the peril which confronts man as he must take on the burden of a dreadful freedom in the face of emptiness. In contrast with them, the madman is an authentic thinker calling out *de profundis*. Do we not still hear his cry, Heidegger asks? May we not also begin our thinking and our search at the point where we realize that all security has vanished because we can find it neither through obedience to a traditional God, nor through that rationalism which, though it has been glorified for centuries, is the stubbornest adversary of thought?

6. Conclusions

A more extensive treatment of Heidegger would have to take account of his essays on Hölderlin, two of which have been translated in *Existence and Being*. For our purposes it is sufficient to point out that Heidegger finds in Hölderlin similarities to what has just been discussed in connection with the madman in Nietzsche's parable. Hölderlin also 'seeks God'; not a God who is dead, but a God who is absent. In a period when traditional certainties have broken down and men have become so preoccupied with things that they have lost touch with the holy, the poet's attitude can only be one of expectant waiting; it can only be a yearning for homecoming. The everyday world is not his true home, yet the old revelations have lost their power to guide him. In keeping with his rejection of rationalism, Heidegger suggests that the poet and the true philosopher stand side by side (on mountains farthest apart) waiting for that word from Being-itself which will enable them to express the mystery. In both Hölderlin and Heidegger this expectancy takes the form of a non-Christian piety; it assumes that 'the word' for our day and for the future has not yet been spoken. On the other hand, one may also see in it an awareness of transcendence, mystery, and freedom which must be recaptured if the meaning of Christ the Word is to be found again. Indeed, Heidegger's hints (for they are no more) concerning the relationships among poetry, metaphysics, and religion have implications much broader than his interest in Hölderlin, and many of us have discovered that some of the poets, dramatists, and novelists of our day have a deeper insight into Christian symbols, even when they reject them, than the analytical philosophers—even when they happen to be theists.

In conclusion we must ask what, precisely, is Heidegger's attitude toward Christian theology, and what is his ultimate position? Unfortunately it is impossible to answer these questions confidently because he has not given us explicit guidance. He admits that to ask 'What is metaphysics?' is to go beyond metaphysics, but does this

186

mean more than going beyond what-is to ask about its relation to Being? Certainly it does not prompt Heidegger to suggest that revelation may supply answers to questions which philosophy can only pose. Although, as we have observed, there are parallels between 'Being' in his philosophy and 'divine self-disclosure' in Christian theology, he seems content to ignore the parallelism. His concern is with Being, and he leaves the question about God to the theologian.

There are, I think, two reasons for this. In the first place, Heidegger seems to assume that in most Christian theology 'God' is conceived of as *a* being. This may be because language often connotes God as personal; it may also be because natural theology has taken categories derived from the world of what-is, such as substance and cause, and applied them to God. In the second place, even if by stressing the transcendence of God theology sets up a sharp distinction between Him and the world so that He cannot be regarded either as a being or as the world-ground, Heidegger does not, apparently, regard it as self-evident that God, as so conceived, is the same as Being.

What, then, is Being according to Heidegger's philosophy? Two contrasting possibilities open up. The first leads to a sort of Stoicism —but without Stoicism's belief in the rational character of the structure of reality. According to this line of interpretation man alone can so transcend time and the external world as to face the question concerning Being, and what he encounters in this metaphysical act is the realization that Being is strange and alien. Let us put the point in quite ordinary language. The things and concerns which seem so important to us, and which seem to give significance to our lives, come from nothing and return to nothing. But it is man's peculiar capacity and vocation to realize this, and to be able to see all that is in a true perspective instead of being deluded into attaching a false meaning to it. This is the only sense in which man can 'transcend' meaninglessness and death. Man can, as it were, become superior to Being by realizing his utter subjection to it; the seemingly nonsensical relationship between *Sein* and *Dasein* can become a triumphant one if man will say 'Yes' to Being instead of to his own illusions; estrangement can be overcome by facing, not evading, the relinquishment of everyday meanings. The only way to outwit death is to be already, in principle, 'dead to the world.'

The second line of interpretation leads to much more positive results. Here the function of nihilating is that of making us aware of the contrast between what-is and Being, and the only way to characterize the latter is to say that it is *not* a particular being or the sum of beings. But does not Christian theology imply something similar whenever it seeks to express the contrast between God as transcendent and the world as contingent? The difficulty, for both Heidegger and Christian theology, is that if no predicates taken from the man-world correlation can be directly applied to Being or God, then these concepts seem devoid of content. One might argue that through its trust in revelation Christian theology has a resource for meeting the difficulty, one which Heidegger needs but does not acknowledge. If one keeps in mind the positive implications of 'Being' as well as the negative implications of 'Nothing' in Heidegger's conjunctive use of these terms, however, his renunciation of everyday concerns can be understood as the entrance of man into a relationship which means *more*, not less, than they do, and in comparison with which they are 'as nothing.' Being, viewed positively as the source of all that is and of human freedom, provides for man the *possibility* of a true home (instead of anonymous domestication) and a true self. The stress falls upon the word 'possibility' because man in his freedom can turn toward either unauthenticity or authenticity; either he can sink into the man-world correlation or he can nihilate it, responding to the mysterious call coming from beyond it, so as to be his 'true self'—i.e. related to Being while remaining in the midst of everyday existence. From such a perspective freedom is not, as it is for Sartre, an absurdity.

In Sartre's interpretation, as we shall later see, human life is regarded as utterly alone and groundless; the only remedy—which admittedly has its limits—is 'engagement' with other men in the enterprise of freedom. This fits in well with the first alternative mentioned above, but Heidegger has declared that Sartre's views do not represent his own intentions. We have already noticed the manner in which Heidegger refuses to regard man as the measure; he is willing to call his philosophy 'humanistic' only in the sense that man can apprehend truth, not as his own invention (as in Sartre) but as coming from Being. For Heidegger the important thing is to recognize that Being is essential no matter what the consequences may be for man and the world. Therefore man is 'important' chiefly, perhaps only, in the sense that through becoming freely attuned to Being he can cast off illusions as to his own self-importance.

Once again we must take into account the fact that mysticism may offer a clue for understanding both the negative and the positive implications of Heidegger's position. Take, for example, his remarks about man's being thrown into existence. They can be construed as meaning that man, with his distinctive endowment of rationality, freedom, and imagination, appears 'for no reason at all' in a universe whose ultimate structure makes a mockery of these endowments. But they can also be construed as reflecting something like the mystic's awareness of the strangeness of the temporal world, its petty pace, the emptiness of its pretensions, the strangeness of man's growing into freedom while he remains conditioned by his body, his physical environment, his age, and culture. The mystic knows that man, while remaining in this world, can enter into relationship with what lies behind and above it. For him, too, man is thrown into an alien world, but in the course of this brief transit which leads inexorably to death, he may discover that existence is a pilgrimage and a vocation. Like Heidegger also, the mystic is keenly aware of the inadequacy of all language fashioned within the man-world correlation (which is of course the only language he believes is available), whenever one attempts to characterize the fullness and emptiness, the 'allness' and the 'emptiness' of ultimate reality. 'Near and hard to grasp is the god,' says Hölderlin, the poet whom Heidegger greatly admires.[9]

And yet Heidegger does not want to use religious symbols for communicating these characteristics, and he persists in identifying the word 'God' with the sort of theology he repudiates which treats God as if He were *a* being. Is it far-fetched, then, to assume that Heidegger is reacting not so much against 'God' as simply against sacrilege? Would not an adequate theological approach have to affirm some sort of genuine equation between Being and God? This line of thought is followed by a thinker such as Gabriel Marcel, whose thought we shall try to expound in the final chapter of this book. But before we trace this possibility we must look carefully at Sartre and Jaspers, by whom in different ways the possibility is explicitly denied.

NOTES

1. Actually the first volume of *Sein und Zeit,* published in Germany in 1927, contains only two-thirds of Part One. The projected scheme for the entire work is as follows: Part One—(1) an analysis of *Dasein;* (2) the temporality of *Dasein;* (3) construction of the resulting ontology. Part Two was to consist of a phenomenological critique of the entire history of ontology. The first volume has not as yet been translated into English.

2. See Werner Brock's account of this essay in *Existence and Being* (London: Vision Press, 1949), pp. 142-83.

3. This passage is directed not only against idealism, but also against the claim of Husserl, Heidegger's teacher, that phenomenology can be presuppositionless. One of the differences between Sartre and Heidegger is that the former approaches ontology via phenomenology whereas the latter aims at a form of fundamental ontology which is prior to distinctions between subject and object, and between theoretical and practical reason, as in Kant. This fundamental ontology is present in the background from the very beginning of *Sein und Zeit.* Heidegger's purpose is to approach Being, not via some particular method, but solely through the relationship which Being-itself establishes with man. Only in this light can his remarks about the failures and accomplishments of metaphysics be understood.

4. Notice that here we have to do, as also in the work of Nicholas Berdyaev, with a doctrine of 'meonic' or uncreated freedom.

5. Quoted in *Existence and Being*, edited by Werner Brock, p. 157 n.

6. See the summary and review of this essay by Brock in op. cit. pp. 218-48.

7. Ibid. p. 392.

8. See the translation by Thomas Common in *The Complete Works of Friedrich Nietzsche* (London: Allen & Unwin, 1909), sec. 125.

9. For the complete context, see the translation of Hölderlin's 'The Patmos Hymn' and 'The Poet's Vocation' in *Existence and Being*, pp. 275, 286.

SARTRE

SARTRE

1. Introduction to Being and Nothing

Jean-Paul Sartre was born in 1905. He studied at the École Normale Supérieure in Paris, and later, in Germany, he attended Husserl's lectures and studied with Heidegger. After he became a teacher of philosophy, first in Le Havre and then in Paris, he began to apply the phenomenological method to studies of 'Imagination' (1938) and 'Emotion' (1939). His first novel, *Nausea*, which quickly established his reputation in the literary world, expounds in connection with concrete situations some of the themes and attitudes which are to be found in his philosophical writings. After being interned in a prison camp in Germany during the war, he returned to occupied France and participated in the resistance. One of his plays, *The Flies*, got past the Nazi censor and conveyed its message through retelling the Orestes story about killing tyrants in order to liberate a people. His plays and short stories depict human beings trapped by social injustice, war, and the spiritual decay of civilization, as well as by their own psychological compulsions—trapped, and yet inescapably responsible for the way in which they deal with the circumstances which confront them. Under the general title of *Roads to Freedom*, he has projected a series of four novels, the first three of which have been translated into English. Here, against the backdrop of the years leading up to the war and into the period of the fall of France, he sketches how the major social forces of our time affect the lives of specific individuals. Because of his talent as a novelist and dramatist, Sartre has reached the public on a wider scale than any other existentialist writer, with the unfortunate consequence that a hazy impression of bohemian decadence has become identified, in some minds, with all existentialism. Naturally far more people are acquainted with Sartre through his literary works than through his big philosophical book, *Being and Nothing*, or even through his essay entitled 'Existentialism.'

Our treatment of him will be comparatively brief, not because of any inclination to dismiss him as unimportant, but due to the fact that we are primarily concerned with the relationship between existentialism and religious belief, and the material in Sartre relevant to that theme is meager compared with the total extent of his thought. An exhaustive survey of his philosophy would have to pay much more attention to his theories of knowledge and aesthetics, for example, than we shall attempt. There have been many intemperate attacks on him, but the most effective critics have concentrated, of course, on his philosophical statements rather than on his personal behavior or the antics of his followers. Thus, for example, Marcel writes: 'To begin with, my attack is not polemical. I consider it important, as well as, in the first place, honest, to admit fully the validity and the power of some of Sartre's premises, and I shall insist on this, perhaps at the risk of shocking some of my readers . . . I believe . . . that Sartre's philosophy [is] much too impressive, particularly to young people, not to be examined with the utmost seriousness and objectivity; though I admit that there is in Sartre a certain taste and propensity for scandal, but this is of secondary importance and I mention it only in passing.' [1]

In discussing *Being and Nothing* [2] we shall leave technical terminology aside so far as possible, as we did in dealing with Heidegger. Once the basic pattern of the work is grasped, its implications for theology become all too obvious. But it must be added that in confining our attention to the basic pattern we are inevitably skipping over those detailed analyses and illustrations where Sartre's combination of philosophical and literary gifts appears to best advantage. Indeed, we are artificially separating the general structure of his argument from that embodiment of it in human situations which is, for the existentialist, his major means of 'verification.' Even so, what we find is in certain respects impressive. In the history of Western thought there are (at least) four great dichotomies, and Sartre's aim is nothing less than the overcoming of all four. These are: (1) a dichotomy of substance, mind vs. matter, which has led to idealistic and materialistic attempts to subsume all reality under one category or the other; (2) an epistemological dichotomy which has separated reality from appearance, the noumenon from phenomena, physical objects from sensa, etc.; (3) an anthropological dichotomy which has split man into two compartments, e.g. a body subject to determinism vs. a free will; (4) a methodological dichotomy, rationalism vs. irrationalism, where theories which stress logic and the intellect fail to do justice to the will and the emotions, and vice versa. Sartre's claim to greatness as a philosopher rests on his expression of the perennial quest for unification while using a modern method, phenomenology, in attempting to understand why this search has led to a dead end in the past. His failure as a philosopher, if he has failed, is due to the fact that his entire world view rests upon a radical estrangement which is worse than the dualisms he has ostensibly overcome.

Probably it is wrong to say that Sartre uses phenomenology as an approach to ontology; he employs it, rather, as *constituting* ontology. The vision of Being-itself, which Heidegger has criticized past metaphysics for failing to reach, is from Sartre's point of view not only unattainable but superfluous. The latter holds that once the relationship between consciousness and the world has been clarified, the ontological task has been completed; there is no Being-itself which includes and transcends both. In reading the opening pages of *Being and Nothing* one needs to remember that, for the author, there are no meanings except those which man himself posits. Therefore there can be no problem lying beyond phenomenology concerning a possible relationship between human meanings and the meaning of Being. His approach may rest upon an enormously gratuitous as-

197

sumption, yet it is the clue to Sartre's persistent conviction that the non-human in itself is simply meaningless.

One of the strokes—and some may wish to call it a stroke of genius —by which Sartre cuts through the dichotomies listed above is that he exploits in a special manner the existentialist thesis that consciousness is not a 'thing' and that, consequently, mind must not be thought of in terms of substance. He holds that the fundamental relationship which underlies all knowledge is not between one something (a mind) and another something (a physical thing). On the contrary, consciousness is always an awareness of something, and this is accompanied by awareness of itself as *not* that thing.

We must lead up to an understanding of Sartre's position by means of one or two preliminary observations. He rejects any dualism which depends upon contrasting reality with appearance because he maintains that appearance reveals, rather than hides, what a thing is. But the thing is not dependent for its existence upon being perceived or known. Both the subject and the object are 'transphenomenal,' i.e. the existing subject involves more than, and can stand in relationships other than, the activity of knowing, and the same is true of the existing object as regards its being known. In connection with his discussion of the subject, Sartre seeks to correct Descartes' formula, *cogito, ergo sum,* by maintaining that beneath the reflective act of self-knowledge lies pre-reflective consciousness. The self-conscious *ego* rises out of an impersonal substratum—impersonal in the sense that reflection has not yet separated consciousness-of-something into an 'I' and an 'object.' The true starting point is indicated not by saying 'I am conscious of myself,' but by saying 'I am a consciousness.' Sartre's remarks about pre-reflective consciousness mean that there is more to the subject than the perceiving and knowing of the *ego;* yet they avoid and combat the notion that the self is a substance standing behind appearances.

After rejecting various forms of dualism, he adopts a radical dualism of his own. He makes a basic distinction between what he calls *l'en-soi,* the thing as it is in itself, and *le pour-soi,* human consciousness. This distinction is announced somewhat apodictically in the

198

opening section of *Being and Nothing*, but elaborated and defended throughout the rest of the book. It may be variously described; at times it seems to be the difference between inert being and spontaneous being, at others it suggests the difference between finite, self-enclosed being and immanent or inclusive being; but the distinction remains altogether fundamental to Sartre's own view. Hence his position may be summarized in a single sentence: Although I apprehend the real thing only through appearance, what I apprehend is nevertheless utterly alien to me.

Marcel has maintained that in the last analysis Sartre is a materialist, and whether the charge is true or not, it at least calls attention to the fact that he deals with consciousness as a reaction to the objective world which is wholly dependent upon the latter. Inasmuch as consciousness can grasp itself only as *not* this or that thing, its own nature implies the reality of *l'en-soi*. If there were no external world, there would be nothing to be conscious of, i.e. there would be no consciousness. When we ask how two such utterly disparate entities as 'consciousness' and 'thing' can ever be united, Sartre's answer is that the former is not an entity. On the contrary, it is a *lack*. It differentiates itself from the solid content of the world by negation; to be able to characterize consciousness as *not* a property, *not* extended in space, and so on, clearly presupposes the objective world of things, properties, space. Where other philosophers have sought to define consciousness in terms of fruition, holding that many characteristics of the natural world, such as those which give rise to beauty, become actualized only through the emergence of appreciative mind, Sartre says just the opposite. Consciousness is for him a hole, a rent in the otherwise sturdy fabric of being. And no matter how perverse his starting point may be, it must be considered carefully, for everything else, including his views on human freedom and religious belief, follows from it.

That this starting point is perverse can hardly be doubted. If the transphenomenal being of the object is beyond my grasp, how can I know that it is alien and meaningless, that is, how can I be justified in making any assertions about it, positive or negative? How does consciousness arise? The answer cannot be found by looking to *l'en-soi*. As Sartre pictures it, *l'en-soi* obviously cannot be said to 'produce' consciousness. It may be quite consistent with Sartre's atheism to say that consciousness appears for no reason at all, but does not such a conclusion sound the death-knell of all philosophizing, including his own? Does not his view of the truth, regarding it as human projection, undermine his claim to have a view of the truth?

In order to get a fair impression of what Sartre means by *l'en-soi*, we must follow him in his attempt to get back behind ideation and epistemological theory to a direct encounter. Where Heidegger speaks of encounter with 'mystery' in the language of philosophical asceticism, Sartre speaks of encounter with the sheer givenness of a thing in the language of repulsion and nausea. Although reference to a well-known passage near the end of his novel *Nausea* [3] has now become hackneyed, it is unavoidable. In this passage Roquentin, after a long preparation of boredom and emptiness (which might be regarded as the reverse of a mystic's preparation for vision), finally comes face to face with the stark thereness of the root of a chestnut tree. As he sits on a bench looking at it, all the respects in which it is a familiar, appropriate part of man's world fall into the background. The layers of meaning which characterize the ways in which it can be used or appreciated by man are peeled away so that it stands forth as it is in itself. This occurs, not through dialectical analysis or epistemological theorizing, but as sheer encounter. What he comes upon is a radical absurdity which arouses a feeling of nausea. The only basis on which there could be communion between the man and the tree would involve Roquentin's simply being there, with all human meanings peeled away. A glimpse of this fact, and of the sense in which man too is simply 'there' in the world, intensifies the awareness of absurdity. Man's capacity to create and invent meanings comes to birth in an alien environment—for no reason at all. If we were to discuss Martin Buber, we should examine a strikingly different interpretation concerning what can happen when a man has communion with a tree.

200

There are other passages which could be cited to illustrate the same point. For example, Sartre's description of the process of gestation deals in a revolting manner with the transition whereby organic growth 'produces' a person, as if depicting an embryo 'as it is' meant putting aside the human hope, hatred, or tragedy connected with it. There is no question of his attempting to *demonstrate* that existence is absurd on the basis of his feelings about encounter with *l'en-soi*. Like any existentialist, he is primarily concerned with the existing subject in concrete situations. This is Sartre's raw material, and the aim of *Being and Nothing* is to provide an ontological setting which will do justice to it. Nevertheless, does not Sartre expose one of the radical weaknesses of existentialism? If he feels this way about trees and embryos, so be it; one of the legitimate functions of the artist is to make us aware of aspects of reality and of feeling which we might otherwise miss.

It is of course ludicrous to regard Sartre's outlook on life as degenerate merely because some of his characters are. What would we think of a critic who reasoned thus about Shakespeare? To be sure, the writer must have something of the villain inside him in order to get inside the villain. Likewise, however, Sartre must have some sort of religious sensitivity in order to write the passage in *Nausea* about Daniel's encounter with God, even though he puts this experience into the career of one of his most repellent characters. The relevant questions have to do with the *pervasiveness* of the pathological element in his novels, dramas, and stories. Is this simply good reporting of Western civilization in the middle of the twentieth century? And even if it concentrates attention on a restricted cross-section which fits into the Sartrean world, is it not part of the service of the artist that he makes us see our world through his? The same questions can be asked about any writer with a distinctive slant and style.

But what then is the relationship between personal reactions and generalization? It is safe to say that no existentialist regards himself as making purely autobiographical statements. By attending to his own existence, decisions, and emotional reactions, he supposedly

201

apprehends 'what it means to be human' in ways which other philosophical methods miss. But as soon as he goes beyond the autobiographical, he comes up against the fact of freedom which gives other men the right to acknowledge or to deny that a given account of human nature or of 'being' is valid for them. Perhaps all philosophical argument finally comes back to a bare appeal to personal assent wherever the question at issue cannot be settled by formal logic, empirical evidence, or semantic analysis. If so, there is something to be said for the existentialist's claim that his philosophy makes provision for the arbitrariness of commitment, instead of trying to hide behind rationalistic pretensions. But an unsolved problem remains if one can honestly claim to 'see' what a particular existentialist writer discloses, while drawing different ontological or theological conclusions from the same data.

These considerations are pertinent to Sartre's feelings about *l'en-soi*. Granting his atheism, he portrays emotions which appropriately arise in anyone who takes seriously the idea that existence is unqualifiedly contingent and absurd. He makes us aware of the precariousness of all human values. Doubtless it is possible for anyone, through an involuntary mood or through destructive intellectual analysis, through confusion, doubt, boredom, detachment, or anxiety, to find himself in a situation where all meanings have been threatened or undermined. Man, and man alone, can contemplate the possibility that all his reactions and interpretations retouch reality; this, coupled with his awareness that the world persists in being there, even though he may not be able to get at it apart from his retouching, gives rise to a sense of estrangement. Sartre sees how this total predicament provides the motive power for every effort at self-correction, for every scientific and philosophical endeavor to replace illusion by truth. He also sees it as the source of skepticism, bafflement, and metaphysical despair. Therefore he offers one possible version of what happens when a man attempts to come to terms with alienation on an atheistic basis.

But is he right in regarding the connection between alienation and atheism as self-evident as he seems to do? If one cannot feel 'that way' about the root of a chestnut tree without being an atheist, then Sartre and an opponent never really start from the same data and communication breaks down entirely. Against him, of course, stand Christians who have passed through alienation into faith, and atheists who do not share his nausea. Which setting, Sartrean or Christian, illuminates truly the nature and implications of estrangement? Which reaction, nausea or tranquillity, is more appropriate to the implications of atheism?

In *Being and Nothing* data and conclusions are so interwoven that it is impossible to separate them, and the author is so skillful as a dialectician that it is difficult to find any middle ground between swallowing him whole and rejecting him entirely. Nevertheless, keeping in mind the questions just raised, let us examine his view of man. The being of a tree is wholly incorporated in its existence; its reality consists of being just what it is. The distinguishing characteristic of man is that he is never 'just what he is.' He is, of course, one who has a body, a job, a family, a nation; but he is able to stand apart from such characteristics by differentiating himself from every respect in which he is an item in the world. This is Sartre's version of man's capacity for self-transcendence, which some theologians take to be the cardinal mark of creation in the Image of God and as evincing man's linkage with eternity. For Sartre, too, it is the source of man's uniqueness and freedom, but its primary effect is alienation from being, and there is no 'eternity' with which it can be linked. Starting with that awareness of itself which accompanies awareness of things, consciousness becomes personal through negating not merely this or that thing, but the total world in which things stand. At this point opposition between 'I' and 'world' becomes explicit. For the 'I' can only be defined in terms of my possibilities and projects; it can only be defined in terms of what I, regarded as a thing in the world, am not. All human striving, loving, hating, and believing must be understood in the light of our efforts to overcome this opposition; they can take the form of attempting (a) to incorporate the world into the 'I,' (b) to merge the 'I' into the world, or (c) to reach a unified synthesis of the two. Since Sartre concludes that these efforts are *in principle* foredoomed to failure, he regards human life as basically fruitless. The only point at which it ceases to be absurd is where it comes to terms with the fact that it is absurd.

There can be no linkage with eternity because man differentiates himself from the flux solely by negation. Although he exists in the present, consciousness of 'himself as present' means that he is not identical with 'himself as present.' Similarly, he can know his past as 'what he is *not* now' and his future as 'what he is *not* yet.' Here Sartre is only contrasting his previous definition of *le pour-soi* with the respects in which my past, present, or future can be regarded as modes of *l'en-soi*. His position resembles Heidegger's discussion of temporality in pointing out that man's way of dealing with time is very different from the physicist's notion of time. From one perspective my past is as much a part of 'facticity' as any purely physical event, but I transcend my past, and I can relate past, present, and future just because I am never simply 'myself' in the sense in which a tree is simply itself. What transcends time is the negating act of *le pour-soi*. Instead of being a fragment of eternal substance imprisoned in the world of material and temporal 'appearance,' consciousness is a nothingness. Man's attempt to transcend temporality positively instead of negatively, his vision of a 'true home' in eternity, is the product of an effort to combine two intrinsically incompatible factors: (a) the transcendence which characterizes consciousness, and (b) the repose, the complete coincidence-with-itself which characterizes being.

Man's freedom does not mean, then, that his proper aim is to come into harmony with the eternal God or with eternal values; rather, it means that his proper aim is directed toward the interrelationship between his own possibilities and the external world in the future. Man's transcendence of time is a summons to action, not to repose. Like Heidegger, Sartre's approach to the external world stresses the fact that man sees things as tools. Man finds himself in a physical environment where things go their own way and abide by their own laws, but how they operate is fraught with significance for him. This does not mean that we fail to grasp the real object. Wishes and desires can, of course, lead to error and illusion, but they need not do so. A specific interest may prompt us to concentrate selectively on certain qualities, but the qualities are really there. Indeed, to aspire to knowledge of the thing-in-itself apart from the human meanings whereby we approach objects is entirely fruitless. It is to ask for consciousness of *l'en-soi* apart from consciousness. The actual situation is as follows: What is truly known is *l'en-soi*, which is meaningless in itself, but our knowledge consists of human meanings, and nothing else could possibly be the case. Man's task is to actualize his potentialities by using as tools a world of things which is intrinsically alien or indifferent to these potentialities.

2. Interpersonal Relations

Estrangement is the basic characteristic not only of man's relationship to the world but of his relationship to other selves. Sartre holds—I believe quite rightly—that it is impossible to attain knowledge of another mind by observing a man's behavior and then attributing to him inferentially a selfhood like my own. What happens is far more direct than an inference. The reality of other selves is disclosed by an analysis of my own consciousness, for among the objects of my consciousness is a special class which is not at the disposal of my plans and desires in the way things are. The most distinctive characteristic of the other person is that he can look at me, and when he does, something happens within me which is different from what happens when I confront a thing. I do not have to go beyond my own consciousness. By this look, the other person enters into my field as a counter-perspective challenging my perspective. I feel myself entering into his frame of reference as an object related to his interests. Although I can make myself the center where experience of things is concerned, the other person breaks into my egocentric pattern as a threat to its claims. I become conscious of my contingency and of limitations to my freedom by encountering the opposition of other persons. None of this means, of course, that I can 'get inside' the other's subjectivity. On the contrary, that remains wholly inaccessible to me. But what I know directly (non-inferentially) is that through his gaze I enter as an object, a thing, into his consciousness. This awareness of the other-as-subject is as immediate and indubitable as my awareness of myself.

Thus the interpersonal situation is essentially one of isolation from each other and conflict with each other. Even though I were to learn everything which can be known about another person as object, I could never control him because his freedom, his subject-hood, is inaccessible. Yet because the reality of the other person is an unconquerable intrusion into 'my' world which threatens to turn me into his object, my only recourse is to counterattack by trying to turn him into 'my' object.

On the basis of this situation of isolation and conflict Sartre tries to explain the nature of love and hate. Love, like human existence as a whole, is destined to continual frustration. In his novels and plays, love impels his characters to try to engulf the freedom of the other person, for love is an attempt to overcome separation, and it is liberty which separates human beings from each other. The lover tries to become the absolute, the ultimate meaning of life, for the beloved. But in so far as he succeeds, he defeats himself, for then the other ceases to be a free person. Love is intrinsically contradictory. If the other remains a person, separation remains; if the other could be possessed completely, he would cease to be a person. In the extremity of its efforts, love may become masochistic (the attempt to turn myself into a thing) or sadistic (the attempt to turn the other into a thing); but these perversions are merely special forms of the basic contradiction which underlies all sexual relations, namely, the futile but endless attempt to merge two selves.

Incidentally, this sado-masochistic pattern runs all through the work of Sartre. Sometimes it appears as contradiction, but often as a kind of ambivalence or ambiguity. This latter stress will become clearer as we turn to Sartre's conception of human freedom. Simone de Beauvoir in *The Ethics of Ambiguity* and Albert Camus in *The*

Rebel carry forward this particular emphasis. To some extent, at least, the contradiction in man's interpersonal relations is related to his own inner self-contradiction, which both repels and attracts the self, provoking at the same time self-assertion and self-loathing.

We need not deny, however, that Sartre's analysis contains some acute and illuminating observations. Who can deny, for example, that we are made most intensely aware of the ultimate inaccessibility of another self precisely through our relations with those whom we know and love best? But what strikes us as remarkable is Sartre's constant assumption that the impossibility of complete merging with another subject makes any approximation to it tormenting and tragic. He does not, of course, regard freedom as a sheer curse. The source of man's estrangement from things and from other selves is at the same time the source of his creativity. But in his descriptions of love, by concentrating mainly upon Eros at its most egotistical, Sartre writes as though mutual fruition *through* the liberty of others were only a minor variation upon the fundamental theme of frustration by others. He also writes as though the hidden things about myself that come to light when the other 'sees' me are for the most part discreditable and shameful instead of releasing and enriching. In one of his illustrations a man is caught peeking through a keyhole; thus he realizes sharply how the other is looking at him as an object, and it is *shame* which signalizes the reality of the other as a subject. No doubt there is a close connection between awareness of the 'other' and awareness of guilt, and as an analyst of perversion, frustration, and the impulse to dehumanize, Sartre has few equals. But has he given an adequate account of what love can mean and be?

Something in Sartre prompts him to feel that it is an indignity for man to find himself circumscribed by the existence of the physical world and the freedom of other selves. It is as if man, born an egocentric infant, forever resents the fact that he has to grow up, and instead of growing up, hangs onto impulses and illusions of god-like omnipotence in so far as he possibly can. The point is that Sartre's disgust concerning the meaninglessness of *l'en-soi* is possible only because he shares (or at least imaginatively re-inserts himself into) the infant's resentment toward things and persons which resist being incorporated satisfactorily into 'my' world. There is nothing in his outlook which enables him to affirm anything remotely resembling the Christian teaching concerning the 'goodness' of Creation, or to stress the blessedness of the fact that one man cannot possess the selfhood and freedom of another. As many writers have pointed out (e.g. Archbishop Temple), Christianity has its 'materialistic' side in so far as, in affirming that the Word was made flesh, it takes a sacramental view of the universe. To be sure, some of the implications of an affirmation of the physical world and the body might surprise many Christians, especially sacramentarians. Yet Christianity has always regarded resentment toward creatureliness as one ingredient in that desire to be 'like God' which is the essence of sin. The pertinent question to raise about Sartre is whether he regards the alienation between man and being, which he describes so acutely, as remediable. Of course, even if what he uncovers is irremediable, it is the duty of the philosopher to tell the truth. Nevertheless the import of Sartre's description of the human situation cannot be discerned until we know what he expects to accomplish by means of it.

In this connection we must observe that although he takes 'We-feeling' into account, he regards it as derivative and superficial compared with the given isolation of one subject from another. Many of the illustrations of togetherness he uses reflect those conditions of industrial society where people are united more as cogs in a machine than as communities. He also shows how the operation of mob psychology can throw into action on a mass basis the same dynamics of love and hate which he has analyzed in connection with the frustrations and antagonisms of the individual. Hence the 'We' stands primarily for an escape from responsibility not an enhancement of it. Even that sense of solidarity of race which characterizes monotheistic religion, basing the unity of mankind upon the fact that we are all created by one God, is regarded by Sartre as an attempt to treat 'humanity' as an entity—an object with a given essence which is complete or at all events completable. Hence belief in God is also an attempt to escape freedom, although religious fellowship can no more abolish the incurable isolation of the subject than can any other interpersonal relationship.

In so far as an *ontological* question is involved, we cannot settle disputes concerning the primacy of communion or conflict by making psychological remarks about Sartre's temperament. But an inquiry concerning his own temperament, or perhaps his character structure, becomes relevant when one observes that there is a spot in his ontology which might have been developed quite differently. I refer to his doctrine that pre-reflective consciousness is more fundamental than self-consciousness. So far as I can see, Sartre fails to develop the implications of this doctrine in connection with 'We-feeling.' For his illustrations of human togetherness he turns mainly to a description of those aspects of modern life in love, work, and politics which leave man swinging between the two poles of isolation and dehumanization.

3. *Freedom*

We have seen that freedom is a summons to action. Primarily, action implies a lack; there is a need to be fulfilled or a possibility to be realized, and therefore the motivation for action comes from the future. Sartre does not attempt to represent freedom as any sort of faculty or aspect in man distinguishable from other faculties or aspects. Freedom, he thinks, goes hand in hand with consciousness. For it is the nature of consciousness to distinguish itself from past and present and to posit future ends as not yet actualized. Consciousness is *as such* projection toward possibilities. Instead of saying man has freedom, it is more accurate to say that human existence is freedom. Motives cannot operate except in connection with projection, and I alone am the source of the projecting. Therefore to hold that human motives and ends can be exhaustively accounted for by referring to nature or society or God is to treat man once more as if he were a thing. The conditioning factors of life undeni-

209

ably supply raw material for motivation and for projecting ends; they furnish the situations, the setting, in which man exists, but consciousness is *not* these. It means separation from whatever has been and is. If man were identical with the sum of his conditioning, he would never act; he would be like any other item in nature which undergoes change. Sartre's technical formula for this whole interpretation is that, in the case of men, existence precedes and conditions essence.[4] Whereas a tree is an instance of being in the world, freedom means *lack* of being; it means that man has to choose and make himself whatever he becomes. A philosophical attempt to define freedom is bound to fail if it begins by looking at man as a being in the world and then tries to find some faculty or region where freedom can be located. On these premises, determinism always wins. Against such premises Sartre sets his own version of meonic freedom, his insistence that freedom is a transcending and nihilating of being rather than an aspect of being. The strictly interminable character of this transcending is such that even after I have succeeded in achieving a project, I am never identical with what is actualized. Freedom means that I can never coincide with any form of being no matter how much I may transform myself or my environment. There is no resting place for man because he cannot become a thing in the world. The *lack* which is freedom is interminable except by death; then man finally becomes a thing.

What is more, freedom is incurably arbitrary. Because, in consciousness, I am separated from the world and from my own presence, how I am related to the world and to myself cannot be automatic. I take up attitudes toward both. To be conscious and to choose are identical. The value I attach to things, the opinions I have of myself derive from choice. I am responsible for the whole fabric of meaning within which I live, but since the choice could be different, my mode of living and my world view are arbitrary and precarious. Arbitrary in the sense that I cannot demonstrate their 'rightness' by showing how they conform to norms, structures, or authorities beyond my freedom; precarious inasmuch as nothing except freedom itself can prevent me from turning, at any moment, in directions which undercut everything I have believed and accomplished.

Sartre does not and need not deny any respect in which man is 'made'—as a thing in the world, by heredity, childhood experiences, habits, family, class, nation, or culture. These physical, biological, and psychological factors constitute my situation, but cannot make me identical with my situation. I can still project what I want, even though I may not get what I want; I can initiate action aimed at a certain goal, whether the goal can be reached or not. Perhaps the crucial illustration of this is a man's relationship to his own past. Sartre acknowledges, of course, that the past is strictly unchangeable and that a man's present self stands in physical and psychological continuity with it. Yet he rejects deterministic theories based upon these facts because he holds that consciousness transcends both the past and the present self; a man can take up attitudes toward both—condemning here, affirming there, concentrating on one strand of experience, ignoring others, being motivated by 'unalterable' past events in such a way that they profoundly influence the future. A man is responsible for his past not only in the sense that his projecting made it what it was at the time, but also in the sense that he can choose what meaning it shall have in relation to his projects now. So far as necessity operates, independently of all human meanings, a man does not 'make' his situation, but he does make whatever meaning it has for him, and for this he is responsible. Even when he tries to renounce his freedom and slip back into the peaceful irresponsibility of being a mere thing, he has to *act;* and to decide to deny freedom is very different from simply not having it.

Early in this chapter we mentioned the dichotomy which divides man into a 'free will' and a 'determined body' as one of four dualisms Sartre seeks to overcome. For him there is no problem as to how two disparate orders of being can be related. One and the same order, the world, is from the point of view of *l'en-soi* meaningless and from the point of view of *le pour-soi* fraught with significance. Being and nothing are indissolubly joined *in* my awareness of their alienation. And I cannot avoid the contrast between being and not-being, nor can I avoid seeing things and situations according to the significance they have for me, even though they do not have that same significance 'in themselves.'

The reality of other persons has, of course, a special bearing upon the individual's freedom. It is obvious that, from Sartre's standpoint, no theories put forward by naturalistic determinism can actually destroy freedom; they become plausible only when, for some reason, man wants to regard himself as a thing in the world. This atmosphere of depersonalization is created by social and cultural forces. I am surrounded not only by things, but by human meanings which have been built up and passed on without reference to my projects. This is the 'everyday' world of Heidegger where anonymous, standardized, public assumptions dictate what I should become and how I should evaluate. In so far as I participate in this world, I tend to become depersonalized because I live by what 'one' does instead of by my freedom. Yet I can resist this tendency in so far as I take responsibility for investigating the interrelationship between everyday meanings and personal ends, just as I have to investigate the interrelationship between natural law and my projects.

Learning how to use nature and anonymous meanings so that they will facilitate instead of engulfing my freedom is often difficult, but easy compared with coming to terms with the freedom of the other person. For when he sees me as an object, part of the meaning of my own life is taken out of my hands in a radical way. When he sees me as a Jew, a coward, a professor, a waiter, he apprehends me in terms of meanings which I cannot choose or accept. I cannot separate such characteristics from the way I live through them, yet he sees them without having access to what it is to be 'me.' Thus this alien knowledge of me—which is sometimes so heartless or prejudiced that it seems an utter caricature—nevertheless intrudes itself into my consciousness. I react with rage, resentment, fear, or pride to a picture of 'me' which I have not chosen. In this sense the mere existence of each man is a sort of violation of the existence of every other; the liberty of each is a threat to every other. As Sartre writes trenchantly in *No Exit:* 'Hell is other people.' I can neither accept being an object nor can I avoid the fact that this is what the other sees. Therefore it is almost impossible to will the liberty of others, for it involves accepting that they see what they see, without accepting what they see.

Thus the individual, who is not responsible for being or for being conscious, and who is hedged about by nature, society, other individuals, and death, must nevertheless take sole responsibility for whatever *meaning* life may have. In Kierkegaard and Heidegger we observed a close linkage between anxiety and freedom. For Sartre, anxiety arises primarily in connection with the fact that my choosing, by marking the whole of reality with my seal, requires that I decide not only the meaning of my life, but the meaning of human life. The individual, without help from outside sources, must take upon himself the burden of all mankind. Christian doctrine has always had to struggle in trying to combine an awareness of solidarity in guilt with the fact of personal responsibility. On an atheistic basis, Sartre arrives at the same combination, for he writes: 'I am as profoundly responsible for the war as if I had myself declared it.' [5]

What is man trying to become? Sartre's answer is that man is constantly moving away from the meaningless absurdity of *l'en-soi*, and seeking to reach a condition which would be like 'being' in its repose and completeness, but the opposite of 'being' in its fullness of meaning. Consciousness aspires to be united with what is akin to it instead of alien to it. The significance of belief in God is that it gives expression to these aspirations. In the idea of God freedom and consciousness are incorporated in 'Being' rather than remaining alien to it. God is both freely creative and forever at rest. He is both the source and a Being. He is consciousness, but the only content of His consciousness is Himself. Human desires, motivations, and projects must be understood in light of the fact that man wants to become God. For Sartre the goal is of course unattainable because God does not exist. But he seeks to show, on the basis of his phenomenology, why the desire is aimed at something intrinsically impossible. Since desire and liberty always imply a *lack* of being,

213

they can never be incorporated into a fullness of being. Consciousness which was identical with itself would not be consciousness. What man aims at is a perfect harmony of *en-soi* with *pour-soi*, but since the two are irreconcilable, and man is in a sense both, human existence is therefore futile.

Sartre illustrates his thesis by referring to specific human accomplishments. Art seeks a coincidence between aesthetic meaning and the external world; science seeks a coincidence between intelligible order and the external world. These activities succeed within limits, but after they have done their utmost, the world, as it is in itself, remains other than consciousness and indifferent to the meanings which arise in relation to our projects. The ultimate goals of both art and science involve a merging of the 'I' into the objective world, or an incorporation of the world into the 'I,' or a unified synthesis (God); and these goals are contradictory. That is why the human thirst to possess, to appropriate, the world is insatiable. That is why, at the deepest level, political and religious strivings coalesce. In a world where 'God is dead' men must invent God by the religious illusions whereby they seek to worship him, or by the titanism whereby they seek to become God. 'Thus man's passion is the inverse of Christ's, for man loses himself as man in order that God may be born. But the idea of God is contradictory and we lose ourselves in vain; man is a useless passion.' [6]

4. A Critique of Belief in God

Thus far we have examined Sartre's philosophy without attempting to challenge his atheism except in incidental ways. Now we must scrutinize it in more detail. In the first place it must be pointed out that he takes the notion of 'divine mind' quite literally and anthropomorphically as implying what his phenomenological investigation has uncovered concerning consciousness. As we have seen, there is no 'consciousness' apart from the world, for consciousness is always 'consciousness-of' something. Accordingly, Sartre dismisses the doctrine of *creatio ex nihilo* because it presupposes the

214

existence of a subject (God) before there were objects. And the idea of a consciousness which creates its objects contradicts the nature of consciousness in any case. But this argument against theism, like his ontology as a whole, depends upon an initial acceptance of Sartre's assumption that consciousness and being are mutually exclusive.

Quite apart from the philosophical strength or weakness of arguments for God, I find it impossible to take this step. As I have suggested, Sartre's ontology undermines its own claim to be true by making all meaning into something which the subject projects. And what of those instances of conscious life, i.e. animals, which cannot be classified under either *l'en-soi* or *le pour-soi?* One is reminded of Descartes' inability to make animals fit into his dualism. Even if we take Sartre's description of alienation as expressing an important truth (as I for one am willing to do), can we deny that it is utterly one-sided? Is not everything in the world above the inorganic level—and possibly even including it—an instance of that fusion of 'inner' and 'outer' which leads to man as a psycho-physical being? Consciousness rests upon and issues from objective structures; it does not read a kinship into nature which makes meaningful interplay possible.

Furthermore, Sartre fails to take account of the sense in which a man can be self-identical yet free, because he always construes 'identity' in terms of his conception of *l'en-soi*. If being and consciousness are not as completely antagonistic in nature and man as Sartre takes them to be, the force of his argument against the reality of God is greatly reduced. This is not to say it has no force at all. It applies quite cogently to crude religious anthropomorphism. If God's consciousness is supposed to be like ours in any univocal sense, then it is impossible to conceive of Him creating the world.

Here Sartre touches upon a central theological problem. How can the ground of Being be personal? If He embraces all being, then He is beyond the split between subject and object, and that means He is not conscious, not a self, in any fashion we can imagine. On the other hand, if He is personal then the world is distinct from

215

Him and He is limited by it. The ancient and contemporary dispute between various forms of absolutism and personalism in theology shows that a momentous problem is involved. But one can hardly contribute to a serious discussion of it by assuming with Sartre that whatever is true of human consciousness must be carried over unmodified into the connotations of the idea of God. Granting that *man* cannot entirely overcome the split between consciousness and Being, it does not follow that the split cannot be overcome at all. It does follow from Sartre's starting point that if God is real then He, as a union of consciousness and Being, transcends human knowledge and experience, and that therefore we have no right to apply such terms as 'personal,' 'mind,' 'consciousness,' 'will,' 'living,' 'loving,' to Him univocally. But no theologian worth his salt has ever denied this last statement. On the other hand, Sartre never claims that his ontology can *demonstrate* the truth of atheism. The issue calls for genuine decision; a man must proceed by choosing; and Sartre feels that it is more consistent with the nature of choosing to postulate atheism.

The most important reason why he rejects belief in God is found at this point. He simply regards it as irreconcilable with belief in human freedom. Yet his entire argument proceeds as if there were only two alternatives. The first is rationalism, which attempts to deduce existence from essence. He assumes that if all finite existence is dependent upon God, then an all-embracing determinism is inescapable. Everything is rationally intelligible in the sense that both things and persons can be understood in the light of the relationship between 'what they are' (essence) and the ground (God) which has caused them to be as they are. But freedom has disappeared because 'what it means to be human' is determined by God alone. The second alternative is, of course, Sartre's atheism which he *equates* with existentialism. The equation is certainly unfair to Kierkegaard, who combined belief in God with belief in human freedom and attacked the kind of rationalism represented by the first alternative. Moreover, Sartre's definition of existentialism—resting upon the thesis that (in the case of man) existence is prior to essence—is highly misleading. He argues that in a universe created and ordered by divine providence, God would produce men in the way that an artisan produces a particular item in accordance with a preconceived plan. This is his own example of what 'essence prior to existence' implies. Man is created with a given nature, and there is some sort of fulfillment toward which he must move in the process of becoming his true self.

On the other hand freedom means, for Sartre, that man falls into existence and then finds that he must make himself whatever he is going to become. Man must create his own values. Surely, however, we do not have to choose between these two horns of a dilemma. We do not need to accept a definition of essence which excludes freedom or a definition of existence which means that it always 'precedes' essence. Instead, we should define freedom as integral to 'human nature.' Undeniably the doctrine of predestination has been expounded in ways incompatible with belief in freedom, and if the predestinarian nevertheless affirms human responsibility, as he usually does, then the inconsistency needs to be pointed out. But this can be done without abandoning belief in God.

Moreover, what does 'essence' mean in Sartre's definition of existentialism? It leaves the origin of freedom utterly unaccounted for. This is partly a consequence of his failure to do justice to those processes and structures in nature which provide a foundation for the emergence of consciousness. Whether we think of the individual or of the race, man's distinctive capacities do not simply happen to come into existence. They are 'already there,' grounded in a unique relationship between consciousness and nature, before man can begin to exercise them. No one denies that the presence of freedom is only potential until the individual begins to exercise it. But Sartre can give no account of its presence even as potentiality.

And even if it rejects belief in God, philosophy should be able to do better than this. Of course Sartre is right in holding that man has a hand in making himself what he is to become. But his statement to this effect constitutes a doctrine of human nature, and such a doctrine can be developed without falling into the theory of soul-substance. Sartre is cheating when he refuses to talk about essential human nature. He is willing to talk about 'universal human conditions' in connection with the fact that all men have to exist in the world as mortals along with other people. But this concession does not meet the most important point. He persists in associating 'essence' (as applied to man) with the idea that selfhood is an eternal entity with which I am endowed by a power beyond myself. The notion, when held in this form, is undeniably objectionable, but it is objectionable because it has been separated gratuitously from freedom.

What we really need, and what Sartre fails to furnish, is a definition of human nature which includes freedom instead of being 'prior' to it. It is compatible with such a definition to say that man receives *the power to be free* from God, and that his exercise of freedom is always a fulfillment or an abuse of this gift. From a Christian standpoint the basis on which the dignity and worth of human life rests is *given;* it is the context within which we exercise our freedom, and although freedom can violate human nature, it can do so only at the cost of tending to destroy itself. From Sartre's standpoint human life can also have a certain dignity and worth, but these are only 'inventions'; freedom alone is *given*—man is not free *not* to be free—and moreover it is a surd datum, a gift from nowhere.

A word must be added concerning Sartre's account of the linkage between anxiety and freedom. Since, according to him, I must create values and an image of man not only for myself but for all men, I experience anxiety in connection with the fact that I am compelled to go forward without any assurance that I am on the right track. Even if an unearthly voice told me what to do, I would still have to decide whether the voice was divine or demonic. And even if there was proof that the voice was divine, I would still have to choose to obey it before anything could be put into effect. Nevertheless, he adds, we must not allow inescapable anxiety to paralyze us. We have to choose without justification and to hold back merely guarantees that the consequences of inaction will come to pass. Sartre admits that he is not happy about having to face life without divine support, and he has no patience with philosophies that attempt to claim essential norms of honesty, progress, justice, etc., even though God is dead. He finds it 'very distressing that God does not exist' because this means that anything can happen so far as man is concerned. 'Man, with no support and no aid, is condemned every moment to invent man.' [7]

If he is being honest and not merely ironical in expressing this attitude, then there are two things to be said about it. First, it calls attention to the important fact that if God is real, He communicates with man through inwardness, conscience, and decision, and there is no *human* means of removing the misgivings which arise when one contemplates the gulf between 'God Himself' and 'my consciousness of Him,' between 'revelation' and 'religious experience,' between the word of God and the words of man. Sartre is right in holding that these misgivings cannot be overcome by proofs, norms, or axioms which tell me what I am, what I ought to believe and do, apart from my decision. In the second place, however, Sartre's ontology prompts him to make the mistake of thinking that human decision is the whole story. He *assumes* that what goes on in religious belief is projection, not communion, but if the reality of God is compatible with freedom, then Sartre's account of man's longing to be (like) God may take on a quite different significance. One can admire him for rejecting something he would like to believe in so far as his motive is honesty. And contemporary life gives plausibility to his statement, derived from Dostoievsky, that so far as man is concerned anything can happen.

Indeed, if the main reason for believing in God is one's fearful reluctance to face the fact that human life is threatened by insecurity, frustration, and meaninglessness, we must range ourselves on Sartre's side of the argument. Faith, like atheism, is indefensible if it is evasive. What should constrain us to oppose Sartre is that he fails to give an adequate account of the world, human nature, meaning, and truth; our opposition must be based upon affirmations we could not evade without lying. If the ontology which excludes him from believing in God is mistaken, it seems a pity that he is not familiar with forms of faith stronger than those he mentions. His critique validly refutes any version of theism which rests upon crude anthropomorphism or rationalistic determinism, but it leaves many versions of Christian faith virtually untouched, notably many existentialist versions.

5. Ethics

We have left to the end a consideration of the ethic that Sartre builds on the basis of his atheistic doctrine of freedom. The trouble with most ethical theories, he declares, is that they provide only general principles and fail to solve those problems which arise when it is possible to have a good motive for turning in alternate directions. A young man wants to stay home to look after his aged mother, but he also wants to go off to join the French underground. No matter which way he turns, he will be doing something he honestly believes is good, and yet he will also feel guilty for not having done the other. Sartre tries to solve such problems by saying that we should trust the feelings which push us in a given direction. And he is right in suggesting that those who try to follow reason alone are not as free as they think they are, because they often fail to carry their whole selves, including their impulses and intuitions, into a decision. He goes further, however, when he asserts that it is impossible rationally to justify an action in advance. This statement reflects his conviction that man must create values 'alone.' Until one acts, the values in question have not come into existence, and a man cannot foresee how his deeds are going to turn out. Consequently the only possible moral judgment is the one which asks how fully a decision has expressed the freedom of choosing oneself. The existing person, including his instincts and feelings, really determines the norms he appeals to, and the kind of man he is impels him toward the kind of standards he sets up. He cannot escape responsibility for inventing these standards.

It might be interesting to compare Kierkegaard's *Sickness unto*

Death with Sartre's treatment of the same theme. For the latter, despair arises in connection with two facts. First, I cannot count upon anything that falls outside my own will. Thus I have to act without being able to determine what will happen when the effects of my action become mingled with the effects of the deeds of others. Secondly, I cannot hide behind the comfortable thought that there are all sorts of possibilities in me which might have been fulfilled if it had not been for hampering circumstances. (Here Kierkegaard makes a similar point.) The only possibilities we have a right to talk about are those which get actualized. Hence the limits which undeniably surround freedom provide no excuse for denying responsibility. Instead of explaining a coward by appealing to environmental, biological, and psychological determinism, Sartre describes how a man makes himself a coward by his acts.

Since anything can happen because God does not exist, it is up to man to create his own middle pathway between slavery to preestablished axioms on the one hand, and sheer caprice on the other. In this respect morality is comparable to aesthetic creativity. When an artist begins a painting it is silly to judge it in advance by a priori norms; whether it turns out well or ill depends on whether the result adequately expresses the artist's intention.

Thus the one person Sartre seems willing to condemn is the man who will not face honestly his own motives and intentions—the man who will not see himself as he really is. He distinguishes between 'good faith' and 'bad faith' in a manner roughly comparable to Heidegger's distinction between authenticity and unauthenticity (despite the fact that Heidegger disclaims any intention of passing moral judgments). Sartre sees that in an effort to run away from the dignity and dread of freedom most people organize their lives around various forms of self-deception. The anti-Semite blames everything on a scapegoat-race. The Freudian blames everything on his parents and his libido. The Communist justifies the use of ruthlessness and lies in the present on the ground that it will lead to happiness and justice later on. All of these are 'faiths' because such

221

people come to believe their own excuses, but they are 'bad' faith.

Sartre singles out for special attention what he calls 'the spirit of seriousness.' This attitude pretends that the difference between right and wrong has already been settled axiomatically, so that no kind of creative ethical venturing is necessary. In its secular form the spirit of seriousness can be seen wherever business men or officials regard certain economic doctrines or rules of procedure as so sacrosanct that they must not be questioned. The reason a man will fight so furiously in defense of such assumptions is that wherever they prevail he can ascribe his actions to 'the way things have to work.' Anyone can so take on a role, so fit himself into the social mechanism, that he does not have to ponder the ultimate question concerning what it means to be himself—apart from his role. Thus the ticket-collector, the waiter, the stenographer—anybody—may have to find some sort of distractions to fill the empty time when they are not playing their roles, for these empty moments threaten them with the possibility of having to face themselves. The spirit of seriousness can also be found, however, in a religious form. Here the individual who immerses himself in the service of God avoids having to grapple with the problem of life for himself. God gives all the answers, and in exchange for the promise of ultimate security the believer yields up his birthright of freedom.

If all these are examples of bad faith, what constitutes good faith? Primarily it means, for Sartre, being lifted out of egotism through the discovery that in wanting freedom for myself I must also want freedom for others. His substitute for religious commitment is what he calls 'total engagement'—e.g. in action which gives a man solidarity with lovers of freedom against its enemies. In the French resistance the lonely individual had to face torture and death, yet each man, deciding alone, was either supporting or betraying his unseen comrades. So far so good. But one has the right to be puzzled as to how Sartre jumps from affirming his own freedom to affirming that of others. He has already shown that this is well-nigh impossible. He has no conception of essential human nature on which to base the assumption that what is good for one individual is good for men generally. His phenomenological description of interpersonal relations puts the major stress on egotism and conflict, and represents 'We-feeling' primarily as a threat to freedom. How does he make the transition to a position which presupposes that fellowship and love can become the fruition instead of the frustration of freedom?

6. Conclusion

Using theological language for a moment, we are compelled to say that although his analysis of 'sin' is acute and penetrating, his doctrine of 'salvation' trails off into a void. Against secularized versions of religious hope, Sartre has the merit of rejecting the notion that human beatitude can be identified with temporal goals. He contemplates no future earthly condition of the individual or the race that will 'make life worthwhile.' For him 'salvation' is a sheerly autonomous and yet self-contradictory act. It means accepting estrangement from the world and other selves without accepting it. Good faith consists in recognizing why I yearn for the ultimate goal (en-soi—pour-soi), and why it is in principle unattainable. One is reminded of Kierkegaard's description of the defiant man who wills to be himself—apart from God. What Sartre asks us to affirm is utterly indeterminate because, having no basis, it must be invented from one moment to the next, and having no goal, it is impossible to specify what we should be moving toward. Human existence becomes a bare striving to affirm what it cannot possibly avoid. He has no basis for believing in the possibility of that community-in-freedom which alone can save integrity, courage, and kindness from being mocked by the nature of things. He asks us to undergo the painful process of outwitting our own egotism, will-to-power, moralistic shibboleths, and idolatrous illusions for the sake of a freedom which has no point other than itself. He calls for sacrifice of a sort, not in the service of a cause which transcends man, but in the service of man's self-transcending as a surd datum. Heretofore I have refrained from emphasizing the sado-masochistic character structure which underlies Sartre's ontology. But can one doubt that he is reading it into his picture of reality?

In such a view there is no answer to the question as to why human consciousness has arisen. The character of *l'en-soi* is such that it cannot account for itself, and initially man does not produce himself. Human life simply happens, and the only category which covers both *l'en-soi* and *le pour-soi* is absurdity. Nevertheless his philosophy is in one respect salutary, for it sharpens fundamental issues in a poignant, urgent manner. Does existence seem absurd to him because it really is or does it seem absurd because his ontology cuts human life off from the ground of meaning? It is not fair for Christians to cite Sartre as a horrible example of where atheism must lead. To do so is to use the old technique of crying: 'Always keep ahold of nurse for fear of meeting something worse.' One can be an atheist without adopting Sartre's philosophy; for example, its view of *l'en-soi* is defective on purely cosmological grounds, and its view of *le pour-soi* is reconcilable with much that psychology, especially animal psychology, has uncovered. Furthermore, an atheist who is acquainted with the history of theology will not attach much weight to Sartre's refutations of belief in God. These refutations depend for their plausibility upon an acceptance of his ontology, and they repeatedly fall into the genetic fallacy that how a belief came about explains just what the belief is and means. Even if Sartre is right, psychologically, that the idea of God reflects man's loneliness, his yearning for harmony, his desperate attempt to find human solidarity in the presence of a Transcendent Starer, it does not follow that God is unreal, though it may follow that all human responses to Him are far from perfect because they are inevitably tinged with wishful thinking.

Nevertheless, despite these defects, Sartre compels both atheist and theist to re-examine their accounts of the relationship between being and freedom. He compels both to grapple with the bearings of the ultimate ontological question upon those provisional meanings and accomplishments which human existence undeniably can embody. The question he makes central deserves the position he gives it, even though, unfortunately, he fails to distinguish between desiring to *become* God and desiring to be restored to fellowship with God. Indirectly he performs a valuable service for the theologian by protesting against any doctrine of divine grace which does less than justice to freedom. He stimulates a reformulation of the perennial Christian conviction that human freedom reaches fruition in grateful response rather than in defiant independence. On the other hand, he does throw the onus of proof on atheists to show that the cards are not appallingly stacked against the human race. He forces them to come out from behind the protective shelter of scientific determinism so as to face squarely the fate of ethics and ontology in a godless world.

Sartre's final word is that life just happens, and remains absurd. Yet the illuminating and bracing thing about him is that he has the courage to follow the consequences of his atheism to the bitter end. By doing so, he inadvertently offers us one of the strongest arguments for faith in God that can possibly be conceived. One thinks again of Pascal's Wager. If I am deceived when I choose to believe in God, then I lose nothing of any real value, since if this kind of atheism is true, all values disintegrate completely. Thus the choice is put before us in the sharpest possible form.

NOTES

1. Gabriel Marcel, *The Philosophy of Existence* (New York: Philosophical Library, 1949), p. 32f.

2. *L'Etre et le néant: Essai d'ontologie phénoménologique* (Paris: Gallimard, 1943).

3. Translated by Lloyd Alexander, New Directions Press, 1949. The passage cited has also been translated as a whole in *The Partisan Review*, vol. 13, 1946, with the title 'The Root of the Chestnut Tree.'

4. *L'Etre et le néant*, p. 515: 'To say that the *pour-soi* has to be what it is, to say that it is what it is not in not being what it is, to say that in it existence precedes and conditions essence . . . is to say one and the same thing . . . I am condemned to exist forever, apart from my essence, apart from the springs and motives of my acting. I am condemned to be free.'

5. Ibid. p. 641.

6. Ibid. p. 708.

7. *Existentialism* (New York: Philosophical Library, 1947), p. 28.

JASPERS

JASPERS

1. A Preliminary Glimpse

Karl Jaspers was born in Oldenburg, Germany, in 1883. He studied both law and medicine, and his first professional work was in psychology and psychiatry. For a time he was a psychiatric assistant at a clinic in Heidelberg, and in 1913 he wrote a book entitled *Allgemeine Psychopathologie* which became a standard text on the subject. In 1916 he became professor of psychology at the University of Heidelberg, but even then his researches were broadening to include philosophy, and his book *Psychologie der Weltanschauungen* (1919) marks his transition from one field to the other. In this book he also shows appreciation for the importance of Kierkegaard at a time when the Danish writer was little known. In 1921 he switched to a professorship in philosophy at Heidelberg and retained this position until 1937 when he was driven from his chair by the Nazis. After the war he was re-instated and named rector or 'honorary Senator' of the University. Since 1948 he has taught philosophy at the University of Basel, where Karl Barth teaches theology.

In 1932 he published a three-volume work entitled *Philosophie*, and he is now engaged in writing an enormous work in three volumes on *Philosophische Logik*, the first of which has already appeared under the title *Von der Wahrheit*. These are the main sources for getting a glimpse of his world view. He has also written books on specific philosophers, such as Descartes and Nietzsche, and on specific problems, such as reason, existence, guilt, and the interpretation of history. Unfortunately most of his books that have been translated into English are of a brief or introductory character, although his inaugural lectures at Basel, *Der Philosophische Glaube* (published in English under the title *The Perennial Scope of Philosophy*),[1] contain much that is important for our particular theme. In these lectures he seeks to show that although the philosophical task cannot be carried through by speculation, it can be completed by means of faith.[2]

Jaspers' reflections revolve around three main concepts: the objective world, the existing self, and Being-itself (Transcendence). He claims that philosophy differs from the natural sciences because what it seeks to grasp, Being-itself, is not an object. There is no direct way in which philosophy can reach its goal. As a Kantian, Jaspers regards rational knowledge as confined to the phenomenal world, and as a Kierkegaardian he realizes that every concept of the Absolute is refracted through the existing of the individual. Whenever we try to reach Being-itself by generalizing on the basis of one aspect of reality—either matter or mind, either the world or the self—we make the mistake of attempting to explain the whole by means of a part.

Therefore Jaspers' philosophy begins with a dilemma which is never solved; it has to be accepted in a quest which is both illuminating and frustrating. For Being-itself must be differentiated from objects and subjects, somehow embracing both while lying beyond the split between them. Nevertheless, he holds that even in ordinary experience the split is not complete; we never encounter thinking without objects, and we encounter objects only with and through the subject. Hence reality cannot be made up of subjects alone (idealism) or of objects alone (naturalism). What we start with is a relation where the terms are different but not sundered. This inescapable starting point imposes a severe difficulty on metaphysics because as soon as we form a concept of Being-itself that concept becomes an object of thought for some subject. There is an unbridgeable chasm between the concept and that to which it tries to refer. Because of the seeming futility of metaphysics, men may be tempted to re-nounce it altogether. For Jaspers, however, this means attempting to regard ourselves simply as parts of the objective world and do-mesticating ourselves wholly within it. The consequence is that we try to attach absolute significance to finite goods. Man, as such, seeks the Absolute, and if he does not do so with open eyes, then he will turn fanatical and follow some spurious substitute.

The man who persists in the philosophical enterprise will find himself engaged in a search which never accepts some static, objec-tive structure, which would make decision superfluous, as its vision of Being-itself. Selfhood, as existing-in-time, is never finished; con-sequently it finds truth a *way* of thinking rather than a final posses-sion. This 'way to wisdom' (the title of Jaspers' recently published introduction to philosophy) opens up as we become aware of the limits of thought, for when we reach these limits we feel the impact of the distinction between finite things and Being-itself and we realize that the latter must be approached not by knowledge but by 'transcending thinking.' Since this sort of thinking seeks to surmount all forms of objectivization, it has affinities with the *via negativa*. It is directed toward 'Nothing' (i.e. *not* any object), and has no results or solutions to offer. Yet it changes our whole attitude toward experience, for now we no longer take the familiar world (*Dasein*) for granted, we no longer regard it as final. This does not mean that we have come into contact with a second, supernatural world be-yond this one. It means simply that we stand critically above this one world, remaining in it without being altogether of it. Philosophy can never get away from concrete situations for precisely in them man's search for the Absolute takes place; yet it takes seriously the fact that these situations point beyond themselves and can therefore become the limited forms within which Being-itself is manifested.

As we have seen, Jaspers realizes that the attempt to characterize transcending thinking by means of words and concepts is both inevitable and contradictory. To use a word is to objectify what the word stands for, yet the whole aim of his discourse is to call attention to the fact that Being-itself is not an object. We can overcome this contradiction only by a special attitude that makes the existing individual aware of the limitations of words and thoughts. The important thing about transcending thinking is not the ideas it unavoidably uses, but the inner change in a person's consciousness of Being which it involves. This inner change does not consist in a new connection among ideas, but in an act of freedom. It is a break with immanence. Its justification is that I cannot avoid it without merging myself as a thing with the objective world and thus becoming dehumanized.

2. *World, Self, and Transcendence*

This preliminary sketch of Jaspers' approach to philosophy must now be explained in more detail. Man's first task he calls 'orientation to the world.' The world is already there (*Dasein*) and the self must emerge out of it. By means of science and philosophy man transforms the flux of experience into his apprehension of a meaningful world. Science provides knowledge, philosophy has to do primarily with the limits of knowledge, but there need be no conflict between the two. The philosopher should utilize available knowledge, and he can agree with the scientist that nothing is to be shielded by dogma or custom from disinterested inquiry. Philosophy can accept the results of objectivity, even though it is not a form of objective knowledge. Jaspers' outlook, at this point, can be stated with clarity and simplicity, but confusion can easily arise unless his special use of two terms is taken into account. He uses the word 'understanding' (*Verstand*) to refer to the capacity that enables us to deal with the objective world and to obtain phenomenal knowledge. This he distinguishes sharply from 'reason' (*Vernunft*) which plays an important role in transcending thinking. Confusion arises because 'reason,' as he defines it, is continually breaking through the fetters of 'rationalism.' It seeks to penetrate beyond finitude; it refuses to limit itself to any one mode of Being; it is the organ of metaphysics because it asks why there should be something instead of nothing. Instead of staying within the confines of immanence, as 'understanding' does, 'reason' seeks whatever may lie beyond the grasp of concepts—including the contradictory, the mysterious, the repellent. Thus it drives beyond the surface knowledge of things which science can provide and also beyond those common-sense, conventional meanings which we attach to everyday life when we avoid ultimate questions. Reason challenges all accepted truths, not with the nihilistic motive of making life absurd, but with the metaphysical motive of finding the authentic ground of truth and value. Jaspers, however, recognizes that one may have to pass through the 'nihilating,' which sees the transitoriness and vulnerability of all finite objects and values, before finding a relationship between the self and Being which cannot be destroyed by doubt and anxiety. Therefore nihilism can have a transitional, purgative function in the process of philosophizing as it discloses the precariousness of every attempt to construct a total interpretation of life within the confines of objective knowledge.

Science cannot shut itself up in a sphere of pure objectivity, for the scientist must be motivated by a sense of the worth and the wonder of knowledge, and unless the meaning and purpose of his work have a subjective foundation, neither the contributions nor the limits of science can be seen in proper perspective. Because each science is relative to its particular methods and axioms, and because all data, from one standpoint, fall within its purview, one can easily forget the partiality of these methods and axioms. Yet the fact remains that science cannot reach a comprehensive, unified view of reality because the existing individual is never simply the sum of what can be objectively known about him. Even if all phenomenal knowledge could be drawn together into a single, consistent system, man would not fall wholly within that system. This is not due to temporary ignorance, which may be removed by some future refinement of method; it is due to the nature of subjecthood, i.e. freedom. Freedom cannot be grasped as a datum of phenomenal knowledge, although its effects and the organism through which it acts may be scientifically studied.

Jaspers' critique of naturalism is one of the weightiest to be found among existential writers because he attaches such high importance to science, admitting that without it philosophizing becomes groundless speculation detached from the fact of man's embeddedness in the world, and also because he possesses firsthand acquaintance with scientific work, especially in the field of psychology. He accuses naturalism of being anti-philosophical because it espouses a superstitious kind of 'unfaith.' It *wills* not to pay attention to anything that lies beyond the reach of objective methods, and therefore it calls a halt to investigation at precisely the point where philosophy, properly speaking, is realizing its own problems. Jaspers insists, of course, that metaphysics should never claim to possess the same sort of evidence which characterizes empirical science, or the same sort of abstract certainty which characterizes logic. But when he encounters the assertion that there is 'nothing but' natural process, which he takes to be the primary basis for naturalistic rejection of belief in God, he replies that the assertion does not rest on knowledge of any kind; on the contrary, it involves what might be called 'a venture of unfaith.' The attempt to hold our account of man within naturalistic limits means that we study only the physical, biological, and historical manifestations of man's uniqueness without throwing any light on the origins of that uniqueness itself. At no point in the naturalistic view of evolution do we make a transition from dealing with objective processes to 'being a subject.' Yet if the latter is ignored, the philosopher must protest that man is always more than the empirical self which can be known scientifically. Cognition operating within the world cannot grasp the primal ground (*Ursprung*) of human existence and freedom. If freedom is ignored, the blunder is not merely a theoretical one; it has ominous practical consequences. There is a direct connection between scientism and dehumanization. It is not only technology which tends to destroy personality and community. The sciences of man, when they claim to tell us the whole truth about ourselves, substitute impersonal concepts for a firsthand awareness of responsible existence. They view the individual as the resultant of psychological forces, and they deal with him as one statistical item in the operation of mass movements, social and cultural.

The force of this critique of naturalism depends, of course, upon the soundness of Jaspers' views of selfhood and freedom. What he calls *Existenz*, as contrasted with *Dasein*, is really synonymous with selfhood, but in order to understand his use of these terms they must be divorced from idealistic connotations. Jaspers' starting point is a solid affirmation of the reality of the external world and of the fact that man is, in one sense, an object interrelated with other objects. It is on the basis of and in the midst of *Dasein*, both natural and human, that the possibility of 'existence' (*Existenz*) appears. By 'self' Jaspers does not mean a Cartesian *res cogitans*, but the total, unique individual including will, emotion, the body, and the unconscious. Yet the self is more than biological and psychological forces since it is not merely a congeries of objective processes. What it implies is best grasped in the face of tragedy, suffering, and death, when one realizes that what 'I am' is inseparable from decision and deed.

The 'I' cannot be grasped by means of universals; it is missed so long as a man tries to view himself as a particular instance of man-in-general. Therefore its origin is unknowable, and since the 'I' is always an unfinished task, one cannot see it as a whole. We can know universal structures and conditions in connection with which everybody develops, but the general principles of maturation do not explain how *I* fulfill or fall short of *my* true self—and no other. Therefore there are no objective criteria for determining exhaustively what I should become. But although I cannot grasp my authentic existence by means of conceptual knowledge, I can throw light upon it. The latter task Jaspers calls *Existenzerhellung* ('lighting up existence'). Admittedly there is no direct way whereby another man's illumination of his selfhood can become legislative for me, but through existential communication one man's attempt to carry out the task for himself may strike up resounding chords in others which prompt them to undertake the same task for themselves. At this point Jaspers is obviously drawing upon Kierkegaard's views, al-

235

though as we shall see he attempts to break through some of the barriers which indirect communication erects.

Once again, the fundamental characteristic of selfhood is freedom. But Jaspers is not interested in the controversy between determinism and indeterminism. That controversy has to do with whether spatio-temporal processes are or are not uninterruptedly causal. They are. Our freedom consists in the fact that although we are in the causal sequences, we are not simply a bundle of causal sequences. This comes out in the fact that I can negate, at least in thought, every mental and bodily process and say truthfully, 'I am not simply that,' even though of course I cannot exist apart from these processes. For example, the fact that a man may have attempted to achieve a 'merely animal' existence, by trying to renounce responsibility, shows that he is not a 'merely animal' existent. Furthermore, he can differentiate himself from every social role even when, because of cultural conditioning, it is impossible to discard the role. Even character, which when once built up we cannot wholly escape, is not something given, a pure datum; it is something we have a hand in making and for which we feel responsible.

But if freedom is different from our thinking, our bodies, our psychological conditioning and our characters, what is it? If it is groundless, Jaspers can hardly avoid Sartre's position. He declares, however, that 'I come to myself as a gift.' Freedom can be ignored and evaded, but never effaced so long as man remains human. Yet its ground is not a knowable structure; it is rather a mysterious origin which I can choose only in the sense of acknowledging and accepting it, not in the sense of producing it. Jaspers insists on thinking of this origin in concrete, individual terms. That is why he refuses to speak of the ground of freedom as a universal structure from which the freedom of individual persons is derived. Nevertheless his refusal is puzzling, for if every man is a 'possible existence' and not merely an object, then human nature can be universally defined accordingly without denying that freedom and 'authentic' selfhood must be fulfilled or missed by each individual.

In Jaspers' philosophy freedom is the end as well as the origin of selfhood, and it accompanies every stage. Though I receive it from the beginning, I must keep moving toward it if I am not to lose it. Hence the fundamental form of freedom is being able to choose oneself, and this is a continual struggle, not a single decision. Such choice, as we have seen, does not involve any break in the chain of causal connections at the level of empirical events. Even when I am compelled by circumstances or conditioning to act in a certain way, there is a difference between being master of such influences and being subject to them. Human action is not mere occurrence; it is occurrence plus the meanings which I impute.

Because Jaspers holds that a man becomes an authentic self only by choosing himself, not by looking at some kind of external norm, his attitude toward moral law has certain affinities with Sartre's. Both writers recognize that it is impossible to live without moral norms, but both emphasize the fact that a norm cannot be genuine and effective unless it springs from within, having been adopted by man's freedom. Hence both writers admit that freedom is perilous. Although it may lead to disciplined self-discovery, it can also lead to the destruction of all standards. Jaspers points out that it can lead to an infinite regress where, in the process of cutting through successive layers of selfhood in search of a sincere core, I trail off into nothingness and become unable to act or decide. But we cannot evade such dangers by trying to subjugate freedom to outside control. Such an attempt is itself an exercise of freedom turned against its own nature. Our only recourse is to take the risk of freedom, and here Jaspers seems to be more hopeful than Sartre by regarding man's ability to question everything as resting upon a positive capacity. We never cease trying to take hold of life instead of falling into endless drifting. We bring our tendencies toward ceaseless doubt into the service of clarifying decision, and this is the essence of reasonable faith.

Furthermore, we reach total commitment not by breaking away from psychological determinants, but by seeing, understanding, and accepting them. Jaspers' position thus combines an admission that the knowable, empirical self presents a deterministic picture with

237

an insistence upon the fact that man is responsible and that the source of his responsibility is unknowable. 'Unknowability' here means simply that the self and its possibilities cannot be objectified. He claims that in many instances when, in a given moment, a person literally cannot do such-and-such, that person is nevertheless partly responsible for the character which makes such-and-such impossible. Although psychiatry can help some compulsions, his writings suggest that psychotherapy should take responsibility as its basic category. Admittedly, responsibility can be lost, but only pathologically. Therefore we should not take the *unreality* of responsibility as a basic assumption, as some psychiatry does, and then apply it not only to psychotics but to neurotics and normal people. Freedom can be lost involuntarily as in the case of psychotics, although even they may be partly responsible for their lives up to the moment of the onset of psychosis and afterwards. It can also be lost, in a sense, voluntarily. Here Jaspers has in mind the destruction of freedom which is brought about by the evil will. A person can will the egotism and hatred to which he becomes incurably enslaved. This, however, usually takes the negative form of refusing to see himself as he actually is. Only a good man can bear to be completely transparent to himself.

In the presence of a crisis, therefore, we should radically 'open' ourselves instead of running away from doubt, perplexity, anxiety, and recognition of our conditioning. We must run the risk of falling into despair in order to move toward the possibility of authenticity. After having taken the risk, one either fails to 'come to oneself' or enters into the actualization of one's true self. Getting stuck in despair is the result of failing to reach complete sincerity. On the other hand, where freedom is fulfilled, effort is no longer necessary. Thus Jaspers tries to combine the sense in which I must 'create' myself with the sense in which I receive true selfhood as a gift. Because man is free he transcends *Dasein*, yet his freedom relates him to transcendence. At the height of freedom one feels that something inescapable and compelling is the basis of life's meaning. 'Where I am completely myself I am no longer only myself.' Yet the distinction between man and transcendence remains. Man is not in any sense to be deified. At this point Jaspers comes very close to a Christian conception of grace, but because he is suspicious of theology, he prefers to call his faith 'philosophical.' He continually associates revealed theology with the notion that God is objective and that the divine will is externally normative; these views he of course regards as incompatible with freedom.

Since certain affinities between Jaspers and Sartre have just been pointed out, it may be well to underscore their differences by surveying Jaspers' defense and critique of nihilism. As we have seen, he regards it as a phase which philosophy may have to pass through in order to reach faith. Pass *through* it, he says, not around it. According to him, it makes more sense to wonder how anyone today can avoid falling into nihilism than to overlook the experiences which lead to it. At some level every contemporary man confronts the void; everything in which he tries to believe collapses. Friends betray; the state becomes demonic so that one cannot be loyal to it; the scientific outlook, which begins as a humble love for truth, becomes perverted through a sense of superiority and power into a supercilious dogmatism based on pseudo-axioms such as: 'the world could be well-ordered provided there were clear understanding and good will.'

Modern man, having lost touch with transcendence and finding rationalism patently incapable of coping with existence, becomes enslaved to various forces in nature and in himself. Wishing to become a law unto himself, he mystically affirms his 'destiny,' only to become shackled to the irrational vitality of racial myths and unconscious archetypes. Placing his whole destiny in worldly fortunes, he falls into despair and madness when they are shattered. Regarding others in the same way as he regards himself, he treats men as puppets because he has forgotten that the soul is rooted in eternity. Humanism, which begins as a serene philosophical substitute for God, is unable to prevent itself from being turned into a deification of man, for when the Absolute is ignored, human resources in some form must be invested with a significance they are

239

unsuited to bear. Since the whole enterprise is based on a lie, it easily passes over into a cult which must insist on its legitimacy in fanatical ways. European Protestantism has tried to meet fanaticism via counterfanaticism without being able to restore religion to its earlier purity. Roman Catholicism combines modern totalitarian methods with an escapist adherence to medieval philosophical patterns.

Hence nihilism is useful when it cuts away rubbish—destroying the illusion that the world is a harmony pervaded by intelligible laws and fully acknowledging the peril of those forces before which rationalism stands either heedless or helpless. But its untenability as a stopping-place becomes obvious as soon as one attempts to be positive and nihilistic simultaneously. One wants to be brave and dispense with all meaning; hence one represents a calculated meaninglessness as the only meaning. Knowing that all commitment is absurd, one holds that the only justifiable thing is to do whatever one does with complete commitment. But nothing can relieve the basic mood of meaninglessness. Since God is dead, the only possible sources of meaning must be found in the world and these are incapable of carrying the burden of absolute meaning. Thus nihilism bears inverted witness to a religious significance which life ought to possess. The events of temporal existence, if man's search for transcendence is a 'useless passion,' are at bottom utterly trivial; against this inescapable fact Sartre's interpretation of human freedom can win only a Pyrrhic victory.

3. Existential Communication and Boundary Situations

The contrast between Sartre and Jaspers comes out most forcefully in their views of interpersonal relations. Jaspers' leading concept is that of 'existential communication.' The word 'communication,' as he employs it, has a special connotation. He is not concerned merely with the fact that the development of specialization has made it difficult for experts in one field to understand those in another. Nor is he thinking mainly of the obstacles created by cultural differences. He seeks to go beyond problems which have to do with semantics and with the exchange of ideas in order to describe a situation where the giving of the whole self is involved. Against the doctrine of indirect communication, which Kierkegaard himself finally abandoned, Jaspers holds that direct person-to-person participation is possible. But it rises above ordinary communication when dealing with people in terms of their roles and functions. In existential communication the uniqueness of each participant is fully revealed and recognized. Each retains his independence and therefore his solitude, for only where independence is respected can there be complete relatedness. Existential communication stands between the extremes of isolation (what Kierkegaard called 'shut-upness') and symbiotic merging. Neither extreme permits a man to become fully himself.

In such communication, or communion, I do not simply reveal what I already am; I become something new and deeper in the process of self-revelation. And though openness is possible only in a context of love, this love is not sentimental or uncritical. On the contrary, within a solidarity which cannot be broken it finally becomes possible for two people to tell each other the full truth. My blind spots are removed not only because it is safe for me to be honest, but because the other can tell me frankly about my limitations and defects. Such a relationship is impossible, of course, unless it rises above ordinary competitiveness and resentment. These natural human attitudes may be present, but they can be conquered only by being admitted and faced.

The special meaning of this key-word in Jaspers' thought must be emphasized because in many circles today it is taken for granted that 'communication' is at its maximum wherever individual differences and emotional involvements can be eliminated. Such an outlook puts a premium upon those respects in which an exchange of thought can be conducted by means of objective rubrics: scientific laws, value-standards held in common, and a rationality that operates similarly in all men. In so far as the other person abides by such rubrics, we say that we can 'understand' him. Jaspers admits, of course, that ordinary communication is the subsoil in which existential encounter has its roots, just as *Dasein* is the foundation of *Existenz*. But there is a kind of authentic understanding of another person which can easily be lost if we dismiss what he says because we cannot gain access to it by following the usual rules of objective intelligibility.

Throughout his treatment of this theme, Jaspers' experience as a psychiatrist plays an important part, and some of the most recent experiments of psychotherapy with psychotics (e.g. H. S. Sullivan and Frieda Fromm-Reichmann) tend to support the point that was just made. But interesting implications follow if one looks at psychoanalysis as a specialized technique within the general framework of existential communication, regarding the latter as that form of interpersonal relations which enhances the discovery of true selfhood. Psychoanalysis starts with a situation in which the participants are not equal. One is ill and dependent, and the traffic of self-revelation does not flow both ways. If Jaspers is right, the goal of psychoanalysis should be the achievement of mutual equality; a mature human relationship should replace the helper-helped situation with a reciprocal person-to-person situation. Any love which is not strong enough to stand the test of *mutual* frankness is sentimental and incomplete. Psychoanalysts today, for good reasons, do not disclose their own beliefs and commitments—let alone their own unsolved emotional problems!—into the course of treatment if they can help it. But may this not mean that the treatment remains incomplete? Many patients, to be sure, complete the treatment after they have terminated psychoanalysis by carrying its gains into everyday life. And many psychotherapists do discuss their beliefs, commitments, and problems, not with patients but with colleagues. Nevertheless, Jaspers is probably right that in a complete process of psychotherapy a point should come when the patient is so mature that the doctor can cease being a permissive listener, and both together pass over into the reciprocity of what Jaspers calls 'loving struggle.' Such a procedure is not wholly practicable at present, but it deserves the attention of psychiatrists as an ultimate goal because it might expose hitherto unrecognized power motives on their part.

Jaspers assumes that existential truth can be imparted only through I-Thou confrontation. This sort of truth does not consist of propositions which are valid before and apart from their expression. Rather, it comes into being when the interpersonal relationship has reached the requisite level of openness and insight. It can be reached only by being lived. Yet we can, secondarily, enter an existential struggle with philosophers and writers of the past so that instead of merely appropriating propositional truths we are helped by them to actualize living truth. Thus Jaspers regards faith (trust) and love as prerequisites for *philosophical* truth, whereas these are usually regarded as concomitants which distinguish religious from philosophical 'knowing.'

Because the individual thinker is not 'universal mind,' his philosophizing is historically conditioned. Moreover, true selfhood cannot be achieved through the cultivation of inwardness at a safe distance from participation in political and social struggle; it requires action in history at the level of empirical events. Indeed, according to Jaspers, we become fully aware of selfhood only because of the 'boundary situations' with which historicity confronts us—conflict, suffering, guilt, and death. If life were endless and its possibilities infinite, nothing would ever be decisive and we would not develop wills. Hence the limits circumscribing autonomy are at the same time indispensable to the development of autonomy. Time makes us realize that we can irretrievably miss becoming authentic selves, and the inescapable presence of conflicts we cannot solve and of obstacles we cannot surmount drives us beyond a passive acceptance of the empirical world as it is. Jaspers' stress upon man's embeddedness in *Dasein* makes him an opponent of mysticism, if the latter means flight from the physical world and from history. On the other hand, his stress upon the connection between freedom and transcending makes him an opponent of positivism and any other philosophy which seeks to domesticate man wholly within the external world.

243

A specific example of the consequences of this position can be found in Jaspers' attitude toward the State. The State is both indispensable for freedom and a threat to freedom. The individual must recognize the manner in which it determines his destiny, and part of his struggle to achieve his *personal* destiny must take the form of political action. These requirements spring not merely from considerations of practical expediency; they reflect Jaspers' general thesis that no one can become himself in isolation. I cannot fight for my own freedom without at the same time fighting for the freedom of others. Yet the inescapability of political responsibility does not mean that the claims of the State are absolute. Its actions and policies must always be criticized, especially in an age when the drift toward totalitarianism is omnipresent, and the criticism must be based on a conception of human community that attaches importance to individual self-realization rather than standardized mass behavior. In politics, as in morals and philosophy, the 'exception,' the rebel, the man who refuses to conform, may do more to keep the function of authority in true perspective than the man who capitulates to it under pressure.

Like Heidegger, Jaspers distinguishes between a dispassionate and an existential approach to history. In the former, the historian is not personally involved in the events and struggles he studies; he may treat even the present in a detached way. But in the latter, one participates actively in events and tries to influence their outcome; one's reaction to these events manifests the fact that one belongs to a given tradition and operates within its presuppositions. Knowing and being are inseparable. Although a historian needs objective knowledge to grasp his own situation accurately, unless he also has existential concern he is not apprehending history as it really occurs.

The question arises, however, as to whether Jaspers' views can provide a stable position *vis-à-vis* the problems we are now discussing. His basic thesis is that if I try to leap out of my conditioning to reach some absolute vantage point, I miss both the nature of selfhood and of Being, for I can apprehend myself only as conditioned, and Being only as operative in and through history. Relationship between freedom and transcendence occurs in the midst of empirical reality, not apart from it. I have no 'self' in abstraction from my concrete activities, purposes, and goals, even though my self is not just a congeries of external processes. Parenthetically one may ask how Jaspers can so steadfastly reject mysticism while retaining his principle of openness. At times he seems to admit that there may be a truth in mysticism which he cannot fully appreciate. The parenthetic question is only one illustration of a basic dilemma, for in general Jaspers seeks to combine awareness of fallibility with decisiveness, and historical relativism with unconditioned concern. His interpretation of decision requires that I make absolute commitments even though I can never gain access to the Absolute in its essence, i.e. behind and beyond historical phenomena. Thus he tries to steer between the opposite extremes of fanaticism and indecisiveness. All credit should be given to him for his vivid articulation of a problem which none of us can evade, even though it may be insoluble. But the question remains of whether his inveterate habit of keeping certainty and uncertainty engaged with each other in an inconclusive struggle may not leave him, and anyone with similar views, in a weakened condition before the ominous power of those contemporary political forces which he is most anxious to oppose effectively.

His view of the relationship between the temporal and the eternal is like Kierkegaard's in so far as both writers claim that the Moment unites the two. The meaning of life is neither wholly transcendent nor a simple affirmation of immanent process. The Moment must not be misunderstood, of course, as signifying an Epicurean 'living in the present.' It means binding past and future together, through decision, in the presence of eternal meaning. According to Jaspers, this eternal meaning is present not as a datum resident within events but as something to be decided. The decision reflects not simply what we want to promote as the next temporal phase, but what we affirm for all time.

What is the relationship of the 'present charged with eternal significance' to the ordinary continuity of events? From one standpoint the Moment is just a fragment of time in the on-going continuum. We do not live from one disconnected eternal decision to the next. These decisions are high points arising out of an unbroken continuity; hence they are connected with each other and they throw light on the whole expanse of everyday living. Between such high points we must live by means of faithfulness, especially by faithfulness to the light which has already been given. To do so does not destroy growth by suffocating it under the weight of tradition. Indeed, the only way in which tradition can be kept alive is by a vital renewing and deepening of what it incorporates. New experience should enrich our appreciation of our past instead of destroying it. Fidelity to one's heritage, family, nation, and religious community is directly implied by acceptance of our historical conditioning as finite creatures. Thus Jaspers is able to regard the Bible as an indispensable source for his philosophizing and faith, holding that in order to recover the inner vitality of the Christian tradition one may have to break with its external expressions in institutions and dogmas. Sometimes fidelity may even require a large measure of resignation. When there is no 'high point' which can reveal a solemn and meaningful background for daily life, we face the alternatives of outright despair and a seemingly ungrounded hope.

We have seen that historicity is an indispensable condition for, and an obstacle to, freedom. Man confronts another boundary situation when he realizes that freedom must seek self-realization, yet cannot without involving itself in guilt. Jaspers writes of guilt as an original *condition* out of which particular instances of guilt issue. And he seems to regard the condition as inevitable because it is connected with finitude. Finitude forces us to participate in economic and political struggles; whether the individual acts or refrains from action, he contributes to patterns which result in some measure of injustice. Every ethical choice requires a man to fulfill one claim by rejecting others, and the others usually have some degree of legitimacy. Every friendship is entered into at the expense of close and sympathetic relations with others who may be equally admirable and worthy of attention.

Despite the fact that guilt is inevitable, Jaspers holds that we must take responsibility for it. This does not mean, of course, that we should indulge in the morbid fiction of pretending that we directly willed a given form of injustice, prejudice, or cruelty when in fact we did not. It means, rather, that we must take responsibility for our whole lives, and not just the 'voluntary' segments, because the whole self is present in every act. Yet Jaspers does not introduce here a doctrine of divine forgiveness. Instead, he teaches that man must have the courage to accept his guilt, and lets it go at that. To any critic who says that if guilt is inevitable there is no sense in trying to be good, he replies that a thorough awareness of guilt stimulates us to remedy those evils which we can correct. So long as we feel that an evil is entirely the fault of others, we can say that it is up to them to do something about it.

The importance of 'boundary situations' in Jaspers' philosophy is due to the fact that they make us supremely aware of the possibilities of *Existenz*—of what it is to be a human being. Standing at the edge of the boundary, man comes in sight, as it were, of the Transcendent. In Jaspers, as in Kierkegaard and Heidegger, our attitude toward death brings out the sharp contrast between objective knowledge and awareness of *Existenz*. Objective thinking may ignore the problem of death entirely or simply record as a matter of scientific fact that animals and men die. On the other hand, existential thinking squarely confronts the death of the 'I' in connection with self and friends; thus it realizes that a question hangs over the whole extent of empirical life which cannot be answered by means of information. I *must* answer the question. To evade it by burying myself in temporal pleasures, or by regarding myself as merely a complicated animal, or by letting life drift by without having really lived, is actually to answer the question. The same is true if I feel that because of death life is incurably meaningless. But another kind of answer is possible, one which Jaspers calls 'courageous faith.' He rejects belief in immortality if that means continuance of human life

247

as *Dasein* in some temporal future beyond the grave. Belief of this sort refuses to acknowledge our finitude and historicity. Yet he does not believe that sheer nothingness stands beyond the boundary. He holds that Lucretius was wrong in thinking that acceptance of annihilation could remove the fear of death; on the contrary, annihilation is the most dreadful threat of all. The real truth in doctrines of eternal life is not that we shall go on existing temporally, but that there are values and decisions which are not merely temporal because they incorporate an indestructible significance. We should not be concerned with some illusory future existence but with the spiritual struggle whereby the Moment can unite the temporal and the eternal. The threat of nothingness is real, and it cannot be circumvented by a doctrine, but it can be actively conquered in the present by courageous faith.

Dasein, everyday life, is destructible, and we should not even desire its indefinite continuation. But *Existenz,* authentic selfhood, can be entered into now and its meaning is imperishable. Only by facing death realistically do we become formed, decisive, resolute, and reconciled to finitude. The threat of missing true selfhood is worse than the unavoidable fact of physical disintegration. And the reality of the latter makes me alert to the former. It is because I am going to die as a biological organism that I may miss true selfhood. Because I do not have forever, the question hangs over every moment: 'Are you living, feeling, realizing, choosing yourself or some feeble caricature of what you could be?' One who has lived for ends-in-themselves and who has entered into existential communication with others knows that what is important in his life and in the life of his friend cannot be annihilated by death.[3]

4. Metaphysics, the Ciphers, and Shipwreck

By its very nature, Transcendence cannot be defined or known, for it cannot be grasped by the understanding that makes the objective world intelligible, nor is it accessible to pure subjectivity. How, then, can Jaspers say anything about Being-itself? How can he refer to it as beyond the split between subject and object, and as somehow uniting *Dasein* and *Existenz*? His reply is that we must think of Transcendence not as something grasped but as something sought. 'Transcending' indubitably takes place. We seek Being-itself *through* world orientation by coming up against the incompleteness, finitude, and transitoriness of *Dasein*. We seek it *through* the clarification of existence which presses to the outermost edge of boundary situations. We seek it through metaphysics and belief in God.

At this point a wide gulf seems to open up between Heidegger and Jaspers because the latter renounces ontology, but the difference turns out to be mostly terminological, especially if Heidegger's later writings are considered. Jaspers assumes that ontology attempts to formulate a conception of Being-itself on the basis of empirical reality and the nature of human consciousness, and he objects to the notion that Being-itself can be grasped directly by means of a system valid for all men. Universal validity is possible, he claims, only in the sort of objective knowledge which excludes existential factors. Heidegger, however, also stresses the contrast between Being-itself and both the empirical world and human subjectivity.

At first glance the two writers seem to take opposed attitudes on the relative merits of 'metaphysics' and 'ontology.' Heidegger suggests that a faithful pursuit of the ontological task will lead to an undermining, correction, and transcendence of past metaphysics. Jaspers, rejecting ontology, writes as if metaphysics, mainly by following the *via negativa,* could be the supreme instance of transcending. But here again the difference is largely terminological, for Jaspers also feels that the true significance of past metaphysics can be entered into only if we regard it as a mode of witnessing the Transcendent by means of symbolic language, and only if we discern in it a manifestation of inescapable search. It is wrong to look on these systems as having set forth literal, objective truth whereby the nature of Being-itself can be apprehended directly.

From a formal standpoint, Transcendence in Jaspers' philosophy is Being-itself. From an existential standpoint, it is 'God'; and the expression 'the hidden God' points to the fact that Transcendence

249

cannot be grasped by means of knowledge. When he comes to discuss Being-itself, neither an objective nor a subjective approach is adequate, yet each strives to be incorporated in that 'third way' which cannot be specified. Every attempt to specify it, of course, has to be expressed by means of objectivation. On the other hand, since Being-itself cannot be known our only *positive* relationship to it must be a non-objective, existential encounter. Formal thinking can make a negative contribution by preparing for this encounter. We do not come in sight of Transcendence by running away from objective knowledge, but by pursuing the latter to its furthest limits. We take every finite category, such as cause, quality, and quantity, and realize that they cannot be applied to the ultimate. Then we 'think' about Transcendence not as an object, but as the presupposition of all finite categories whose limits can only be defined in relation to this presupposition.

Beyond positive knowledge of the world lies this awareness of antinomies which gives us a proper perspective on knowledge we can possess. The antinomies Jaspers has in mind are Kantian. We cannot conceive of the world as having a beginning or as not having a beginning. We cannot conceive of the transition from nothing to something, and yet we cannot conceive of there not being such a transition. Thus the supreme achievement of thought is to reach and to acknowledge its limits. Then we are ready to take seriously the fact that what is logically meaningless—e.g. the identity of Being and Nothing or of Necessity and contingency—may nevertheless have to be presupposed.

By setting up and negating every positive statement we can make about Being-itself, we get a glimmer of Transcendence, and thereby realize the difference between Being-itself and every historical manifestation through which it operates. Strictly speaking, Jaspers should negate, as well as affirm, his own term 'Transcendence,' for it too has spatial and relational connotations.

What his position comes down to, then, is that Being-itself, although it transcends every finite mode, is nevertheless encountered in the midst of finitude. He insists that philosophy must incorporate the existential factor, the concrete ways in which Being-itself is experienced, by means of what amounts to personal confession. A philosophical faith can keep us aware of the remoteness as well as the nearness of God, of His strangeness as well as of that kinship which makes Him 'my' God. That such an outlook distinguishes Jaspers' position from speculative rationalism is clear enough. But it leaves him open to attacks from two sides. Philosophers can claim that he has really abandoned their ranks by exalting faith and personal confession above rational discourse. And theologians can claim that he pilfers an essentially anti-philosophical position, mainly from Luther, and then puts it on display as the true essence of philosophy. One of Jaspers' reasons for calling his faith philosophical instead of theological is that the latter speaks of God as personal and therefore falls into the mistake of regarding Him as *a* being. He also holds that if God ever literally appeared in history freedom would be destroyed. Only because He remains transcendent is man impelled to seek Him through free activity. If the answer to the meaning of life were available apart from search and struggle, man would have no part in making himself what he is to become.

Because Being-itself is the ground of all existence, both terms of every antinomy are rooted in it. Hence both sides must enter into our search—the dark, destroying forces as well as the orderly, constructive ones. As Jaspers writes of 'the law of the day' and 'the passion of the night' he reminds one of Jung. Plainly, he wants to see those forces which issue in clarity, communication, and fidelity win out, but he believes that this can happen only if those other forces which want to break out of the confinements of order and stability, and which can plunge man toward nothingness and death, are incorporated into courageous faith. Sometimes this may take the form of a willingness to renounce the world in favor of death. In any case, unless the dark passions are allowed to come into the open where light can struggle with them, they will break loose in wholly destructive forms. Political and religious fanaticism show all too clearly how man's readiness for renunciation and sacrifice can serve nihilistic revolt under the guise of noble intentions.

251

We have already seen that the two approaches to Being-itself, by objective thought and by inward attitude, are inadequate. Only because man transcends *Dasein* and objective knowledge can he come into relationship with Being-itself, yet what he is thus related to also transcends him and his necessarily concrete, historical, subjective ways of approaching it. Jaspers seeks to ameliorate these difficulties by means of his doctrine of 'ciphers.' This use of the word is derived from the fact that messages are sometimes put into codes which have to be deciphered. Jaspers holds that ordinary finite events can point beyond themselves in a symbolic manner, but the message must be decoded, and the key to the code is not a form of knowledge. What is required is a free decision of the whole man in response to the message which comes from Being-itself.

Although what the cipher points to transcends ordinary experience, one pole of the relationship always falls within ordinary experience. In principle anything and any event can become a cipher so long as it points, not to some other finite entity or event, but to Being-itself. If the Transcendent has *no* connection with the world, we would not even be aware of the intervening gulf. On the other hand, to identify Being-itself with anything finite, or with the totality of the world, is to remain trapped in immanence and thus to deny freedom.

The cipher is a unique symbol. Ordinary symbolism in science and philosophy takes for granted that the symbol indicates a reality which, in principle, might be known non-symbolically. By the latter knowledge we can test the adequacy or the appropriateness of the symbol. But ciphers cannot be verified in this way since what they point to cannot be reached by knowledge. To assume that there is some other way of getting at Transcendence, by means of which the cipher can be tested, is to reject that claim of a particular experience or event to be a manifestation of Transcendence—i.e. to reject its cipher-hood. Thus the cipher must be self-authenticating. The only thing that can give us a more authentic relationship to Being-itself than an ostensible cipher is a genuine cipher.

When we try to communicate *about* the situation of being related to Transcendence we naturally have to use universals, but the language best suited to express being in the relationship is religious myth. Speculation which attempts to form a concept of Being-itself apart from ciphers makes the mistake of cutting itself off from the only way men can be related to it. On the other hand, an approach which studies all myths empirically but believes in none of them cannot remain purely empirical, for its own basic concept, Nature, is constantly employed as identical with or as a substitute for Being-itself.

Although Being-itself is independent of man, how it manifests itself is related to the responsiveness and perceptiveness of the self. The cipher cannot mediate, cannot be what it is, unless man is receptive. Hence we can take attitudes which block off and resist what Transcendence offers. We can stay within the confines of immanence; we can set up rationalism as the sole test of truth; we can fall into a relativism in which nothing is regarded as unconditional. In all of these instances we are refusing to acknowledge and decode the ciphers. Receptiveness requires personal commitment, admission of the limits of knowledge, and search for the truth as 'the truth for me.'

Because the ciphers are historical, they reflect the way in which existence changes in its relationship to the eternal. Real fidelity to them requires a continual readiness to abandon one form for another. Only so can the finite, historical pole of the relationship be properly subordinate to Being-itself. Therefore Jaspers insists that no cipher is final. But it is difficult to reconcile such an attitude with his teaching that the cipher is self-authenticating. How can he say that no cipher is final without setting up a criterion, not itself a cipher, by which the multifarious claims of myths and symbols can be judged? Does not the assertion that no cipher is final presuppose a relationship to Being-itself which is final?

These questions are important because Jaspers' teaching about ciphers is his substitute for a doctrine of revelation. His reiterated complaint against the latter is that it makes claims of finality which ignore man's fallibility and finitude, destroy openness, and put a stop to the ceaseless quest. Yet revealed theology often occupies positions similar to Jaspers'. It also holds that God's essence is not objectively knowable. It affirms that He transcends and is real apart from man, even though we can only be related to Him in and through faith. It declares that God manifests Himself in concrete, historical events, and it can acknowledge that the myths and symbols through which men have expressed the experience of being encountered undergo continual changes. It claims that revelation, like the cipher, is self-authenticating, and that the only adequate remedy for defective religious beliefs is an authentic response to God Himself. Even though most theologians admit that philosophical criticism can help us get rid of defective beliefs, it cannot of itself establish authentic response, which is really synonymous with saving faith. Theology must admit, finally, that men are able to take attitudes which block off or resist what God offers, although theologians differ in their views on how grace overcomes this resistance, and their differences come out crucially in connection with the doctrine of predestination.

The one aspect of revealed theology which Jaspers cannot accept, and which has no parallel in his doctrine of ciphers, is its claim to finality. More will be said about this matter shortly. Suffice it to say here that Jaspers is right in discerning that it is very difficult to accept a final criterion in such a way that spiritual growth is constantly fostered instead of blocked. It is difficult to hold any belief, doctrine, or formula in such a way that its historically conditioned character is always remembered and paramount importance is not attached to the human belief, but to the reality of God to which it points. Let us also grant that Jaspers may be right in feeling that revealed theology has for the most part failed to strike the delicate balance which might overcome these difficulties. Nevertheless, are not these difficulties intrinsic in the human situation as Jaspers himself has described that situation? Are they avoided by renouncing revelation? Does not Jaspers himself remain entangled in them so long as he asserts that his own doctrine of the ciphers is in any sense true?

Perhaps Jaspers achieves a strange consistency by holding that no positive cipher is final because the final cipher is negative. 'The ultimate,' he says, 'is shipwreck.' [4] It may be characterized as a situation in which no cipher appears, and by which all ciphers are to be tested. We come closest to Transcendence when all approaches to it have been shattered. Our attempts to construct a metaphysical system have dissolved into antinomies. Our attempts to find an intelligible pattern in history have been engulfed in the chaos of events. Freedom has turned against itself and destroys freedom. Even the religious quest has trailed off into silence and emptiness. The individual is in a state of inner collapse, frustration, isolation. No philosophical or religious 'doctrine' can help him. Something must happen inside him and yet it does not happen. This realization of the utter precariousness of existence, when we have literally nowhere to turn, brings home as nothing else can the difference between our world and Transcendence. By cutting off every analogy, every meaning which might tempt us to think of Being-itself in familiar, manageable terms, it makes us aware of the unattainable character of what stands behind and above all our approaches. Where nothing is left to us, Being is there. 'The non-being of all that is accessible to us, that non-being which reveals itself in ship wreck, is the Being of Transcendence.' [5]

Jaspers believes that the possibility of shipwreck is a condition of freedom. Unless human existence is thus precarious, we could domesticate ourselves in the world at the level of *Dasein* and cease to be fully human. The experience of shipwreck may teach us that our true destiny lies above the level of empirical events, and some of us cannot learn this until the course of empirical events has become utterly catastrophic. Instead of learning the lesson, however, we may simply confront meaningless destruction without hope. This moreover actually occurs. Suffering may lead to the complete destruction of the personality instead of to strength and wisdom; the death of a little child after long torment, the wholesale slaughter of warfare, the spiritual putrefaction of the concentration camp—none of these facts can be fitted into a meaningful pattern of history. Hence they make every philosophy questionable. The outcome does

255

not depend on the ability of a philosophy to provide explanations; these are unobtainable. It depends rather on the ability of the individual to become related to Being-itself by means of shipwreck. Philosophy, in all ordinary uses of the term, has come to a dead-end, and personal faith has taken over. Yet the faith is not directed toward any object.

As soon as we try to teach someone else, by means of language, how to cope with shipwreck, we have left the situation itself and passed into the region of universals and logical discourse. All Jaspers can say, by means of such discourse, is that destruction of the world cannot destroy Being-itself. If my cipher can express this fact, if it can remain standing after all human potentialities have been shattered, then it is authentically a window through which the light of Transcendence shines. But there is no way of reaching the peace of this affirmation except by passing through anxiety and hopelessness.

How does man have the power thus to stand fast? How does he have the courage to affirm Being? One cannot say 'through his freedom'; for the situation Jaspers has described is one where freedom itself falters. Neither can one say 'by saving grace beyond freedom,' for then it is a puppet who is saved instead of a man. Jaspers believes that when we have relinquished all illusions, all false optimism, all this-worldly hopes, all unrealistic confidence in our own strength, then a new kind of strength comes to us because freedom can destroy itself but cannot destroy its Ground. At that point we can enter freely into the faith which declares: 'It is enough that Being is.' [6]

What Jaspers has described is at the opposite pole from a Freudian death-instinct which actively seeks and desires shipwreck. A premature willingness to give up the ship pretends that tragedy does not matter because everything is hopelessly obscure anyway. Shipwreck is authentically faced only when we struggle against it with all our strength yet still recognize that it cannot be avoided. There is no legitimate renunciation of the world which does not issue in a return to the world. One must really care about the values which are destroyed; one must be faithful to whatever is meaningful and normative in life; and then one must face the destructibility of everything that can be cherished. It is only when, through struggle and sadness, we have let go of everything temporal and finite that the Eternal appears in temporality and finitude.

5. Philosophy, Religion, and Faith

Jaspers is convinced that all truth is one because it is grounded in Transcendence, but he is equally convinced that no one can reach this truth in a static or exclusive manner. Our approaches must take the form of a constant movement, and we must remember that all of them are historically conditioned. This throws the emphasis on the individual's search. Existential truth may come to us in 'exceptional' ways, i.e. which go against the general or universal patterns of thought and morality. What makes the Exception valuable is not his unconventionality; the deviant may be a criminal instead of a prophet. And it is possible to break with the conventional inwardly while outwardly living a quite orderly existence. The distinguishing mark of the Exception is that he finds himself subject to an unconditional claim which is not objectively demonstrable. A scientific truth remains valid whether we accept it or not. We do not appropriate it by means of loyalty, but by means of a rational process of verification which any other mind in principle can also follow.

But fidelity to the unconditional claim should not encourage scorn for scientific truth or everyday moral standards. The Exception is compelled to go beyond them, but always with the agonizing awareness that he may be wrong. And since persecution may befall him whether he is right or wrong, persecution cannot in itself be regarded as a vindication. Spiritual heroes and pioneers are often executed by men who think they are defending order and civil righteousness against a dreadful threat, but usually the latter have some portion of the truth on their side which the Exception, in his singleness of purpose, has ignored. Moreover, it is misleading to divide humanity into two groups, the exceptional and the conventional. The struggle between these two can go on in the breast of any man,

257

because everyone can share in collective responsibilities and yet everyone can also have a unique way of reacting to life which incorporates values that no one else can fully appreciate.

Therefore the individual search must be balanced by a principle which Jaspers calls 'authority,' meaning that through our traditions and communal heritages we receive riches far greater than any isolated individual could spin out for himself. Authority makes its impact not merely through rational suasion, but also through laws and institutions. The Exception may come into conflict with its coercive power, but his revolt should be intended to reshape traditions and institutions, not an attempt to annihilate them. The legitimacy of authority can be tested by the extent to which it is inwardly, freely appropriated instead of having to maintain itself through threats and coercion. Indeed, the real test is the extent to which authority is based on Transcendence. Since this can never be 'known,' the scientific study of governments and cultures can merely describe how they operate; it can never tell us the extent to which these patterns reflect the Eternal. Thus political judgments about ends, as contrasted with technical questions about means, must be based upon religious confession. The validity of these judgments can never be demonstrated; they can be implemented only by loving and serving what they imply. All too often authority becomes tyrannical, relies on force instead of devotion, and deifies itself in ways that are an outrage against Transcendence. Nevertheless, if the bearing of the reality of God upon human society is to be found at all, it must be found in connection with historical traditions and institutions which seek to point to Him, and He must be served through serving relative, historical movements and earthly authorities.

Thus in his search for truth Jaspers swings continually between two poles, unconditional faith and openness. Fanaticism arises whenever unconditional faith tries to base itself upon a truth which is regarded as objective and universally valid. In the attitude which Jaspers calls 'catholicity,' truth is regarded as static and finished, and as the exclusive possession of one group. He holds that existential truth cannot come to anyone in this form. It comes as 'truth for me,' and therefore it is inconsistent to try to force anyone else to accept truth on the basis of dogma, demonstration, or in any other non-existential fashion. Whenever Christianity claims to have exclusive possession of the final revelation, purports to be able to transmit it through creeds and doctrines, and then declares that those who reject it are damned, it is falling into 'catholicity.' Here authority has forgotten its proper role and has turned tyrannical. Finite, fallible men claim that they have come into possession of a finished truth, thereby forgetting that God transcends all the historical manifestations through which He reveals Himself.

Openness requires me to remember that my personal faith is only one among many. I must be ready to die for it, but only in the effort to convince others *freely* of its truth. I cannot serve it by killing them for rejecting it. Nevertheless, Jaspers has to face the question as to whether openness may not lead to a tentativeness which undercuts all vital faith. He contends that it does not if openness is incorporated as an essential ingredient in faith itself. Trust can include readiness to meet risk and change. Firmness can include willingness to enter into existential communication with alien points of view. Since my own faith can only be understood from the inside, it follows that I am not in a strong position for passing judgment on other faiths so long as I have to view them from the outside. Yet Jaspers does not suggest that by studying all religions sympathetically, we can arrive at a syncretistic view which is more adequate than any one of them; for the syncretist, if he is committed to none, fails to get inside any. The instant he gives his commitment to some rationalistic or eclectic amalgam, his so-called 'universal essence of religion' is really just one sect among others and at logger-heads with others.

There is then no escape from historical particularity. Faith is always both absolute and relative. It is absolute in the sense of being unconditional; it is relative because it is individual and historical. The only way to meet this situation is to strive ceaselessly for communication. Having no faith at all is not openness, but emptiness. Readiness for communication means that in some hitherto alien outlook I may find a manifestation of God to which I have been blind. Nevertheless, Jaspers recognizes that an ideal solution is impossible. Today we confront substitute religions which spread their ideologies not merely by means of sacred books, rites, and doctrines, but through dictators, storm troopers, and secret police. The conflict among faiths competing for the minds and souls of men therefore takes forms where loving communication is out of the question, especially when the opponent is a wartime enemy. Yet we become completely dehumanized unless, in fighting the war, we are struggling to preserve or to re-establish the sort of human dignity and spiritual freedom which loving communication implies.

It should now be apparent why Jaspers stands as a mediating figure within the existentialist movement. There are existentialists who have remained, however restively or iconoclastically, within the traditions of revealed religion, Protestant, Roman Catholic, and Jewish. There are other existentialists who are atheists. Jaspers rejects both alternatives, seeking to transform aspects of each and to blend them together into a philosophic faith. His efforts give rise to a dialectic of defiance and surrender. If it is only through a full exercise of freedom that man can enter into authentic trust, then the doubts and questions which arise in our minds must not be silenced.

The first step must always be the achievement of independence. Only a man who has learned to trust himself can believe that Being-itself is trustworthy. Any honest man is so revolted and baffled by the tragedy of life that he is tempted to rebel against existence. By rejecting pseudo-solutions, he finds that there are no remedies for evil, suffering, and guilt except those which man can achieve by his freedom. If life can be made worthwhile, it is not through practicing some sort of metaphysical or religious *legerdemain* which makes tragedy unreal, but through becoming something we can affirm despite man's precarious and vulnerable situation. There is, then, a truth in atheism. I must become my own answer instead of expecting the answer to be furnished by tradition, society, or the church. Here Jaspers finds atheism on the side of honesty when it refuses to call evil 'good' for the sake of retaining theodicy, and he finds

260

that conventional doctrines of God often go hand in hand with timidity and dishonesty. But he adds that insistence upon truthfulness is an authentic way of standing in the presence of God even when an individual, as an atheist, does not realize what he is doing. God, the ground of freedom, does not want blind and craven capitulation.

On the other side of defiance, however, lies a form of surrender which is strength, not weakness. Through an acute sense of righteousness and justice which prompts us to cry out against the world as it is, we come into communion with a righteous and just God. Through asking God the most embarrassing questions, we seek Him. Through rejecting rational or traditionally pious conceptions of Him that cannot stand the test of criticism, we express our need for an authentic relationship. At that point we realize that we could not defy God unless He had already given us the power to do so. By accepting and exercising this gift, the atheist accepts God without knowing it. Once we can affirm the source of that freedom which enables us to rebel, to doubt, and to make our own answers to life, we can be ready for whatever duties and tragedies may come to us.

From Jaspers' standpoint, then, atheism is a complex phenomenon and it is superficial to reject it wholesale. At least three different attitudes may be found under the same label. The first strives to find sufficiency by complete domestication within the world. Instead of exercising the tragic freedom of entering into true selfhood, it immerses the self in immanence and settles for such goals as enjoyment, prosperity, or power. This atheistic conduct of life can be found not only among those who consciously reject belief in God, but also among many who belong to churches and regard themselves as religious people. The second form of atheism is nihilism, and Jaspers' attitude toward it has already been discussed. Against the first form of adjustment to the world it has the merit of insisting upon the exercise of freedom, but it regards freedom itself as absurd. The third form of atheism, which may sometimes be combined with the second, is really a religious protest signifying, albeit indirectly

261

and unwittingly, the transcendence of God and man's yearning for truth, justice, and meaning.

Jaspers' relationship to his own Protestant tradition is even more complicated than his attitude toward atheism. For purposes of exposition we have sometimes used 'Being-itself' and 'God' interchangeably in the foregoing because Jaspers comes close to doing the same thing himself. But the latter word has many religious connotations which cannot possibly be read into his philosophy. This becomes clear if we examine his use of another term, *Das Umgreifende*, 'the Encompassing' or 'the Enveloping.' He applies this term to each of seven different horizons, from any one of which we can look at the whole of reality. These are: (1) Empirical existence (*Dasein*); (2) consciousness in general (*Bewusstsein überhaupt*); (3) creative mind (*Geist*); (4) existing in inwardness (*Existenz*); (5) reason, as defined earlier (*Vernunft*); (6) world, as defined in connection with world-orientation; and (7) Transcendence. In an effort to simplify our discussion, these have been grouped under three main headings—world, self, and transcendence. Yet everything can fall within any one of the seven. For example, I can be viewed as incorporating the universe, or the universe can be viewed as incorporating me. The world can be regarded as excluding selfhood (and, as a consequence, selfhood may be ignored), or it can be regarded as including the ego. Nevertheless, 'that which envelops' really lies beyond any closed perspective.

The most puzzling aspect of this scheme is encountered at the point where Jaspers treats the seventh, Transcendence, as *primus inter pares*. He seems to be indicating that if Being-itself holds all modes of reality together, we can never reach a unifying perspective from which we see how this is done. Being-itself is manifest to us through various unifying perspectives, but absolute unity—or, as some theologians might wish to say, God as He is in His essence—forever transcends us, and the seventh mode can merely point to that fact.

Jaspers himself recognizes certain affinities between his position and that of Plotinus when the latter speaks of the ineffability of the

One. Jaspers' meaning is that no predicates derived from the way we seek to organize knowledge and experience are applicable to Being-itself. We cannot legitimately speak of it as either personal or impersonal, determinate or free. But since Jaspers does have to denote what he is speaking about by using one term, Being-itself, the question arises of whether the latter can then be differentiated— as it must be, if it is transcendent—from connotations which make it merely a summary name for that in which everything real participates. If all ciphers are *merely* inappropriate, then Jaspers' affirmation of transcendence, and his accompanying rejection of pure immanentalism, is undermined. No matter what conclusion we reach on this issue, we can at least understand why, when Jaspers uses the word 'God,' anthropomorphic connotations must be excluded. At the same time, because the relationship of the individual to Being-itself must be existential, our mode of approach cannot divest itself of anthropomorphic coloring. If someone reproaches Jaspers with having ended with incoherence, since he says in effect that what he and every other man *must* do is at the same time inappropriate, I suppose he could reply that this situation illustrates precisely what he has been trying to call attention to all along—the inaccessibility of Being-itself.

Now let us turn to the relationship between philosophy and religion. Jaspers recognizes that since both deal with the whole of life and with ultimate questions, commerce between them has always involved both kinship and enmity. He is willing to admit that philosophy could not long survive, at least as a vital enterprise, unless religion trained people from childhood onward to orientate their lives toward transcendence. And he vigorously opposes efforts to reduce tension between philosophy and religion by arranging some sort of division of labor; he is not willing, as some philosophers are, to turn over such matters as faith, absolute commitment, and existential concern to religion on the ground that their presence is likely to interfere with the rigor of those methods which have first claim on the philosopher's allegiance. For Jaspers, precisely because philosophy must be based upon a faith of its own, it cannot accept the

263

claims of special revelation nor submit to ecclesiastical authority.

He rejects special revelation because he sees it as an attempt to turn something which must remain individual and existential into something direct, objective, and universally binding. He does not, of course, reject the belief that revelation occurs in history; what he denies is that a particular cipher can at the same time *be* the Transcendent. He also denies that religious truth can be appropriated by accepting dogma, inasmuch as it cannot be passed on from one generation to the next as scientific truths are, nor can it be comprised in a rationally ordered system. Furthermore, whereas Christianity fixes on only one cipher as final, philosophy must try to see how all ciphers point to God. Whereas Christianity demands the acceptance of a particular book, institution, and Saviour, philosophy appropriates freely from any religious source without capitulating to exclusivistic demands. Thus, according to Jaspers, the philosopher can remain more faithful to the transcendence of God than the theologian, for the latter always wants to identify God with something finite. And where Christianity thinks it has some basis of certainty which cannot be questioned, philosophy insists on questioning everything and anything.

The dilemma between openness and decisiveness thus appears once again. In order to retain his philosophical integrity, Jaspers must remain aloof from religious belief, yet to be genuinely open and ready for communication he needs to be susceptible to such faith. He admits that in his effort to take account of whatever is true in all religious traditions, the philosopher becomes incapable of entering fully into any. Therefore there is no way out of the dilemma. If a man incorporates the value of one emphasis, he will cut himself off from direct experience of the value of the other, and there is no third possibility able to synthesize both. The split is not between philosophical detachment and personal commitment. A conflict goes on, within Jaspers, between two irreconcilable forms of existential faith. When either philosophy or religion loses its existential character, it has deteriorated. The one may be led by endless questioning into an intellectual and spiritual paralysis called suspended

judgment. The other can fall into mechanical, external belief in revelation. But even when both are at their best, there is one ineradicable
difference. The philosopher surrenders to God only via independence and autonomy; the religious man subordinates his freedom to
some kind of superhuman guarantee. Jaspers clearly believes that
the philosophical venture shows a higher kind of trust and comes
closer to the truth by taking account of the threatening, as well as
the affirming, character of Transcendence. In short, he seeks to
retain and to reformulate what is best in Christianity by relinquishing precisely those claims of certainty, finality, and uniqueness
which many Christians regard as forming the indispensable core of
their truth.

Yet Jaspers would like to persuade philosophers that the Bible
should permeate their thinking. He explicitly takes over the way in
which it affirms monotheism, preserving a dialectical relationship
between the transcendent and the historical. He also accepts, in his
own way, the belief that man is created in the image of God. He
holds that ethical distinctions are grounded in divine love which
transcends moral relativism, and that history as a whole has meaning and is not fragmented into particular moments and epochs possessing only transitory meaning. Although he regards most prayer
as superstitious because it attempts to view God as a finite person
who can be persuaded to satisfy our selfish desires, he holds that
prayer, in a purified sense, is the only appropriate manner whereby
man can 'think' of God. It is a living relatedness to the Transcendent
instead of talk about such a relationship. Thus prayer can mean the
building up of one's strength through meditation on the source of
creativity and freedom; seeking only an inward transfiguration and
expecting no external results, it can save worship from being corrupted by mixed motives. Closely related to this sort of prayer, to
which the philosopher turns in times of stress and isolation, is
Jaspers' conviction that suffering may become a means to communion with God. He sees in the aged Jeremiah a man who has
been deprived of all earthly support, who has encountered shipwreck, and who finds, nevertheless, that it is enough that God is.

Hence there is no doubt about Jaspers' receptiveness of the Bible. But he is convinced that inasmuch as revealed theology has continually blocked a free appropriation of the Biblical message, it is up to the philosopher to recover its living appeal by cutting through all accretions of dogma. As he undertakes this task, Jaspers is compelled to regard Christian belief in the Incarnation as incompatible with the absolute transcendence of God.

He expresses his attitude sharply in the following passage: 'It is among the sorrows of my life spent in the search for truth, that discussion with theologians always dries up at crucial points; they fall silent, state an incomprehensible proposition, speak of something else, make some categorical statement, engage in amiable talk, without really taking cognizance of what one has said—and in the last analysis they are not really interested. For on the one hand they are certain of their truth, terrifyingly certain; and on the other hand they do not regard it as worth while to bother about people like us, who strike them as merely stubborn. And communication requires listening and real answers, forbids silence or the evasion of questions; it demands above all that all statements of faith . . . should continue to be questioned and tested, not only outwardly, but inwardly as well.' [7]

Jaspers rejects special revelation, therefore, on the ground that it blurs the distinction between finite things and God Himself. Precisely because the Word of God is not the word of man, the Christian doctrine of the God-man is unconvincing. He admits that often, in the conflict between faith and reason, Christianity has rightly reminded philosophy of polarities which the latter was trying to ignore. He admits that instead of purifying religious truth, much philosophical criticism has made the mistake of trying to destroy it. But he steadfastly resists the exclusivistic claim of Christianity on the ground that it tries to treat the content of faith as though it were universally true. The theologian has to claim that revelation has lifted him above the exigencies of human finitude and fallibility. Thus will-to-power is introduced into a religion which supposedly nurtures the opposite. When this happens, philosophy cannot remain neutral. To do so would imply that intolerance is harmless.

Belief in the Incarnation is incompatible not only with Transcendence but with freedom. Since the center of value is in the individual, not in the genus, the primary task of becoming oneself must not be made subordinate to a universal model of perfect Manhood. To regard Christ the Pattern as of supreme importance is to treat the individual as though he were expendable, and to violate the principle that every man is an end in himself because he is a source of ethical creativity. The most any human being can do is point to Transcendence. No man can *be* God. If there were an event in history where God had finally revealed Himself, then man would no longer be called to the venture of finding his own way through the darkness of life. He would merely need to accept, as universally binding, what the God-man tells us to do, and to receive, through atoning transaction within the Godhead, a salvation which makes struggling and groping superfluous. Hidden beneath the doctrine of the God-man, Jaspers feels, is a fear of freedom and a contempt for humanity. Indeed, theology can take a form akin to nihilism when it relinquishes the faith that God can work creatively in history through all men. Then the belief that He can bring about salvation through a special, sinless man, who as such cannot really be part of our dark and tragic history, is merely a device for escaping the hopelessness which attends the initial defeatist attitude toward man.

Once the elements which he regards as idolatrous have been removed, however, Jaspers affirms that the spirit of Jesus can help each man reach his own authentic selfhood. But this spirit appears in many other ways in human history and Jesus has no monopoly on it. Jaspers cites Matthew 19:17 where Jesus asks 'Why callest Thou me good?' as an attempt on the Master's part to reject the attribution of deity to Himself. Jesus, like other prophets and martyrs, was an Exception with a special vocation. But we cannot make Him into a standard picture of the whole man for every man. He refused to take up the ordinary duties of marriage and the state, and He paid but scant attention to knowledge and culture. Thus

267

there are many values we have a right to pursue which a rigid worship of Him would exclude. Finally, a literal following of Him becomes not a way of life, but a way of death. He stands as a symbol for the fact that man must be ready to suffer and die for his faith, but this readiness must be combined with a responsible attitude toward the on-going processes of history, political action, and institutions. The message of Jesus must be freely, not slavishly appropriated. By criticism and independence the philosopher can serve the cause of Transcendence, which Jesus also served, against those who have turned belief in Him into idolatry. Philosophy must continue to fight revealed theology in so far as the latter results in defensiveness and special pleading, puts a stop to critical inquiry, destroys communication between believer and unbeliever, stresses eschatology at the expense of historical endeavor, and tends to induce a martyr complex.

6. Critique

Jaspers' criticism of theology applies with considerable force whenever a doctrine is not held in a genuinely existential way. Thus it can apply to a theological outlook originally existential but subsequently hardened into a form of dogmatism which tries to treat the supernatural or the supra-rational as furnishing a form of objective certainty. A doctrinal scheme can be as rigid as any speculative system, whether it rejects philosophy (e.g. Barthianism) or whether it regards philosophy as compatible with revelation (e.g. Thomism).

The problem remains as to whether Christianity, in being faithful to itself, must take forms which Jaspers rejects. He contemplates only two possibilities. The first is universally valid, objective knowledge, which is confined to phenomena, non-existential, scientific. The second is unconditional commitment, which is 'absolute' in the sense that it calls for total response on the part of the whole man, but which is at the same time inescapably individual, historically conditioned, and engaged in endless striving. He holds that the Transcendent manifests itself through various historical media, but points out that our individual apprehension of God is only one among others, that our religious tradition is only one among others. Yet as we have seen repeatedly, it is impossible for Jaspers to regard his own philosophy, in so far as it is true, as falling under either of these alternatives. Clearly he does not claim for his statements about Being-itself the sort of universal validity which characterizes scientific propositions. Neither does he put them forward merely as private opinion which reflect the peculiarities of his individual subjectivity. What, then, is their status? Even if he could succeed in confining himself entirely to the *via negativa,* his negative statements, in order to be true, would have to occupy a position which avoids both alternatives.

In short, Jaspers must presuppose that, in his case at least, some sort of fusion has taken place between the universally valid and the existential. He cannot assume, without undermining his own philosophy, that because all individuals are historically conditioned they are equally far from a right orientation toward Being-itself. It is difficult to avoid the force of Joseph de Tonquédec's remark: 'Jaspers deprecates every "philosophic system," every universally valid "doctrine," every teaching that can be objectively transmitted. And after having made these statements, he writes three volumes of philosophy. Whether he admits it or not, he certainly attempts to teach his contemporaries the one and only way of truth, the only correct attitude regarding reality, the only way to attain to being and to relate oneself to Transcendence.'[8]

The general difficulty in which Jaspers finds himself at this point has a direct bearing on his remarks about Christology. He teaches that Being-itself can be discerned with varying degrees of adequacy through the ciphers and that the eternal and the temporal can be joined in the Moment. But he regards it as incompatible with the nature of both Transcendence and history to say more than that they can be connected. He holds that to regard them as pervasively identical is pantheism, and that to believe they are identical at one unrepeatable point is arbitrary. One must acknowledge, in his defense, that many arbitrary and foolish beliefs are impossible to disprove. But if he believes that Being-itself is manifest at all in history, why does he assume that no such manifestation can take the form of identity (God-manhood)? Here he brings 'already finished' assumptions about the nature of Transcendence and the nature of historicity to bear upon the Christological problem. How did Jaspers reach them? How can he hold that one cipher may be more adequate than another, but that no cipher is final, without claiming for his own views concerning the possible connections between Transcendence and history some sort of real finality? How has he attained enough certainty about Being-itself, despite his own finitude and fallibility, to declare that no man can be God? Why is it consistent with humility and freedom to subject all searching and faith to the transcendent illumination of Being-itself, which must reach me in history if it is to reach me at all, yet inconsistent with these same qualities to subject searching and faith to the Transcendent as Incarnate in history?

Jaspers takes the statements in which Jesus points beyond his humanity to God the Father as irreconcilable with belief in His deity, whereas for some of us these same passages enter directly into the conviction that here humanity has become a transparent medium through which deity shines. Thus, for example, Paul Tillich writes: 'Final revelation does not destroy reason; it fulfils reason . . . In the New Being which is manifest in Jesus as the Christ, the most concrete of all possible forms of concreteness, a personal life, is the bearer of that which is absolute without condition and restriction . . . Final revelation is not logical nonsense; it is a concrete event which on the level of rationality must be expressed in contradictory terms . . . The paradox of final revelation, overcoming the conflict between absolutism and relativism, is love . . . The absoluteness of love is its power to go into the concrete situation, to discover what is demanded by the predicament of the concrete to which it turns. Therefore, love can never become fanatical in a fight for an absolute, or cynical under the impact of the relative.' [9]

Jaspers is right in holding that the doctrine of the Incarnation has been put forward in ways which violate freedom, obscure the precariousness of human life, put an end to search, and falsely deny the element of risk. But these ways of holding the doctrine can be criticized just as sharply on the basis of revealed theology as they can on the basis of his philosophy. Indeed, so long as theology remains existential, its fusion between Being-itself and historicity is comparable to that fusion which Jaspers has to presuppose for his own 'truth.' He excludes God-manhood on the basis of a general notion concerning connections between Transcendence and history, which cannot be reconciled with his insistence that there is no finality.

The Christian theologian, if he is wise, claims finality for *Agape*, not for his propositions about it nor for his personal measure of participation in what *Agape* is. The Christian position is not a trick whereby one remains 'terrifyingly certain' and arrogant while pretending to be very modest about the claims one makes for oneself. In God's presence every claim we make for our beliefs and our lives becomes precarious indeed; the task of actually participating in what we talk about becomes endless, and faith in Christ offers not a *substitute* for living out our lives, but a call to self-realization. The forgiveness, the release from guilt, the entrance into fellowship with the Eternal which Christ offers cannot be actualized in me apart from me. If Jaspers really believes that Being-itself manifests itself in history, and does not regard commerce between man and Transcendence as a one-way process in which man must do all the searching and climbing alone, then he has already assented to what might fairly be called the Christological principle. Finitude, sin, and the on-going process of life mean that we never reach 'finality' in the sense that the way *we* hold or embody the truth is perfect or legislative for other men.

But what about the truth itself? If it is manifest to us at all, it is manifest in the midst of these conditions, for we cannot jump out of them. And if Being-itself in any sense takes the initiative, so that there is a two-way process of meeting which man may accept and which he may also resist or evade, then how does this initiative express itself and what sort of God does it reveal? 'Being-itself savingly

271

manifest in history' is a religio-philosophical phrase not wholly incompatible with Jaspers' views. One suspects that it is neither consistency nor his admirable and persistent honesty which prevents him from translating this as 'the Word became flesh.' Apparently theologians have successfully blinded him to the possibility of a form of Christian faith which might cure what is, in Jaspers, a really intolerable form of indecisiveness without destroying the commendable aspects of his openness. All our symbols and doctrines may be inadequate, just because they are ours, to express God's self-revelation in history. But it does not follow from this that God has not revealed Himself in History, uniquely, in Christ. And if He has, that does not mean that all non-Christian doctrines and symbols are repudiated and destroyed. It means that they, along with non-Christian doctrines and symbols, can be illuminated and judged by what He is. Accordingly, a pagan or an atheist who seeks the truth in love can undeniably be nearer to God than a Christian theologian with a proprietary attitude toward the deity and who utters Biblical doctrine with arrogance toward his neighbor. This can be the case precisely because God is present to man as love and in love.

Jaspers' position really implies that although human love may collaborate with the ultimate in various ways and at various levels in history, the two are never fully united. From a Christian standpoint, this is the same as saying that God has never fully expressed His love. To this one can only conclude by replying that if Jaspers is right, it must be just as frustrating to be Being-itself as it is to be human.

NOTES

1. Translated by R. Manheim; published in New York by Philosophical Library, 1949.
2. In English, in addition to the work cited above, we now have these other works by Jaspers: *Man in the Modern Age* (London: Routledge, 1933), *The European Spirit* (London: Student Christian Movement Press, 1948), *The Way to Wisdom* (New Haven: Yale, 1951), and *Tragedy Is Not Enough* (Boston: Beacon Press, 1952).

3. Jaspers' distinction between *Dasein* and *Existenz* may be noticed primarily in *Philosophie* (Berlin, 1932), pp. 15-23, and in *Von der Wahrheit* (Munich, 1947), pp. 77-9.

4. *Philosophie*, III, p. 220.

5. Ibid. III, p. 234.

6. See, for a further development of this important point, *Tragedy Is Not Enough*, pp. 41-2.

7. *The Perennial Scope of Philosophy*, p. 77.

8. *Une Philosophie Existentielle: L'Existence d'après Karl Jaspers* (Paris, 1945), p. 100.

9. Paul Tillich, *Systematic Theology*, I, pp. 150, 151, 152.

CHAPTER VII

MARCEL

1. *His Life*

2. *The Ontological Mystery*

3. *Two Types of Truth*

4. *Personality and Freedom*

5. *Transcendence*

6. *Faith*

7. *Community and Freedom*

8. *Grace and Freedom*

9. *Faith and Reason; Testimony*

10. *Evil and Death; Hope and Salvation*

MARCEL

1. His Life

Gabriel Marcel was born in Paris in 1889. His father, an official in the French government and at one time ambassador in Stockholm, belonged to a Roman Catholic family but early became an agnostic. Because Gabriel's mother died when he was four, he was looked after by an aunt. She was of Jewish stock, although her family was indifferent to religion; finally she adopted a non-dogmatic form of liberal Protestantism which placed great stress on self-discipline and service to others. As he looks back on it, Marcel attributes three characteristics of his thought to the circumstances which surrounded his childhood. First, the differences of temperament and opinion to which he was exposed in his family made him realize that some of the deepest incompatibilities in life cannot be reconciled merely by means of intellectual formulas. Second, the religious aridity of his environment at home and at school aroused in him an obscure discontent which set him forth on a spiritual quest which was finally to culminate in his conversion to Roman Catholicism. Third, the fact that his mother 're-mained present' with him, despite her death, gave rise to an awareness of 'hidden polarity between the seen and the unseen' which he regards as a major influence in his writings.[1]

Although he was a brilliant pupil, Marcel was repelled by the academic approach to life because it tended to stifle creativity. Too much importance was attached to his grades, and he came to feel

277

that he was being valued for his scholastic output instead of for himself. He found his relationships to courses, teachers, and fellow pupils 'abstract' in the sense that they were remote from his inward needs for growth and expression. The methods of instruction employed in the classroom often made a great book seem disgusting instead of attractive. The same discontent followed him when he took up the study of philosophy. An opportunity for travel had given him a chance to explore some of the beauties of the world and the meaning of friendship at first hand, yet his personal quest seemed to have little connection with the textbooks. At the age of eighteen he wrote a thesis on Coleridge and Schelling, and subsequently became a teacher himself. Yet he has steadfastly refused to write systematic works. He began his own line of reflection by keeping a 'Metaphysical Journal,' and most of his other books consist either of journal entries or of essays and lectures which read as though they have been built up from meditations written in a notebook. This is true even of his two volumes of Gifford Lectures on *The Mystery of Being,* which provides the most comprehensive and consecutive statement of his philosophy.[2] Perhaps his most 'academic' book is a study of Royce's metaphysics, written in 1917, not yet translated.

In his philosophical studies he was influenced by the idealism of Hegel, Bradley, and Royce, but their preoccupation with the epistemological problem of the reality of the external world and their search for solutions to order and rearrange the content of *thought,* seemed to him to overlook the central issue, that of the real *existing* of the person. He became suspicious of system-building and tried to find a point of departure in sense experience, but he discovered that empiricism could be as heedless of metaphysical implications as idealism is of concreteness. His interests, then, were both existential and ontological, and since at this time he had not read Kierkegaard, Heidegger, or Jaspers, he was obliged to launch out on his own. One of his main concerns took the form of trying 'to discern the transcendental conditions of faith . . . without committing myself in any way or prejudging . . . the metaphysical value . . . of such faith.'[8] As he looks back on it, he realizes that he was trying to discover whether there is an essential core in faith which cannot be explained away by psychology and sociology. He never expected that, if such a core could be found, it would turn out to be anything but intimately personal. He was not searching for some sort of *Glauben überhaupt* standing beyond confessional differences as Esperanto stands beyond all living languages. At the same time, he felt that faith actualizes a linkage between man and reality which transcends the empirical self. Faith cannot be treated merely as a mode or aspect of the empirical self because our knowledge of the latter is at many points objectively determinate.

The shock of the First World War gave new urgency to his reflections. Like most of his European contemporaries, he was suddenly made to realize that the material and cultural conditions of life which had seemed so secure were actually very precarious. Because his physical condition excluded him from military service, Marcel worked for the Red Cross, and part of his task made it necessary for him to inform relatives about those who were killed or missing in action. His revulsion against everything which seems to treat human beings as data on a file card or as statistical groups stems partly from these experiences, and it has, of course, been greatly deepened by the developments of the ensuing decades.

Among the other influences which inspired his version of existentialism was Bergson's philosophy, from which he learned to accept a stress upon intuition and creativity without going as far as Bergson in the direction of anti-intellectualism. Marcel also became intensely interested in parapsychology and spiritualism, and he still regards them as useful safeguards against several prejudices to which philosophers are subject. One such prejudice tries to regard the self as a closed, rational entity. Another takes a narrow, confident view of what is natural and normal and then tries to hold its definition of reality strictly within these limits. Yet if parapsychological data are valuable because they break through such assumptions, they may also give rise to a danger—that of thinking that the interior transformation on which religious fellowship rests can be brought about by a technique and come entirely under human control. 'The only genuine inward mutation,' Marcel adds, 'is . . . inconceivable without . . . grace.'[4]

He is also a dramatist and a musician. His philosophical themes are often illustrated by analogies drawn from aesthetic experience; he sees man's religious response within the setting of creativity generally; a playwright's instinct prompts him to keep as close as possible to specific situations and individuals; and his musical sensitivity keeps him aware of meanings which go beyond the causal, the visual, and the verbal. Hence his attitude toward art is more positive than Kierkegaard's. To be sure, Kierkegaard held that faith merely dethroned the aesthetic and did not destroy it, and Marcel would certainly grant the peril of remaining at the aesthetic level. But in Marcel's writings art blends effortlessly into philosophy and religion. As he says, 'the dramatic mode of thought . . . illustrated and confirmed in advance all that I was later to write on the purely philosophical plane concerning knowledge in its capacity to transcend objectivity.'[5] In general, however, his plays are more somber than his philosophical books. It is as if through the plays, which he began writing at the age of eight, he located the issues concerning loneliness and frustration which he later dealt with more reflectively in his journals.[6]

Marcel's conception of his philosophical task is best expressed in his own words: 'The supreme mission of the philosopher cannot consist in proclaiming a certain number of official truths liable to rally votes at international congresses . . . The imperishable glory of a Kierkegaard or a Nietzsche consists . . . mainly in this, that they have proved . . . by their trials and by their whole life, that a philosopher worthy of the name cannot be a man of congresses, and that he deviates from his path every time that he allows himself to be torn from the solitude which is his calling . . . In an [academic] examination there are clearly formulated rules and the stage has been set in advance, whereas in the real world . . . there is nothing of the kind. The stage always remains to be set; in a sense everything always starts from zero . . . The temptation for a congress

280

man is always to refer to an earlier congress where it was established that . . . This perpetual beginning again, which may seem scandalous to the scientist or the technician, is an inevitable part of all genuinely philosophical work . . . The conviction that reality cannot be "summed up" [in a work which] needs only to be expounded and memorised paragraph by paragraph . . . came to me very early . . . My effort can be best described as an attempt to establish [an ontology] which precludes all equation of being with *Ding* . . . My aim [is] to discover how a subject . . . is related to a reality which cannot in this context be regarded as objective, yet which is persistently required and recognised as real . . . The undertaking [has] to be pursued within reality itself, to which the philosopher can never stand in the relationship of an onlooker to a picture . . . Experience . . . has to become . . . its own beyond . . . The error of empiricism consists only in ignoring the part . . . of creative initiative involved in any genuine experience . . . Its error is to take experience for granted and to ignore its mystery . . . The deepening of metaphysical knowledge consist[s] in the steps whereby experience, instead of evolving technics, turns inwards toward the realization of itself.' [7]

In 1928, Marcel found that this sort of perspective placed him on the side of religious faith in a debate with Léon Brunschvicg. Then François Mauriac wrote him an open letter, saying, 'Come, Marcel, why are you not one of us?', and through this question Marcel, recognizing a personal call, decided to seek baptism into the Roman Catholic Church.[8] He has retained his intellectual independence, however. He regards his work as strictly philosophical, and though naturally he thinks it is compatible with revelation, he acknowledges that other thinkers can share many of his philosophical views without accepting Christian theology. Often he is quite critical of Thomism, and one constantly has the impression that he is pursuing his reflections wherever they may lead, without worrying about the orthodoxy of the outcome. At the same time his Roman Catholicism goes hand in hand, as we shall see, with many of the distinctive emphases of Marcel's rendition of existentialism.

2. *The Ontological Mystery*

His essay 'On the Ontological Mystery' may well serve as an introduction to his thought as a whole. In this essay what he means by 'Being' is suggested rather than stated. It is suggested positively by the qualities which are associated with a 'sense of being,' and it is suggested negatively by the conditions which arise when man fails to exercise this sense or has lost awareness of it. Marcel feels that, generally speaking, modern man has cut himself off from the ground of creativity, freedom, and meaning, and that many of the most disturbing psychological and social conditions of our age can be understood only by restoring awareness of this ground. In other words, the main trouble is *not* that men find it difficult to adapt themselves to certain environmental and cultural conditions; the main trouble is, rather, that these environmental and cultural conditions themselves often prompt men to ignore their deepest spiritual needs and to repress that sense of significance and value which is indispensable to being a person.

Marcel gives three illustrations of the estrangement he is seeking to describe. In the first place, 'the individual tends to appear both to himself and to others as an agglomeration of functions.' [9] Marcel does not question the applicability of scientific methods to the study of individual and group behavior, but he suggests that if this approach is the only one adopted, the net result is to see man as one through whom physical, biological, economic, and political forces work, and to regard the personality as a mere resultant of these forces.

The second illustration is more concrete. It pictures a man—a conductor on the subway—who is virtually identical with his functions. His existence is almost wholly routinized. It is that of a timetable, not only in his job, but in his role as a member of a union, in his voting, in his habits of eating and sleeping. An expert on industrial hygiene might even be able to specify how much recreation he needs, what kind and at what hours, in order to function well. Of course sickness and accidents can disturb the routine, but even then there are hospitalization schemes for overhauling and repairing this machine-man. And when he dies, the company replaces him much in the same manner in which it might replace worn-out machinery. Probably the most 'human' characteristic of this man is an obscure unrest which lurks in his heart, indicating that the patterns of modern life violate his own nature. His existence is essentially empty; hence despair, or the need to avoid falling into despair, appropriately reflect the fact that some appalling mistake has occurred and that our so-called civilization tends to stifle instead of to nurture what is distinctively human.

The third illustration describes the way in which modern men approach life exclusively in terms of problems and allow no room for mystery, and this distinction between problem and mystery is a most fundamental one. The problematic approach assumes that everything which occurs is 'purely natural' and that in so far as events can be understood they fit into a cause-effect pattern. Such an outlook, when applied to birth, love, and death, goes hand in hand with the attitude which was described in the previous examples. These phenomena are regarded as understandable because they represent the performance or the cessation of certain functions. Naturally, anyone has to admit that there are some things we do not fully understand and hence cannot fully control. But the problematic approach assumes that the proper way to handle difficulties is to press forward along the lines already laid down by scientific discovery in the hope that by means of further research and new technical developments, present maladjustments and unforeseeable disturbances will be gradually eliminated.

What Marcel means by 'Being' involves a reaction against this whole pattern. In the 'brave new world' the person has disappeared and so has the sense of wonder. Existence is basically empty instead of full. The need for Being is a need to participate, as contrasted with fitting into a routine. The despair which lurks below the surface of modern life and sometimes breaks through into consciousness signifies that such participation should be possible although, in the circumstances, it is not. Participation in what? Marcel answers that 'Being' is what remains standing after we have checked off (by analysis) all the elements of experience which do not possess intrinsic significance and value. If one says that, in view of death, nothing can withstand this test, then the result is an absolute denial of Being.

Marcel notes that contemporary positivism takes a negative attitude toward Being by renouncing all metaphysics, but that in the process of ignoring the transcendent, it is also compelled to ignore the personal and the tragic. Indeed, there is outright collision between what Marcel regards as 'meaningful' and the connotations which logical positivism attaches to the same word. The latter confines itself to verification by means of technical operations which refer to the external world. Thus it fits in with the dehumanizing patterns which have already been illustrated. On the other hand, Marcel holds that functions and operations, being instrumental, are quite literally meaningless unless they serve some value to which they are subordinate. Thus 'meaning,' for him, is directly connected with what he calls *presence*—the disclosure of ends-in-themselves. Awareness of and response to such presence is at the opposite pole from verification by an examination of sense data, even though neither the presence nor the response is disembodied. The difference arises, rather, because awareness of presence requires an inward realization through love. Marcel acknowledges that his remarks are more an appeal than an argument. They are a protest against an arbitrary definition of 'meaning' which, when carried through, mutilates the life of the spirit. They will not, therefore, have much force with someone who has no inkling as to what he means by the life of the spirit.

Precision at this point is difficult because the methods we use in argument are well suited for dealing with problems, but not for dealing with mysteries. When we formulate problems, the knowing subject stands over against what he is thinking about. In the case of Being, however, this is impossible. I cannot stand over against it or outside it. Hence, I cannot deal with the ontological question without *at the same time* dealing with the question 'Who am I?' Since the latter has to do with the whole self—its feelings, its body, its will—instead of with the ego merely as an organ of cognition, Descartes' *cogito* does not help at all. Descartes' method presupposes a thinking subject standing over against objects, whereas we are asking about the whole self as contained in, not over against, Being. In short, the bond between the self and Being cannot be uncovered by means of the problematic approach, for this bond is sundered as soon as the subject-object split arises. The nearest analogy, perhaps, is direct communion between one person and another, but even this analogy is defective because I cannot fully be contained in the life of another person. At any rate, Marcel is postulating the primacy of Being over knowledge. In metaphysics, such thought as we can engage in must derive from what is already given through participation in the bond. 'Knowledge is, as it were, environed by being; it is interior to it in a certain sense . . . Knowledge is contingent on a participation in being for which no epistemology can account because it continually presupposes it.' [10]

These remarks throw light on what Marcel means by 'mystery.' It is different from a 'problem' because I am involved in what I am trying to understand and therefore cannot stand over against it. One example is the union of soul and body. Here one's starting point is an indivisible unity. I can, to be sure, regard my body as one object among others, but I can do this only by artificially abstracting from the crucial fact that what makes it *different* from all other objects is that I am present to myself in it. Then, by similar abstraction, I can treat the mind-body relationship as a 'problem' and seek a universally valid answer. Indeed, almost any mystery can be treated as though it were a problem. Take the so-called 'problem of evil,' for example. The philosopher or the theologian reflects on disorders which he views from the outside and for which he tries to discover the causes. He may conclude that the disorders are to be found primarily in the operation of the world or primarily in man's point of view. In either case, his attitude is that of the observer seeking explanations. 'But the evil which is only stated or observed is no longer evil which is suffered . . . I can only grasp it as evil in the measure . . . in which I am *involved*.' [11]

Perhaps the best illustration of mystery is that of love, which obviously cannot be real unless I am involved. Yet the problematic approach may be applied to it also. The personal reality of being-in-love can be replaced by a discussion of how psychosomatic entities carry out the functions of the libido, will-to-power, etc. But none of the deliverances of the problematic approach can constitute the personal reality, and they should not be permitted to devalue it.

Consider one final example, that of an encounter with another person which has become a deep and lasting influence. 'Causal' explanations as to how the two persons happened to meet may be offered; they may have been drawn to the same spot by a similar taste in scenery, or they may have struck up an acquaintance which flowered because of temperamental affinities. But one cannot really stand outside such a relationship, weighing the respects in which it looks as though it were predetermined or the respects in which it looks like a lucky accident. For the *meaning* of the relationship is not grasped through such reflections. It is grasped only by being the person who in some measure has been fashioned and brought to self-realization through this encounter.

Let us follow this analogy for a moment. Response to Being is in some respects like the inward development which occurs when I enter fully into a relationship of participation with another person. Have we any right to suppose that the connotations thus aroused are legitimately applicable to Being? If so, Being must be more than an abstract idea and it must be more than a content of thought derived from sense experience. To recover the bond which modern life tends to break or to ignore, an inward development must take place. One must be capable of recollecting himself, i.e. of taking hold of his life instead of being at the mercy of it. Marcel stands in what might be called 'the ontological tradition' because he holds that in the case of Being, and in this case alone, we cannot dissociate the idea from the reality. 'Because this idea *is* certainty, it *is* the assurance of itself; it is, in this sense, something other and something more than an idea.' [12]

But, unlike the traditional ontological argument, Marcel's appeal is not to the nature of rational thought, presupposing its relationship to the order of Being. His appeal is rather to a recollection of the self as a unity wherein awareness of the bond with Being is restored. It is only from the vantage point of such an inward recollection that the priority of Being over knowledge, and the consequent relationship between 'the real' and 'the idea,' can be appreciated. His version of 'the ontological argument' is neither rationally coercive nor is it an argument. It is rather an attempt to point to a relationship which underlies all knowledge and argument in philosophy, and which quite transcends the split between subject and object.

In one sense it is impossible to convey what he means, because he must try to communicate it through words as though the ontological bond could be an item of knowledge. Nevertheless, by description he can hope to evoke a response of recognition in the reader. Accordingly, he describes recollection as both an *act*, and as 'relaxation and abandon.' [13] My 'being,' as participating in Being, is not simply the sum of my empirical life. I can judge my empirical life because I encounter, within recollection, Being beyond all possible judgment and representation. Two further comments throw some light on the matter. In the first place, what Marcel means by recollection is the opposite of self-sufficiency. Since 'my being' can be entered into only through its bond with Being, the 'I' ceases to belong to itself. He quotes with approval the words of St. Paul: 'Ye are not your own' (I Cor. 6:19). On the other hand, Marcel does not believe that we have an intuition of 'Being-itself' which is distinct from other intuitions and from other items of knowledge of experience. We are dealing, rather, with an assurance which all thought, intuitive and discursive, presupposes. He calls 'primary reflection' the sort of thinking whereby we deal with experience as it comes to us. He calls 'secondary reflection' the act of recollection whereby we seek to become aware of that bond which makes the first sort of thinking possible, and which such thinking presupposes without knowing that it does so.

The ontological need can deny itself. 'Despair is possible in any form, at any moment and to any degree, and this betrayal may seem to be counselled, if not forced upon us, by the very structure of the world we live in. The deathly aspect of this world may, from a given standpoint, be regarded as a ceaseless incitement to denial and to suicide.' [14] Yet neither academic philosophy nor modern science can cope with despair. Academic philosophy cannot help at this point because in its discussions 'tragedy has simply vanished.' [15] And the scientific outlook, by fostering optimism concerning technical progress, has unwittingly contributed to a form of disillusionment which becomes a sort of trap. Let us see how this occurs. Despite the triumphs of technics, we now realize that man cannot save himself by such means. Actually, man is 'increasingly incapable . . . of *controlling his own control.*' [16] Yet having started down the pathway of technics, it is as though man cannot turn back. He admits there are areas outside his control, but he clings to the assumption that he has good credentials for obtaining as much control as possible, and he takes it for granted that if he can gain greater technical mastery over objective phenomena, he will use such power well. This outlook is really based on an illusion, and the only way to remove the illusion is to take a totally different view of reality, one which is not limited to the world of objects and which recaptures the significance of the person by recovering man's bond with Being.

In other words, the real victory over despair must in the first instance be inward. I can be in despair concerning reality as a whole just as I might be in utter despair concerning a person; similarly I can hope in Being as sustaining the worth of whatever deserves my wholehearted allegiance. Because the struggle between despair and hope takes place at the level of freedom, we cannot assume that the rightness of either can be demonstrated in advance. So far as the objective structure of the world is concerned, we can only say that it both permits despair and can give rise to an unconquerable hope. Sometimes the loftiest affirmation comes about only through being prepared for and elicited by despair. It must be made clear, however, that since hope is here directed toward Being, it rises beyond the plane of empirical eventualities; it is directed toward salvation, i.e. the affirmation that man can be meaningfully related to Being, as contrasted with an attitude which makes hope depend upon some specific and eventual success. For example, when I hope for a friend who is seriously ill, my fundamental affirmation is that reality cannot be indifferent to this stricken person. Of course I also hope specifically for his recovery, but the fundamental affirmation is not destroyed if my friend does not recover.

Now contrast such an attitude with the problematic approach when the only relevant questions are factual. On the basis of the best medical information available, I form an expectation concerning whether my friend will survive the disease. I must not allow wishes to distort my expectations. From such a standpoint, which is entirely appropriate for the spectator, a great deal that is called 'hope' is merely desire wrapped up in illusions. But when I ask about the value of my friend's life, I am at the same time asking about the value of my own life, and on both counts the spectator attitude is transcended. The hope which arises at that point goes far beyond both factual information and illusions concerning empirical eventualities.

Hence it is possible to characterize quite succinctly the difference between technological and ontological hope. The former is confined to results which man can bring about by manipulating the objective world. The latter 'does not depend on ourselves'; it is 'hope springing from humility and not from pride.' [17] By pride Marcel does not mean (as he takes Spinoza to mean) an attitude wherein we have an exaggeratedly good opinion of ourselves. He defines it rather as consisting 'in drawing one's strength solely from oneself. The proud man is cut off from a certain form of communion with his fellow men.' Pride, as so defined, 'is in no way incompatible with self-hate.' [18]

Then is practical action to be condemned because it implies a human self-confidence which is akin to pride? Does Marcel's ontological hope lead to a form of quietism? He answers that the idea of inert hope is contradictory. It 'is not a kind of listless waiting; it underpins action or it runs before it . . . Hope . . . is the prolongation . . . of an activity which is . . . rooted in being.' [19] It arises when the whole of one's will comes to bear upon what does not depend on man. Instead of being a Stoical stiffening of the soul, it is relaxed and creative. The real contrast is that between a withdrawal into self-sufficiency and a forthgoingness which results from a renewal of the bond with Being. All creative work, both scientific and artistic, really excludes self-sufficiency. It requires a free dedication of those powers of knowledge and initiative, which man indubitably possesses, to that which 'does not depend on ourselves.'

Thus Marcel seeks to cut through the antinomy between self-sufficiency on the one hand and slavish dependence on the other. As we shall see, this attempt has an important bearing on his discussion of freedom and grace. He also seeks to cut through the antinomy between spontaneity and deadly conformism. His key concept, in the latter connection, is the idea of fidelity. Fidelity to Being requires the active recognition of something permanent, but since what is thus permanent is a presence rather than an abstract, timeless idea, we may easily ignore or forget it instead of maintaining communion with it. Inert conformism arises when we try to treat this presence as though it were a principle. Then in religion, morality, and all other spheres, men try to claim that certain actions or beliefs follow necessarily from the principle. Marcel does not hesitate to say that such an attitude is idolatrous. It takes what is really powerless apart from my affirmation of it and tries to represent this same principle as though it made any decision on my part superfluous. It replaces the continuous, active struggle to be faithful to a presence, a Thou, with the sclerosis of habitual conformity to something which is, so to speak, settled once and for all, regardless of my response.

Genuine fidelity is like the endless effort to understand another person in give-and-take conversation. Therefore it includes acknowledgment of a mysterious incitement to create, to have drawn forth from the self fresh forms of recognition. Besides being like Jaspers' existential communication, it is also like artistic creativity. The world is not present to a painter merely in the sense that he can stare at it as it stands over against him; it is present to his heart and mind *within* him, participating in a bond with him which stirs a vision that he can either strive to express or can suppress and fritter away. Thus 'presence' stands for an impact which is made upon us, and in this sense its uncircumscribed initiative lies beyond our control. But its claim does not destroy freedom and throw us into passivity, for through fidelity we can be deepened and refashioned in our response to it, and through lack of fidelity we can negate its effects and refuse its call.

Our relationship to a dead loved one illustrates how we are able to maintain or obliterate the presence of Being. One can of course think of the death of a person in solely biological terms, as one may do when he reads the obituary notice of some utter stranger. One can also remember the loved one in a wholly subjective way by retaining some picture or effigy of him. But to be permeable to the continuing presence of the loved one is quite different, because in this case there is a mysterious interchange between my free act of fidelity and the gift granted in response to it. The latter, the gift, is something which I cannot create. It is only at the level of mystery, rather than at the level of a problem, that the notion of influence from a dead person can possibly be admitted, for what Marcel means by 'influence' is not exhausted by my awareness or memory of the deceased. At the problematic level we can only talk about an influence which comes either from the outside or the inside. Marcel is trying to describe a situation, based no doubt on his own relationship to his mother, where the dead person can be 'with' me without trying to claim that the deceased is surviving somewhere in space. If one were to hold that the situation he describes can be explained quite adequately by means of the psychology of memory and of wishful thinking, he would reply, I think, that the 'adequacy' of such an explanation presupposes the finality of the subject-object split and of the cause-effect pattern which, as his philosophy attempts to show, cannot exhaust the nature of the personal and its relationship with Being.

If this example of 'presence' seems to make his outlook credulous or superstitious, there is another which may be more easily accepted. The latter example is furnished in connection with his attempts to characterize 'spiritual availability' (*disponibilité*). He says that there are people who can be 'present,' at our disposal, in time of pain or need, while others, despite goodwill, simply cannot. Even a very attentive listener may not be able to 'make room for me in himself.' [20] There is a way of listening which is a giving of oneself, and another way of listening which is a withholding of oneself. 'Presence' reveals itself unmistakably in a look, a smile, an intonation. And for the one who can give his whole self, I am, in return, a presence. One of the difficulties about speaking of person-to-person relationships is that the same principle can cover both 'I-Thou' and 'I-He' (or 'I-It') situations. In the latter case, where the other person observes me as a sequence of phenomena, he is really treating me as an object rather than as a presence. [21]

Unavailability is rooted in some measure of alienation. For example, I may see that sympathy is appropriate, but be able to offer it only with my mind; I may even be sorry that I cannot offer more. In any event, I am unable to treat the other wholly as a presence. Those engaged in humanitarian work, who have to confront an endless number of 'cases' and who have to deal with social problems by means of statistics, continually find themselves in this predicament. Yet the fact remains that if the other is a 'presence' he cannot be a 'case'; and although he presents a problem which falls into a statistical pattern (e.g. the fifteenth alcoholic admitted to the hospital that day), the sense in which his problem is 'he' cannot be dealt with statistically. Because it is impossible to deal with everyone we meet in a fully personal way, each of us—not only doctors and social workers—secretes a kind of shell which gradually hardens and imprisons us. Fortunately the reality of the personal is such that at any moment real encounter may overturn our habitual perspectives and attitudes. Often when something breaks through our armor, we withdraw immediately. We may be terrified because this gap in our defenses endangers the stability of our established patterns of thought and feeling. Nevertheless these encounters are exceedingly precious, for they are glimpses of the real which lies beyond the confines of what we call normal. The truth is that human life has a certain sanctity. It is only by maintaining our imperviousness that we can believe we are getting at reality when we learn methods and formulas which reduce other persons, and therefore also ourselves, to 'natural' processes and functions.

Marcel's critique of self-sufficiency is also relevant at this point. For him the word connotes a person who is opaque rather than transparent to others; it also connotes a continual condition of insecurity. In order to remain self-sufficient, a man must keep aloof from those forms of relationship and awareness which might disturb his equilibrium. Yet this defensiveness actually makes the insecurity worse, for it leads to constriction, and it cannot succeed in shutting out death. Therefore pessimism (sometimes in an unconscious form) goes hand in hand with inability to be at the disposal of others. The man with an open soul is safeguarded against despair because he knows his life is not 'his own'; he knows that the most legitimate use he can make of freedom is to recognize this fact.

Thus far Marcel has been putting forward an existential ontology without making any direct references to Christianity. How is his philosophy related to theology? In so far as theology follows a problematic approach, as it often does, he is of course critical of it. Several contrasts between such theology and Marcel's own outlook might be developed: the contrast between 'giving doctrinal answers' and 'entering into communion with God'; the contrast between following tradition slavishly and being faithful to a permanent Presence Who incites creativeness; the contrast between producing a sacrilegious theodicy in answer to the 'problem' of evil, and engaging inwardly in the struggle between despair and hope over 'reality as a whole.' He also wishes to make it clear that when he refers to mystery, he does not mean that it is utterly impenetrable by philosophy. In short, Marcel refuses to accept a simple contrast between knowledge and faith. He insists instead that there is a form of onto-logical *knowledge* which can be reached only by adopting an approach different from the problematic. It may be intimately related to revelation without being altogether identical with it.

He is willing to admit that the notions which characterize his philosophy could not have been formulated apart from Christian influences, but he denies that they explicitly presuppose Christianity. 'We cannot reason . . . as though there were not behind us centuries of Christianity,' he asserts, but adds that he worked out his leading concepts twenty years before he became a Christian. Since revelation is inconceivable except as addressed to a being who is involved and committed, a philosophy which stresses these attitudes can become congruous with Christian faith. Its findings are not to be confused with revelation itself, however, nor is revelation to be regarded as some sort of 'flowering' of such an existential ontology. Hence Marcel's approach can be adopted without adhering to any given religion. Yet anyone who follows it will have to admit the *possibility* of revelation; he cannot exclude this possibility in advance or ignore it.

3. *Two Types of Truth*

Many of these same ideas are developed in greater detail, along with the addition of some new concepts, in Marcel's Gifford Lectures, *The Mystery of Being*. In order to make good his claim that his existential ontology rests on a form of *knowledge*, he must counteract the assumption that knowledge is confined to objective truths which are in principle anonymous and stand in contrast to private, subjective ideas. The greatness and the limitation of scientific knowledge, he says, consist in the fact that a discovery can be cut asunder from the personality of the man who made it. It is publicly verifiable in the sense that anyone properly equipped can get the same result. In an existential philosophical investigation, on the other hand, the outcome, the truth discerned, cannot be anonymous; it cannot be separated from the inner struggle and the spiritual development of the individual philosopher.

For example, this outcome may involve primarily a transition from inner conflict to inner harmony without any alteration in the objective data at all. Yet this does not mean that it is subjective in the bad sense. There can be aesthetic judgments which are intensely personal and emotional, yet they are not merely private. The fact that there are obtuse people who fail to respond aesthetically does not mean that such judgments are arbitrary. Similarly, there is a form of philosophical knowledge which cannot be verified by 'just anybody' who is able to think straight and to make the necessary experimental observations, as in science. For in order to reach such knowledge the whole self must be engaged in a search which is as much inward as it is outward.

One way to characterize this philosophical search is to say that it is a response to a universal nostalgia which modern civilization has both intensified and ignored. We have to specify its aim by calling attention to the disruptions caused by its neglect. The scientific definition of truth is, perhaps unwittingly, so much in alliance with these disruptions that it cannot provide us with an adequate conception of their cause and cure. The disruptions might be characterized as *both* isolation and collectivization. The scientific outlook can contribute to isolation by depicting the external world as a process in which the human spirit can find no home. It can also go along with the drift toward an 'ant-hill' society run by means of technology, where the only criterion is efficiency and all human passion and creativity have been subjugated. The corrective, whereby the individual rediscovers what he is in himself—as contrasted with being a cog in a social machine—is at the same time directed toward a rediscovery of a sounder communal ethic.[22]

Borrowing a phrase from Heidegger for the moment, let us say that the philosophical truth which Marcel is trying to characterize 'recalls man to himself.' The main point is that it is not objective in the scientific sense, but neither is it private. The surest indication that modern life has broken a bond is the protesting, restive condition of the human creature as he has to exist amidst isolation and collectivization. Marcel does not claim, of course, that estrangement and anxiety are peculiar to modern man. Human life has always been subject to them. But he does declare that the scientific outlook and the conditions of contemporary technological culture have made our spiritual illness especially acute, and have also made especially difficult the kind of philosophical endeavor which aims radically at recovery. The last fifty years ought to have made it obvious that the whole enterprise of an autonomous, man-made culture is a crashing, perilous failure. Yet we persist in retaining those methods which make self-destruction increasingly likely, and by an immense refusal we resist the sort of 'secondary reflection' which would seek a solution on a wholly different level—based upon and drawing strength from the transcendent.

Man's need to heal the inner breach which results in emptiness, dehumanization, and despair is at the same time a need for transcendence. Marcel regards man's linkage to the ground of meaning beyond himself as an essential element in the structure of human nature. It cannot be eradicated by means of scientific discoveries, for it is different in principle from biological and psychological needs. The latter cease at the moment when I have obtained what I require, but the need for transcendence *resists* coming to rest when creaturely demands have been met. Once again, the creative artist provides an example. There is in him an urge to produce, regardless of whether his needs for food, sexual gratification, or economic security have been adequately met. He has a sense of vocation which involves the co-operation of a whole swarm of conditions, not all of which are within his control. And when he 'gets it right,' in producing a poem or a painting, he feels that he has created at a level above himself.

In keeping with his effort to go beyond the subject (private)-object (public) contrast, Marcel declares that although *linkage* to transcendence unquestionably falls within experience, this does not mean that what we are talking about falls within the scope of the self. It is the intrinsic character of this experience—i.e. of the need for transcendence—to point beyond itself, and we encounter this reference within experience. To say this is not to indulge in a form of special pleading. All knowledge involves consciousness of something other than itself. But much modern philosophy makes the mistake of assuming that all knowledge must be similar to sensation where the knower is conscious but the 'known' is a thing. In connection with transcendence we must think, rather, of an illumination which is not wholly within our control, since it depends upon the self-revelation of the known.

At this point Marcel's views remind one of Heidegger's essay 'On the Essence of Truth.' Both are suggesting that the way to break through the dead-end, to which modern epistemological disputes usually lead, is to turn to an ontology based on active interplay between the nature of man and the nature of Being. In such an ontology, man's responses in terms of anxiety, concern, guilt, and decision will not be extruded from the sphere of 'knowledge by confining the latter term to dispassionate operations whereby our sensory-intellectual apparatus is brought into conformity with phenomena. On the contrary, such 'existential' attitudes will be explored with the thought that they *may* be indispensable preconditions for apprehending ontological structures within which phenomena occur.

Furthermore, if the notion of interplay is taken seriously, then knowledge cannot be actualized without initiative or self-unfoldment on the part of the 'object' which complements the subject's activity of apprehension and interpretation. A general pattern which attributes self-unfoldment to the 'object' can make an appropriate place, within the total scheme, for the sense in which an event makes its impact via sensation, without indulging in any pathetic fallacies that seem to attribute volition to inorganic entities. Yet when those levels are reached at which meaning can be communicated only through the self-unfoldment of personalities or significant structures, this general pattern is spared the necessity of trying to reduce such communication to the model of a sensory apparatus taking in and interpreting impressions derived from physical objects.

In a word, the sort of ontology Heidegger and Marcel suggest can make room for different levels of knowledge, whereas much modern philosophy has employed a restricted aspect of knowledge as a dictator, and looks to this dictator to pass judgments concerning what is to be admitted as real or excluded as unreal. Marcel adds that his approach is really more faithful to the concrete situation than the so-called empiricism which offers a collection of anonymous findings. Even in connection with sense perception, knowledge involves being illuminated. The information which science puts at our disposal can be carried with great advantage into the situation where knowledge is firsthand. But since, in the nature of the case, anonymous results are secondhand, they are no substitute for that concrete illumination which is not wholly within our power inasmuch as it depends upon the self-revelation of the known. When one thinks of experience as a whole, realizing that it contains much more than sense perception, the failure of empiricism to be genuinely faithful to it becomes scandalous. For the actual situation of the self is one of encounter with truth revealed from beyond the self; a direct interplay is continually carried on in terms of *Weltanschauung,* standards of value, response, and refusal. Empirical studies which compile information about laws of individual behavior and group reactions may indeed be relevant to this concrete situation, but they consist of abstractions from it; they constitute no substitute for it and they do not in the least justify ignoring or denying the centrality of its importance.

Let us contrast once again two different views of truth. The first concentrates upon the adequacy of ideas to things known. The second has to do with 'truth,' where the meaning of life is at stake, and where one is seeking what he can live or die for. Quest for truth, as conceived in the first definition, is in principle unattainable because new events are continually unfolding which may necessitate the revision of any system of interpretation previously reached. But a man whose thinking perfectly coincided with truth as thus far established, according to the first definition, and who was therefore entirely free from illusions might nevertheless be a person who was suffering from spiritual denudation and insensibility because he had failed to pay attention to the quest for truth in the second sense. Indeed, what makes the lives of some people tragic is that they seem to find existence tolerable only by evading the challenges and agonies connected with this latter quest.

Yet the power to come into touch with truth in the second sense does not come from outside the self. It comes from within the self as derivative from the transcendent source. What Marcel is talking about here is freedom, and it gives rise to a basic distinction within the self. Part of a man can run away from illumination, trying to stay at the unauthentic level. Another part welcomes illumination through those possibilities which reach beyond what he is at present. Yet both parts are 'I.' Notice that in describing the part of the self which is open to illumination, Marcel speaks both of an active quest ('welcoming') and of a passive receiving from beyond. Both expressions are indispensable, and we should not emphasize one to the exclusion of the other. For example, facing the truth about ourselves implies a kind of activity, such as courage. Yet the element of inescapability is present also. If the truth is an unpleasant one it makes its impact upon us despite ourselves. Nevertheless, if the receiving of this unpleasant truth were inescapable and automatic, there would of course be no point in talking about the obligation to face it.

Whatever resistance I put up is directed not merely against facts, though this may be involved, but against myself, i.e. the 'truth-seeing' part of myself. Why should man be so constructed that he cannot reach genuine serenity until he gives up this resistance? Why should even the willful, blind part of the self feel a strange satisfaction and relief in its own defeat? Here the breaking in of truth-in-the-second-sense goes contrary to the way I want things to be, yet there is a marked contrast with the manner in which truth-in-the-first-sense may comprise impersonal facts that go counter to my wishes. In the latter case we get rid of illusions by means of accurate information and logical thinking; in the former case we get rid of them only through inner purification, resulting from a power given to us in exchange for the difficult act of opening ourselves to it.

Admittedly the contrast disappears wherever scientific love of truth takes on a religious quality; where openness to fact involves a dedication similar to openness to revelation; where being willing to die for scientific truth endows it with a sanctity comparable to the claims of one person upon another. But such attitudes operate unconsciously in most modern scientists, if indeed they are present at all, and they often go counter to the scientists' professed views concerning what is real. Moreover, the theoretical possibility of combining objectivity with personal dedication does not carry us very far. Since in practice one can so easily undermine the other, the really important question is not whether a combination is theoretically possible, but whether a man is actually struggling to reach that difficult form of fidelity wherein his desires are made subordinate not only to fact from without, but to spirit from within. Certainly we cannot assume that dedication to truth in the first sense automatically produces dedication to truth in the second.

What Marcel calls primary reflection can be virtually equated with the scientific attitude and with the search for truth-in-the-first-sense. The distinction between primary and secondary reflection may be clarified further in connection with the so-called mind-body problem. Primary reflection tries to treat my body as one among many, and it tries to be detached about the fact that this particular body happens to be mine. It sees that my body follows the same natural laws as all others. Thus information about my behavior might be extended indefinitely without incorporating my own firsthand knowledge of what it is like to be myself. Inasmuch as primary reflection severs the unity of self and body, we cannot look to it to do the reuniting. Philosophy has wasted a great deal of time trying to explain this divorce away by using the analytical methods which caused the divorce in the first place. Hence Marcel challenges the whole mode of thinking that tries to regard mind and body as two 'somethings' that must be related to each other. At the level of objective thinking there is no answer to the question of how I can be an incarnate self. For my body, in so far as it is mine, is not in the first instance an *object*. I is not other than myself in the way that the rest of the external world is. I cannot stand over against it, as

I can stand over against objects, except by an act of abstraction which does not really break the underlying unity.

Therefore, although I can take a detached attitude toward my body and treat it as a problem, such an attitude never can get at the whole truth, and results in distortion unless there is a continual awareness of that direct linkage between myself and my body. Furthermore, since my body exists in the world, it constitutes a direct linkage with Being which is ulterior to any gap between subject and object. In short, there is a way of knowing both my body and, through it, Being, which can only be recovered by secondary reflection. The best way to characterize it is to speak of 'participation' as contrasted with 'forming ideas about external objects.' Admittedly, I can regard my body in a utilitarian way—similar to the way in which I look upon possessions or tools. But besides being something which I have, my body is also something which I am. Since it is not merely a possession or a tool, I cannot treat it merely as a means without treating myself, and therefore selfhood, merely as a means. Once again we come upon the principle: 'Ye are not your own.' In one sense we may have the freedom to do anything we want with ourselves, including committing suicide. But because the incarnate self is not just an instrument, freedom violates its own source whenever it tries to treat any man, including oneself, as though his body and his life were wholly at one's disposal. To emphasize the sense in which 'I *am* my body' may sound like materialism, but for Marcel the unity of self and body means that, in a very important sense, the body is not an object, whereas materialism tries to regard man wholly as an object and leaves no room for what Marcel means by 'self.'

The category of incarnation is the only one which can do justice to the sense in which my body is not an object but a subject. This category applies exclusively to a being whose subject-hood is fundamentally and not accidentally in a body. It brings out the fact that if I think of my body on the analogy of subhuman physical events, I am not thinking of it as it is. This body is a person. What is more, it is not just any person; it is I.

Now let us apply this result to the problem of sensation. A physical event, prior to sensation, is not a datum of my experience at all. How is the gap bridged between something which is not a datum of mine and something which is? One cannot say: 'By means of sense data,' for these stand on one side of the gap. Once again, instead of trying to solve this problem by means of primary reflection, philosophy should challenge the traditional approach *in toto*. When I talk about a physical object as at one spot in space and time, giving off impressions that are related to a receiving apparatus at another spot in space and time, I am not talking about myself. As soon as space and time and their contents are related to my body they are no longer items in an objective continuum. They constitute my personal existence, for I exist only in the here and now. Thus the relationship between a physical object and a receiving apparatus *presupposes* my existence. The fundamental link is not one of transmission but of participation. Unless my knowing were already within reality, no message could ever be transmitted. The approach of primary reflection assumes that there is some sort of break between the knower and the objects. But Marcel argues that at the level of feeling we never are cut off from the known. What participation means, therefore, cannot be described solely in terms of awareness of external objects. For example, what the soil means for a peasant is connected with his inner being, his sufferings as well as his acts. Furthermore, the same piece of countryside can be participated in by a peasant in one way and by an artist in another.

We have already noted how relationship to being transcends the opposition between activity and passivity, and these illustrations serve to reinforce the point. Participation on the part of the peasant or the artist is active, because it involves the feeling that one is being carried along and incorporated. From such a perspective, the purely technical or controlling approach to the world turns out to be sacrilegious. For it tries to attach primary or exclusive importance to an attitude which is appropriate only for dealing with non-sentient entities and which, even then, produces a restricted kind of knowledge.

302

These remarks prompt Marcel to add that the familiar contrast between a spectator attitude and a participant attitude rests upon an oversimplification. The man who wants to control is not a mere spectator; and the participant is not simply swallowed up in his emotions. As a matter of fact, what he calls 'contemplative participation' must be distinguished not only from the spectator's and the technician's approach, to which it is opposed, but also from the romantic approach, with which it may easily be confused. Contemplative participation heals the breach between the external and the internal by a method different from epistemological theory. The method is one of recovering an unbroken affinity which all subject-object knowledge presupposes, and therefore cannot be grasped as an item that falls within the pattern of subject-object knowledge. For example, in so far as I really contemplate a landscape, a certain togetherness grows up between the landscape and me. This involves drawing near to the concrete uniqueness of the scene *and* drawing near to myself. Which self? The self which is able to rise above rage, pettiness, and distraction. What is going on is not so much a piece of introspection as it is a kind of entering into the depths of myself, which at the same time means being able to get out of myself. This way of apprehending reality stands in sharp contrast with traditional metaphysics because the latter assumes that I must strip off the empirical husk so as to isolate a nucleus of pure reason which lies buried beneath it; or it assumes that I must rise above concrete experiences so as to establish a link between my mind and intelligible structure. So far as Marcel is concerned, philosophy should stay close to concrete experience and the concrete self; its task is to do justice to them in a manner which objective thinking never can rival.

4. *Personality and Freedom*

We should not think of concrete circumstances as having independent existence outside the self. They come into our lives only in connection with our free activity, to which they offer obstacles and opportunities. Moreover, the way we handle these obstacles and

303

opportunities must not be thought of in terms of cause-effect necessitation. For example, an artist may have to paint a given scene in a special way; but to say that the scene caused him to produce this particular painting is nonsense, for if the man were merely a reproducing apparatus he would not be an artist. Omit his inwardness and you have passed from aesthetics to physics. In all genuinely personal experience, when we encounter a friend or a beautiful scene or compose a piece of music, the opposition between contingency and necessity is inapplicable. What happens is not a casual accident. I am possessed by admiration, or beauty, or creativity in such a fashion that I am not purely autonomous. But certainly I am not operating at the level of necessitation; for in such moments I am at the opposite pole from being an automaton.

Similarly, the unrealized potentialities I call upon when I turn inward are neither indeterminate nor fateful. A personal vocation is involved. I cannot become 'just anything'; I must become myself. Yet this is not imposed on me as fate; it is addressed to me as an appeal. Thus I may be led to condemn the very life which, up to the present, I have been leading. Likewise a person-to-person encounter is neither an accident nor a necessity, but the beginning of a potentially creative development.

Our belief in the worth of personality should rest on direct awareness instead of upon abstract doctrine. Creativity is basic for ethics in the sense that if my conduct is to be relevant to another man and his situation, he and I must enter into communion. Since the word 'creativity' is ambiguous, however, we must try to specify what Marcel means by it. As he uses the term it does not mean 'self-expression,' as though the individual were a monad; rather, it means growth toward open community. At the same time, the creativity that goes into self-discovery and discovery of others is more like reconnoitering than it is like logical thinking. A man with a very clear mind may be quite unskillful in the art of finding his way through life when it comes to personal relationships. He may base his life firmly upon a certain set of assumptions, so that every judgment he makes is consistent; yet if his assumptions are sterile, his sense of what is important may be completely distorted. Such a man may easily impose wearisome demands on himself without realizing that the demands are in a sense fictitious, and that he would be far truer to himself if he had the courage to relinquish his constricting assumptions. He may take pride in his conscience as a champion of ethical values; but actually this has the anti-ethical effect of prompting him to subordinate persons to principles. Since he also subordinates himself to its principles, conscience has thus become in him a mechanical tyrant, whereas, properly, conscience is always a call to self-discovery.

We are free in so far as we can handle circumstances creatively, but this does not necessarily mean 'action' in the sense of getting things accomplished. A paralytic on a bed may be creative. Neither does freedom mean that we are autonomous; the freer we are, the more open we are to ideas and impressions which we cannot completely control and predict. Openness means being able to understand a new idea without necessarily adopting it; and it is a mark of the insanity of our times that this distinction is rapidly disappearing. For example, in education the student must get his results as quickly as possible, by whatever short cuts, so as to obtain a degree and a job. Thus education is set up in such a way as to defeat the flowering of free intelligence. Openness stands above the dichotomy between blind commitment and skeptical detachment, rescuing intelligence from slavery on the one hand and from irresponsibility on the other.

The inadequacy of objective thinking comes out most clearly when I try to answer the question: 'Who am I?' No other human being has the inner data to answer the question. But neither do I. I grasp my past in such a way as to see things which the child did not; but I also overlook things which the child saw and felt. I cannot grasp my life just as it happened. In trying to do so, I am like the person who tells the story of a journey; his account of the early events is colored by what he now knows is coming. If I try to answer the question 'Who am I?' by pointing to the sum of my achievements and actions, what they mean is inseparable from the responses and

305

interpretations of other people. Who, among them, can be said to get at the core of the 'real' me? And are they to judge me by my habitual line of conduct, or by exceptional acts which rise above or sink below the average level? By my finest accomplishments or my worst failures? To be sure, I hold my life together by some vague sense of purpose; but I cannot really define what it is. Even when I seem to get a clear glimpse of this purpose, my creative activities in relation to it can easily slip into professional routine, and my interest in it can become blunted by weariness or grief. What does give meaning to the lives of people? For some, the answer does not seem to extend much beyond the functioning of their own bodies. For others, it does not extend much beyond a rather petty circle of familiar and routine experience. And all of us, in our freedom, repeatedly *reject* calls made upon us to rise out of these poverty-stricken meanings. We think of life as like an account at the bank which we can spend if we feel like it. We count on having a certain number of years. But it is not really so. We do not have even a given day with any certainty.

It is only at the level of sacrifice that I begin to realize that the answer to the question 'What is my life?' is not wholly mine to give. But sacrifice is a baffling phenomenon, for here the individual gets his life by letting go of it. This seems a flat contradiction, and it begins to make sense only if we interpret shrinking from sacrifice in terms of running away from what we were meant to be. Objectively and externally there may be no difference between self-sacrifice and suicide. But inwardly the two are at opposite poles. It appears absurd to say that I realize my own nature most completely by becoming a corpse. Yet since the statement can be true, the fulfillment it refers to must take place at a level where the continuation or cessation of physical existence is not the decisive factor.

Thus the meaning of my life transcends my conscious grasp at any given moment. I am always partially a stranger to my own depths. And I can fully discover myself only in so far as I respond to a call which comes from beyond what I now am. Yet this call is not imposed upon me from the outside, and I can either respond to it or reject it. Even if I decide that life is pointless, the fact that I can raise the question presupposes that life might have a point. I may feel like an actor who begins reading a play on the assumption that the present lines, which seem silly, must have some function in the total pattern of the drama. Yet the comparison is inexact. I am more like one who has to go out on the stage and improvise; and everything can happen as though there were no director at all. Sartre assumes that I am indeed like an improviser who has to go against the grain of a fundamental pointlessness. But Sartre runs into a contradiction. How can I create meaning for my life through total engagement, if the over-all pattern in which I participate is meaningless?

There is no remedy so long as I picture myself as an isolated ego who has to *make* life valuable; and there is no escape from isolation so long as real communication with others is blocked by hostility. I do not begin to become a real self until antagonism is replaced by an inner bond, so that I can stop being self-conscious and begin to be incorporated into shared ideas and shared feelings. Entering into this selfhood is at the opposite pole from trying to become an observer who watches the stream of experience flow past like a movie film. Thus becoming my true self involves two things: First, a point where my past and my future mysteriously clasp hands in what might be called 'the absolute Moment'; here eternal meaning, though it transcends me, is neither static nor abstract; it is intimately personal and it is operative in time. Secondly, entrance into that intersubjectivity of communal participation which is more our true home than is our physical environment.

The fact that men no longer think of life as a gift has made the second meaning especially dim; for instead of realizing that I cannot become myself apart from the family bond, I regard life in such a world as a penalty, pronounced by nobody and for no identifiable crime. Thus fatherhood and sonship have lost their meaning. The begetting of children becomes a matter of throwing into life infants who never asked to be born. The point Marcel is making is not primarily moralistic; he is claiming that the essence of fatherhood is

307

care for the selfhood of the young life that comes under one's keeping, and observance of the rules of monogamy does not automatically guarantee that such care will be present. The physical-personal bond of the family is a good symbol for man's bond with Being because it is only within the 'We' that anyone ever becomes 'himself.' Thus, in Marcel's terminology, the family bond is a mystery.

Some may feel that since objective information about the history and present functioning of the family is available, the word 'mystery' is inappropriate; to which Marcel replies that a novelist or dramatist can make us aware of what he means, even though a sociologist may not. The presence of a loved-one in the family bond must be distinguished from anything that has to do with spatial relations. For example, a man in the same room with me may be so alien that I cannot feel his presence. He understands my words, but not me; and if he repeats my words to me they may even be unrecognizable. I cannot be myself while I am with him. When the opposite occurs, I can be responsive to the presence of another, whether he is near or far in the spatial sense, and he makes me more fully myself than I could be when alone. Hence the way we incline ourselves toward a presence is essentially different from the way we grasp an object. Presence can only be welcomed or rebuffed. It calls for a response on our part, not a mere noticing. But to say that the family bond and presence are mysterious does not mean that they are unknowable. The unknowable is what lies beyond solution by the problematic approach; but a mystery is neither soluble nor insoluble; it is to be entered into instead of looked at.

5. Transcendence

Marcel admits that his sort of philosophizing confronts a special danger. Since it starts with deep inner experience which cannot be renewed at will, it can easily pass over into talking about such experience instead of existing in it. It can remain true to itself only by *not* becoming an argument for certain truths that can be grasped by learning its content. It must remain an appeal to the individual which can always be rejected, no matter what discoveries may occur in the sphere of publicly verifiable knowledge. This is as it should be, for the acquisition of objective knowledge is never the same thing as becoming myself. He goes so far as to say that even if science had finished its task and the natural order had become completely intelligible, every important philosophical problem would still remain. Take, for example, a sleeping child. Exhaustive scientific knowledge says nothing about the sacredness of this sleeping child, and yet inability to feel something of the sort is a mark of barbarism. It is wrong to say that this sacredness is created by my feelings and attitudes; for when we are confronted with a barbarism devoid of reverence, we are sure that what it ignores has a validity that does not depend upon the presence or absence of any individual's acknowledgment. In short, what gives life its sacredness transcends us; the extent to which we embody its meaning depends, in part, upon our purposes; but the source of meaning remains, whether we recognize it or not, and whether we respond to it positively or negatively. When seized by despair, lust, or ambition we may become blind to it; and when it makes its presence felt we may welcome or run away from the encounter. Yet this meeting with the absolute Thou, beyond the self and beyond other people, takes place wholly in inwardness. God cannot be approached like an objectively existing thing or an objectively demonstrable principle because our bond with Him, as the ground of meaning and freedom, is ulterior to everything we can stand over against.

At many points in the foregoing discussion, the close relationship between what Marcel means by 'Being' and what he means by 'God' has been self-evident. But he denies that their identity can be taken for granted, because it is always possible to reach a philosophical conception of Being which is incompatible with what the believing consciousness means by God. The likelihood of this sort of conflict may be reduced from the side of philosophy, however, by rejecting the traditional approach of metaphysics which attempts to define Being as static, and as reached by abstraction from personal experience. Marcel is avowedly seeking the eternal *in* personal experience and *in* concrete relations with others. His method, so far from leading toward subjectivism, gives a central place to that fundamental characteristic of personal experience which requires real communication. I cannot be cut off from others without at the same time being cut off from myself. Self-knowledge must be *hetero*-centric, and legitimate self-love must be based upon loving relationships with others. The starting point of metaphysics should be the togetherness of the 'We' instead of the *cogito*.

In Sartre, existentialism undeniably takes an opposite form; his philosophy is egocentric in principle and so makes intersubjectivity and openness toward others impossible. Therefore, Marcel is anxious to show that existentialism can break with traditional metaphysics without falling into Sartre's difficulties. Intersubjectivity (like 'Being' in the preceding discussion) is the nexus within which anything is given to me; it cannot be demonstrated because it is the already-present ground on the basis of which we affirm anything else. Indeed, it is not something which can be designated as a 'this' or 'that'; it is living communication.

The word 'existence' should be used in such a way that its primary meanings are connected with first-hand acquaintance with what it is to be a self, while the sense in which 'things' can be said to exist turns out to be secondary and derivative. Such a usage contrasts sharply with the assumption that, starting with knowledge of the existence of physical things, we can then form a notion of the existence of human beings as especially complicated organisms. Marcel rejects the latter approach on the ground that objective knowledge cannot get at the singular existence of anything, although it is this singularity which is, strictly, 'in being.' The only way we become directly aware of the existing of a thing is through its sensible presence to a subject. But science has to abstract from this situation; it has to try to form a notion of the subject, or certain properties of the object, apart from its presence to any particular knower. In short, it has to concentrate upon those aspects in which the knowing activity can be the same for all men and the characteristics of the object apprehended can be the same for all men. In its own

310

proper fashion science can tell us a great deal about the properties of objects, but it abstracts from the situation whereby alone we become aware of the existing of objects. Existence is not a property, although there is no sense in trying to form a notion of anything apart from its properties.

Our awareness of the existing of things is mediated to us through our own bodies. Therefore my body, as existent, is the bed-rock reality which my awareness of the existence of anything else assumes. Yet, as Marcel has already tried to show, my body is not merely a thing. I cannot rightly think of it simply as an object perceived, because it is *through* my body that I perceive. So far from identifying 'existence' with items which may be located in space and time, we should recognize that the bed-rock existent, my body, cannot be merely such an item because it is that *through which* things become localized for me in space and time. My body cannot merely be 'there' for me, because it is through the body that other things become 'there' for me.

These considerations prompt Marcel to make some rather cryptic statements. From the standpoint he has developed the mere thing turns out to be a pseudo-existent. Anything that can be destroyed, taken apart, and reduced to dust never was an existent in the strict sense. But since a person's body as a presence cannot be reduced to a mechanism which disintegrates and ceases to function, it may be meaningless to say of a dead person that he no longer exists. This statement is directly connected with his conviction that a dead person can be present, even after the body has ceased to be an object in space. He applies the same line of reflection to subpersonal things; in so far as a garden has been *existent* to me as 'presence,' it (not just an image of it) retains being even though, in the ordinary sense of the words, the garden has ceased to exist.

Clearly, Marcel wants to regard the nature of existence, in his sense of the term, as an important clue to the nature of Being. The bond between the two seems to be a certain indestructibility. I cannot really regard the existence and non-existence of my self as modes of the same thing. To be able to do so, I would have to stand

311

outside both modes, and I obviously cannot stand outside existence; any transition from non-being to being always comes back to a subject who is. Despite the close affinity of the two terms, however, there is a contrast between experiencing myself as existing and experiencing myself as being. To ex-ist is to emerge, to arise. I can rise up so as to become more readily accessible to others, but I can also withdraw myself into my own inner being. The latter gives me a foundation on which I can stand. But though I can turn toward it, I cannot fully coincide with it. I can take hold of my own *existence;* but my *being* is wholly a gift, and I am always aware, not only of its presence, but of its distance. There are ways of narrowing the gap between that self-realization which I can produce by taking hold of existence, and that rootedness in being which is given to me, but in this life the gap cannot be completely overcome. Furthermore, the difference between what I make of myself and what it is given me to be, may become so great that I would be condemned to losing the latter if it were not for grace.

The nature of my existence of selfhood can rightly be followed as a clue to the nature of Being only if the notion of the self as a monad, a circumscribed ego, is overcome. The more my existence participates in that of others, the closer it comes to Being; and the more one falls into egocentricity, the less he exists. Hence Marcel is not trying to conceive of Being or of God on the analogy of a center of consciousness. He complains that classic ontology has been dominated by static conceptions which stress the perfection and self-sufficiency of Being or God. Rather the kind of fulfillment he has in mind is like the creativity which can go on between persons. It is something *lived,* rather than something timeless and abstract. Moreover, such fulfillment, as for example in the case of mutual love, does not necessarily mean that what we are talking about is finished. Finally, traditional ontology and theology have tried to conceive of *ens realissimum* as made up of attributes which comprise a whole. But it is wrong in principle to try to approach the uniqueness of an individual being as though it were an additive whole. Therefore, it is equally wrong to try to approach universal being in such a manner. God is not a *quid* with a certain number of predicates. But since we have to use predicates in characterizing anything, how can we speak of Him at all?

Marcel's answer is to look upon each human being as a genuine incorporation of Being. We have already seen what this means to him. It means that to try to treat persons and their relations as functions is to miss what is constitutive of persons as well as the *real* character of their relations. A forgetfulness of how each man participates in Being-itself goes hand-in-hand with depersonalization and all its dreadful consequences. Yet we cannot merely think of all human beings collectively and say that they, taken together, make up what we mean by Being-itself. Since each person is a subject, none can be just an item in an aggregate. To refuse to regard Being-itself as substantive leads to a nihilism like Sartre's. We cannot regard men as coming from nothing and returning to nothing, and at the same time regard them as genuinely participating in being.

But since men do die, must we regard individuals merely as transitory appearances of Being-itself, which is eternal? Here the close affinity between nihilism and negative mysticism becomes apparent. In the one case there is no transcendent Being to which man can be related; in the other case the reality of the transcendent Being swallows up the individual. Against both, Marcel wishes to affirm that the real core of the person, as participating in intersubjectivity, cannot perish. This may sound like a Platonic theory of immortality, but it is not. He is not saying that the soul is something which will be perpetuated. Having abandoned all attempts to treat either the individual or Being-itself as objects, and taking his stand on the experienced nature of intersubjectivity, he declares that it is impossible to love someone without affirming that the value of the loved person is imperishable.

Yet no one can look at the world without realizing that everything and everyone he loves may be destroyed. Does Marcel's approach result in a kind of faith which must constantly conflict with objective knowledge? Actually he regards the deliverances of scientific knowledge as compatible either with faith or with the lack of it.

Therefore it is extremely important to examine what inclines a man toward faith or its opposite. The atheist and the believer experience the same evils. What makes the difference? The atheist assumes that since evils occur God does not exist. This presupposes an idea of God so adequate that one can say what He would do if He were real. On what can this idea rest? In the nature of the case, how can an atheist have the right to a theory as to what Deity should do in given circumstances?

6. Faith

When we come to discuss the believer's attitude, it is important to draw a distinction between conviction and faith. 'Conviction,' as Marcel uses the word, means that one puts up a sort of barrier, claiming an assurance that nothing will modify. 'Faith,' on the other hand, means placing one's whole self at the disposal of what is believed in. It is possible to have a strong conviction about another person without pledging oneself to him. The *words* which express conviction may be indistinguishable from those which express faith; yet in the one case we stay within a sort of citadel or enclosure, while in the other case we make a venturesome offer, indeed an 'invocation.' It is difficult to find the right word for pointing to the object of faith when one tries to reply to the atheist, for what faith is directed toward is not an object. Yet what is essential for faith is neither my convictions nor my words. In the heat of an argument it is easy to forget this. I begin fighting for the certainty of something that is mine. Nevertheless, the only thing that is mine is openness toward a reality which is capable of being invoked.

This reality itself is of essential importance, and it is part of the nature of faith to realize that a venture can be lost. We invoke the absolute Thou and there may be none, or there may be no response. Moreover, there may be particular aspects of our belief, which we thought essential, but which can be proved wrong and which we may therefore be compelled to abandon. Many people, having discovered that some of the things they were taught to believe as chil-

314

dren are illusory, leap to the conclusion that intellectual honesty requires the abandonment of faith entirely. Others, feeling that they will find it impossible to live if they lose faith, have clung blindly or uneasily to illusions because they saw no way to abandon them without at the same time losing what they knew to be indispensable. Marcel suggests that what is really essential in faith can neither be proved nor disproved by any sort of objective evidence. It consists in making a way of living out of hope and love as directed toward God. In the case of a specific individual, it is justifiable to continue to hope for him, in the sense of affirming his value as a person; and unless we can do so, our love for that individual is dead. Where faith, hope, and love are present, the self-offering is a humble readiness which is at the opposite pole from trying to develop techniques that will tap divine power for our own purposes.

This humility is linked with a recognition of contingency and dependence as metaphysical facts. In many discussions humility in this sense is lost sight of entirely between two opposite attitudes. This first is a form of mortification in the presence of a condemning Deity which is closely associated with feelings of guilt, impotence, and self-hatred. The second is a form of human self-sufficiency which takes pride in man's creative powers and teaches us that, in view of the discoveries of scientific knowledge, we can and must learn to be dependent only on ourselves. Marcel wishes to repudiate both. There is an awareness of our condition as finite beings which can be sober and appropriate. We miss it when we indulge in masochistic groveling; but we also miss it when humanistic and scientific visions of autonomy have blinded us to a sacredness in nature, in beauty, and in persons of which we are not the source. Hence Marcel sharply repudiates the attempts of humanists to lump all forms of belief in God under the general category of irrational authoritarianism. In our times the individual has become enslaved to the Party or the State through a form of idolatry which relinquishes personal freedom to something inferior to it. But there is no analogy between this irrational authoritarianism and the sort of dependence on God whereby a man turns humbly and *freely* toward

315

the source of his being. The idolatry of totalitarianism must be understood as the Nemesis which waits for men who, in trying to make autonomy work, have left a vacuum where faith in God should be.

7. Community and Freedom

How, then, can dependence be so characterized that the universal validity of God's claim upon our lives is suitably expressed? All the false prophets of our day try to make universal claims for their particular philosophy of history. Since relativistic views are weak in resisting them, we need to rediscover an authentic universalism. Yet our norms cannot be established by seeking ideas which everyone could be persuaded to affirm; an authentically universal claim might be one which many persons reject. One norm Marcel is willing to defend, after certain defects in Kant's formulation of it have been removed, is that persons should be regarded as ends in themselves. But we must see this principle as operating under concrete conditions, not as an a priori axiom. When we do so we realize that it cannot be looked upon as a private, individual attitude. The act whereby persons are regarded as ends in themselves is intrinsically communal. 'Even if I pray alone in my room . . . I am uniting myself . . . to a community which does not belong exclusively, or even primarily, to the visible world.' [23] Thus prayer for another, as an instance where the universal norm is being fulfilled, cannot be dealt with adequately by either a subjective or an objective approach. The former overlooks the element of participation, the communal context in which I act. The latter, which is to be found in sociological studies of religion as a cultural phenomenon, ignores the inwardness of the act itself. Thus the existence of that intersubjectivity which provides the context for a universally valid claim cannot be doubted by one who freely participates in it. On the other hand, its existence cannot be proved or disproved by one who looks upon it from the outside, although the outsider's approach may prompt him to declare that only those aspects of community which

316

can be studied by sociological methods—i.e. institutions—are real.

Exactly what is the role of freedom here? Clearly participation in genuine community depends upon it. But in what sense can the *offer* of fellowship be real apart from individual response? If the offer might be granted or withheld from me, then the actualization of fellowship, although it involves my response, is not brought about merely through the exercise of my freedom. In an attempt to clarify what he means by freedom, Marcel distinguishes it from 'doing what I want.' He points out that it is possible for a person under conditions of captivity to retain and even to deepen inner freedom, despite the fact that he obviously cannot do what he wants. He also insists that inasmuch as many desires are compulsive, freedom may require a certain conquest over them instead of conformity to them. Yet when I yield to a discreditable desire, is it right to claim that since I was acting under compulsion, I was not responsible? The more I succeed in proving my own innocence by such a device, the more I have to admit that I am at the mercy of desires which operate as though they were detached from me and which can therefore reduce me to slavery. I drift toward viewing myself as having the innocence of an automaton. But I cannot convince myself that I am wholly an automaton because the entire course of my reflection shows that I am a being who questions himself. If I were really an automaton, I could not reflect upon, evaluate, and judge myself as I actually do—even when I reach deterministic conclusions.

Indeterminism, on the other hand, presents a radically defective view of freedom because it gives rise to the notion that the purest examples of liberty are to be found in circumstances where the stakes are insignificant. It is only in such circumstances that the reasons for choosing one way or the other are not compelling. We need to reformulate the matter so as to see that freedom has a direct bearing upon what I become. Picture, if you will, a man who is under terrific pressure to commit treason in order to save his own life. If he commits treason, then it is by a free act which reveals what he is. (Marcel does not discuss the use of drugs and torture in this connection; but he might well assert that if, by such means,

317

the personality of the victim has been so destroyed that he is literally not responsible for what he says, then his act is not treason.) On the other hand, if he remains faithful, this can only mean that he attaches tremendous value to freedom itself. In either case, by his freedom he has a hand in making himself what he is to be. Yet it is important to recognize that fidelity can no more be automatic than is treason. A great deal of fortitude and stubbornness may be called for; but genuine fidelity cannot be mechanical because as one confronts the sort of ordeal in question one cannot know in advance what the outcome will be. There may be unrecognized weaknesses which are brought to light under pressure, and triumph over these weaknesses is like a creative act. Moreover, in retrospect one may recognize that hidden resources came to his aid, helping to make him what he becomes—namely, a man who remained faithful.

8. Grace and Freedom

To remain faithful to freedom is to remain faithful to oneself and to that whereby we help to make ourselves what we become; yet everything that has just been described presupposes the *gift* of certain resources as well as the creative act. What is the relationship between grace and freedom? Grace should be thought of primarily as analogous to the gift of *oneself*, rather than as the transfer of some power or property from a donor to a recipient. Moreover, the gift is unconditional; that is, it is not contingent upon the use that the recipient is going to make of it, and it is not offered with the purpose of securing a hold over him by means of gratitude.

If these remarks are applied to God, then they clearly imply that Marcel rejects most forms of theological determinism and predestination. But what guarantee can there be that we receive life as the result of a divine generosity which seeks nothing except the fellowship which generosity itself expresses? The only genuine answer is 'revelation.' It is only as I become gratefully aware that God reveals Himself as generosity, that I can apprehend all life and my own life as gifts of grace. Yet we can find people whose awareness of the sanctity of life presupposes revelation and who nevertheless do not articulate any definite belief in God or may even regard themselves as unbelievers. On the other hand, it always remains possible to deny such a view of life, and to regard all existence, including my own, as absurd (Sartre).

Thus Marcel is brought to a point in his reflections where he raises a question that is momentous for existentialism as a whole. Must we simply make a choice between two conceptions, neither of which can claim rationally to be more true than the other? In that case the affirmation of divine grace and revelation would have only a sort of pragmatic value. It would enable us to retain our belief that the significance of life has an eternal ground, as over against the atheism which says life can possess only the significance which human freedom bestows on it. But the question of truth cannot be evaded. And if atheism is true, then courage and uprightness themselves demand that we refuse to be duped; they demand that we reject belief in grace. Marcel suggests, however, that if we adopt the atheistic alternative we soon discover that the term 'truth' has lost its significance, and so has freedom. Truth has lost its significance because if all the judgments we make constitute a projection of meaning onto a world which in fact is alien to such meaning, then the judgment by which this sort of atheism claims to be true is caught in the meshes of its own theory. Like every other judgment it is an arbitrary fabrication, which is equivalent to saying that it cannot claim to be true.

To be sure, such a line of argument will not succeed in forcing a man like Sartre to abandon his position. It is possible, at least verbally, to be satisfied with intellectual self-destruction, and even to enjoy it in a satanic sort of way. One does not relinquish such atheism unless a minimum of good-will has been aroused, and it is precisely this good-will which is lacking in Sartre's case. That is why 'freedom' also becomes finally devoid of meaning and value in his philosophy. He regards it as an anarchic disposition which runs indiscriminately through every variety of human activity, the worst as well as the best. The only sense in which he can speak of abusing

319

freedom arises when one has failed to exercise it, and since freedom has nothing to be faithful to, being faithful to freedom itself turns out to be a dead end. In fact, freedom in any significant sense clearly vanishes in that culmination of Sartre's outlook on life which equates it with an inescapable, enslaving trap that can only be accepted and cursed simultaneously. Yet this connection between truth and freedom which the believer affirms, and the significance which they derive from being grounded in God, cannot be rationally demonstrated. For the divine generosity in the light of which religious faith sees life itself as a gift cannot be understood, for the very reason that it is at the root of every understanding.

Neither grace nor freedom should be thought of in terms of a causal interplay. So Marcel rejects any conception of grace which regards it as a force or influence distinct from the causality which is proper to the human agent. The question which sets him at odds with Sartre or any other atheist has to do with whether 'my being in the world' is an expression of generosity. The atheistic position assumes that there is nobody qualified to bestow such a gift. On the other hand, the believer apprehends 'being in the world' as a bestowal of the absolute Thou. *Both* the atheistic and the religious position are unverifiable; yet both statements illustrate how men cannot help taking up some sort of position toward the reality, whatever it may be, that lies beyond verification.

9. *Faith and Reason; Testimony*

Since the believer's attitude goes beyond knowledge, in the ordinary sense, what is the relationship between faith and reason? Instead of writing about faith and reason Marcel, following his desire to remain close to the concrete situation of the individual, speaks of a gap between the believing and the reflecting 'me.' He admits that a perfect synthesis is impossible for wayfaring man, *homo viator,* who so long as he exists must forever move forward. This means that reflection will continually bring up difficulties which threaten faith; but Marcel adds that a *modus vivendi* can be found only by facing these difficulties, by accepting them as a test and an ordeal, instead of rejecting critical thought as one might turn from a temptation. In fact, faith undergoes a sort of purification by opening itself to the attack of reflection and surviving that attack. One of the dangers is that conceptual thought will try to substitute progressively abstract terms for concrete ones. This may lead to a static conception of Being-itself which tries to represent it as a 'thing' to be grasped by objectivizing thinking. In order to resist this danger I must recover the direct, living connection between my own being and transcendent Being. This recovery is best illustrated by contrasting the role of the reporter of objective truth with the role of the witness. In the first case the truth which is reported is quite independent of the man who discovers or purveys it. His historical relationship to it is, in the technical sense, accidental. It may be a fact that at a given moment a particular scientist formulated this truth for the first time; but no one regards the biographical circumstances which surround this event as having any crucial bearing on the truth he formulates. In the case of the witness, on the other hand, the historical connection between his life and the truth to which he testifies is critical. He points to the truth with his life instead of by means of an intellectual formula, and the *nature* of the truth to which he bears witness—perhaps by martyrdom—continues to be inseparable from the nature of his testimony. If men become heedless of the sort of truth he has died for, a recovery of the story of his existence as testimony, through a revived oral or written account, can reawaken them to it.

Applying these considerations to theology, Marcel holds that the attempt to demonstrate the existence of God represents Him as though He were an objective truth. On the contrary, Marcel suggests that if the living God can only be approached through the testimony of one's existence, then it follows that God is inevitably incarnate and that testimony must be directed, in the first instance, toward this Incarnation. It also follows, secondarily, that since God is livingly connected with the being of every man, every approach to justice and love is at the same time an approach to God. When-

321

ever God is thought of abstractly, in terms of patterns of justice and love which prevail no matter what we do, freedom disappears and so does sin. I cannot really sin against an objective truth which remains valid, regardless of what I may think or do. But I can sin against a truth which is actualized only through Incarnation, and here also freedom is real; for I can refuse to testify with my life, or I can bear false witness. There is only one way of being faithful to the effect of the Incarnation, and that is to become an embodied testimony to the living God. Once a mathematical truth has been discovered, all subsequent reporters of it are in a sense superfluous. But no past witnesses to Christ makes testimony today superfluous, and perhaps the core of the apologetic task in every age is to be located in lives rather than in arguments.

Nevertheless a philosopher may break with immanence and recognize in some general way the need for faith and transcendence, as Jaspers does, without being able to accept any particular historical religion such as Christianity. Conversion to Christianity cannot be genuine unless it is free; but it is also dependent upon conditions that are beyond the power of freedom to bring about. Conversion is the act whereby a man is called to become a witness. This presupposes that something has actually happened in history in which we can discern the action of the living God, and through which we receive a recognizable call. But it is a mistake to try to localize this conversion in a given moment, and it is a mistake to think that once the call is answered in the affirmative, the believer is then installed once for all in some privileged position from which he can look condescendingly upon the tribulations of outsiders. The call is a constant one, and the possibility of relapse or betrayal is equally constant.

It is difficult to tell whether this is aimed specifically at Jaspers. But regardless of Marcel's own intentions, it illuminates the central differences between the two philosophers with regard to Jesus Christ. From Marcel's standpoint, Jaspers can accept *in general* the interlocking of grace and freedom, and he sees clearly that this interlocking must be concrete and historical. We actualize our relationship to the Transcendent only as we embody it in our lives and testify to it with our lives. In other words, Jaspers can accept incarnation as a general principle without, as he sees it, jeopardizing the transcendence of Being-itself; but belief in the Deity of Christ seems to him to violate both the nature of Transcendence (i.e. God would then not be wholly transcendent) and the nature of the historical (i.e. as the sphere of finitude). Do Jaspers' difficulties arise from the fact that he is still forming his doctrine of the Transcendent only on the basis of what he finds to be characteristic of the historical from his human position within the historical? One might ask: 'Well, what else could he do?' Marcel has recognized throughout that all existential thinking must be rooted in human experience, but he suggests a readiness to let God Himself throw light on what He is. Is it possible to grasp the nature of the historical, without either getting outside it or by generalizing from our position within it, but rather by seeing it in the light which He grants? If so, then it would be wrong to lay down axioms in advance concerning what God could or could not do. In a word, Jaspers affirms incarnation as a general principle which is nowhere perfectly fulfilled, while Marcel sees the operation of the principle in men as testimony to the Incarnation, not as a principle, but as a Person.

Finally, for Jaspers it is a scandal that Christianity, which is only one religion among others, claims to be universally true. This leads, he believes, to arrogance, dogmatism, and false claims of security and finality. On the other hand, Marcel defines testimony in such a way that no final claim can be made for *homo viator*, whose task is to embody this 'universal truth,' and concerning the adequacy of his witness he must never claim exclusiveness, security, or finality. The element of unconditionality attaches not to claims we make concerning ourselves or our human beliefs; it attaches, rather, to the nature of the Transcendent toward whom our faith is directed. To Jaspers, if our faith is thus unconditional it cannot be 'universal,' since he associates universality with that which is objectively valid. For Marcel, on the other hand, universal validity in the sphere of values or religion, as contrasted with science or logic, does not mean 'pub-

323

licly verifiable by anybody and everybody.' Moreover, for him the element of unconditionality means that belief in God which is contingent upon any of our demands (e.g. upon *not* having to undergo certain forms of bereavement, disappointment, or suffering) is, at bottom, superstitious. It makes belief contingent upon the fulfillment of a contract: 'I shall believe in you, God, provided that . . .' Then if disaster strikes the man may assume that the contract has been broken by the other party. What really happened, however, was that the man made his contract with an imaginary being. The more belief is taken to be wrapped up with affirmation of certain concepts, the more likely is it to be shattered when adversity occurs. It is only the presence of God, not an idea of Him, that can be stronger than the presence of catastrophe.

10. Evil and Death; Hope and Salvation

But if this presence of God to faith is a gift, how can a man be blamed when this gift has not been granted to him? Such a query obviously separates grace and freedom in a manner which Marcel resists. God's offer is not an invention of our freedom; but His presence or absence to us is connected with how we have responded to the availability of fellowship. This does not mean, however, that the trials and ordeals which come to us are sent by God, as a sort of celestial schoolmaster, to test our faith. The father in the parable of the Prodigal Son transcends any such notions. The real question is whether we regard the evils which befall us simply as links in a chain of causal circumstance or as having an integral, not an accidental, place in a meaningful whole. The latter approach means that we have been lifted above that anxiety in which life seems meaningless. In connection with any specific ordeal, however, there may be a significant difference between our ability to withstand its impact at that moment and our ability to see meaning in it retrospectively.

In any case we again see the indissoluble connection between grace and freedom, for that which lifts us above anxiety is inseparable from purity of heart. In principle, Marcel suggests, all the evils which destroy faith, and which the unbeliever may try to avoid or surmount by his own power, can be summarized under the category of death. Every particular situation which we feel we cannot live through, because it deprives us of something indispensable, is a reflection of that ultimate situation which we cannot live through and which deprives us of everything indispensable. Perhaps we can imagine a world in which, after each creature had actualized all his potentialities, he would pass into a peaceful euthanasia and death would no longer be an object of horror; but such a world would wholly lack spiritual depth; it belongs in a fairy story. Our real world harbors seemingly inexhaustible possibilities of waste and destruction, and those who reach the highest spiritual fulfillment, instead of being in any sense immune from tragedy and death, often seem to have to undergo trials, persecution, and suffering of special intensity. Hence unless death has its place in a meaningful whole, we cannot be expected to believe that other evils have theirs; but a certain sort of 'spiritualism' makes the mistake of trying to fit death into the picture by denying its *apparent* finality.

The opposite mistake lies in a dogmatic affirmation of this finality; and from this error spring the most terrible evils of our age, which treat men as machines capable of a given output. There is a direct connection between the two errors; for a man who has been offered the too facile consolations of pseudo-religion may be driven into despair when he rightly becomes disillusioned with them. There is a straight line leading from the religious failure of our age to the forced labor camp and the cremation oven. Theoretically, one might suppose that abandonment of belief in eternal life would lead to more loving care for life in this world; but what has actually happened is the very opposite. Life in this world has become more and more widely looked upon as a sort of worthless phenomenon. An increase of slavery, in various forms, is the most glaring fact about our civilization, which has come to look upon death as the final word. The only thing left to such a generation is hope in 'social immortality'; and we have seen how, in such circumstances, the utmost bravery and willingness to sacrifice one's life for a future one will never see have been made to serve not the individual, but the species, in the form of such deified societies as Nazi Germany and Communist Russia.

For it is only on the basis of a metaphysics of intersubjectivity, where persons are seen as freely united in community rather than as subjugated to the mass, that sacrifice can take on a different and inward meaning. At this level, participation in the reality for which one sacrifices himself means that the significance and worth of personality-and-community are indestructible; for Being is indestructible. At the opposite pole is the view that human beings are interconnected by relations of simple succession, appearing and disappearing like an interminable game of skittles. But since the question at stake seems to be one of fact, how can faith or freedom have any bearing on it? Marcel replies that the Christian hope does not rest upon the outcome of a factual inquiry. The factual evidence for survival is not only meager (possibly non-existent), it is religiously well-nigh irrelevant; for the most it could show, even if it were strong, would be the survival of the *ego*, whereas what Christian hope is directed toward is not merely survival, which might still be egocentric, but life in God. Hence, so long as we confine the discussion to whether immortality is a fact or a delusion, we have not touched the heart of the matter. Factual evidence has to do with people in so far as they are objects. Whether the factual evidence is taken to indicate that these objects are destroyed or survive, nothing has been said about the person as a Thou.

Does this mean, then, that when he comes to speak of eternal life Marcel falls into a kind of dualism which he has otherwise sought to overcome? No; he declares that to construe his statement as an attempt to divide the person into a destructible phenomenon and an indestructible noumenon, is to misunderstand the case entirely. For this is to remain within the patterns of objective thinking, separating man into 'parts.' But the indestructibility he has in mind is that of a meaningful *bond* rather than an object. The quality and promise of eternity can be enclosed in the love that exists between two people. What is really important is the destiny of that living link, not the destiny of an entity which is isolated and closed in on itself, provided the human love we now refer to embodies that openness which is characteristic of genuine love and is not an idolatrous form of mutually shared narcissism. Participation in eternity is claimed for such a human bond, not as a closed system between husband and wife, parent and child, or friends, but as reflecting, under conditions of finitude, a divine love which charges existence with infinite possibilities.

Marcel is not suggesting that there is some supra-terrestrial place at which people arrive after leaving this earth. Desire might express itself in the form of such a notion; but desire is to be radically distinguished from hope. Hope does not consist in evading the apparent finality of death; it reaches its zenith, rather, when the situation is fully faced. At that point the ultimate opposition between existence and meaning which death signalizes is dealt with not by consulting factual information (for it cannot be decisive), nor by toying with ideas as to what would be desirable. Either one submits to the ultimate opposition and acknowledges the consequence that life is ultimately meaningless (as in nihilism), or one hopes and believes, on the basis of his present experience of God as the ground of the intersubjective bond, that the opposition is transcended.

Hope might be looked upon as an active reaction against a state of captivity to sickness, exile, estrangement, and meaninglessness. Perhaps this explains why, in those who are assured of a certain sort of material ease, hope so frequently withers, and with it the whole of the religious life. At the back of hope lies the assurance that tragedy is not the final word. Once again we see why the issue at stake turns, not on factual information, but on freedom. The presence of hope depends upon the putting forth of interior activity. But toward what is it directed? If it is directed only toward relief from intolerable circumstances in this world, it may be disappointed. If it is fixed upon some sort of development or state which will begin only after death, it may be an illusion. The answer, therefore, is that hope is not directed toward some finite object or outcome, whereas desire is so directed. Hope is, rather, the driving force behind what it is to be human. As such it is more than a biological urge to survive; for human beings can retain the biological urge, and cling to physical existence tenaciously, after they have become spiritually dead. Hope is akin to what gives life, not its reproductive successiveness through time, but its perennialness and sacredness in time. In totalitarian countries whole peoples have been murdered by those who 'hope' for a new, eternal order. But to call this 'hope' and to call such an order 'eternal' is to fall victim to ghastly lies. Here we really see despair wearing the mask of hope, and we see political movements whose aims are purely historical wearing the mask of 'eternal' claims. We must tear away these masks.

Values really hang together, and it is impossible to promote order, justice, or community at the expense of truth. What matters today is that man should rediscover the sense of the eternal, and withstand those who would make his life subservient to an alleged sense of history. Hope is not to hope *that* such-and-such will occur. It is to direct the driving force which keeps man human to the Transcendent, its source. The context in which Marcel puts forward the appeal of his entire philosophy is strenuously eschatalogical, not serenely speculative. Any views of faith and hope which can be sustained in our day, he believes, must face the fact that we are probably heading for catastrophes even more terrible than those of the last forty years. But the destructive forces are not like earthquakes and floods, since they have enlisted our human instincts and passions. The struggle against them must take the form of diagnosing and of seeking to cure an inward contamination which reaches into the depths of every man. Outwardly the problems of contemporary civilization look as though they called for a gigantic piece of social engineering. But the primary diagnosis and cure must be spiritual; and in the realm of the spiritual, proposals for gigantic programs are intrinsically suspect.

Marcel's philosophy, then, rests upon the indissolubility of faith, hope, and love within a concrete ontology. (He explains that his term 'intersubjectivity' is synonymous with 'charity.') It is aimed at universality, for the terms just mentioned are intended to embrace the whole human community; but his concept of the whole is 'polyphonic' and supra-personal. He thinks of each individual as actively participating, and rejects every arithmetical notion which would try to treat human beings additively as masses. He aims at universality because he seeks to describe a mode of participation from which no one is excluded.

Does this lead him into outright universalism? In reply he points out that we are in no position to know whether all human beings are destined to salvation, and neither are we in a position to take over God's role as judge in excluding anyone. The most we can say is that freedom implies the possibility of spiritual self-destruction, which can take the form of impious self-assertion. Here freedom turns against its own proper nature, for defiance of the ground of Being can take place only through one who has received both being and freedom from this ground. The result is a perversion of being; yet such perversions really occur.

Must not Marcel put forth some sort of argument for the reality of God, however, if faith is to be more than an incommunicable psychic event? His reply is that arguments about God are relatively futile until one has become clear about the motives for being able or unable to believe in Him. A man like Albert Camus who cannot see how the reality of God is reconcilable with the suffering of children is not on the same plane as a man who rejects belief in God because he does not want to face his own finitude and imperfection. Conversely, what men have tried to establish through arguments for the reality of God represent various and incompatible conceptions of what constitutes perfection. Therefore the proofs are ineffectual precisely at that point where they seem to be most needed, i.e. in trying to convince an unbeliever; and in so far as a man has experienced the presence of God, proofs serve no useful function. If the real motive for unbelief is a negative will, can one hope to show the atheist, this Lucifer-man, his mistake? Only conversion will overcome his negativity, and that falls within the domain of grace. One man may be an instrument in the conversion of another, but never the cause of it. Yet Marcel is eager to go beyond Kierkegaard and Pascal in emphasizing the intelligible aspect of faith. The way in which persons and meanings come together in a concrete ontology deserves to be called *knowledge,* because it is closer to the spirit of truth than is mere ratiocination. Whenever faith breaks away from knowledge in this sense it tends to degenerate into idolatry.

Faith is not, then, simply an incommunicable psychic event. Where other writers frequently say that it has an 'objective' reference, Marcel prefers to say that it has an 'intersubjective' reference. The act of opening ourselves to God involves our freedom; but this act does not automatically guarantee that grace is released for us. Indeed, in speaking of both faith and salvation—at least so far as these may be entered into while a man is engaged in temporal life— Marcel is anxious to avoid any suggestion of a static, finished condition. Basically sin consists of taking oneself as center by shutting oneself off against the universal, and the battle against it must be incessant. The collective conditions through which sin operates cannot rightly be conceived either as chosen by the individual or as imposed upon him from without. These conditions are not the *result* of individual choosing, for they enter into the context in which he does his choosing. But neither are they simply imposed upon him from without, for he actively participates in them instead of submitting to them automatically.

So long as man is a wayfaring creature, salvation can only mean a continual entering into that universal community which is grounded in God; it cannot mean some sort of spiritual standstill. From this perspective Marcel is willing to admit that our age may be witnessing a deterioration of the human species. All hopes that history is moving toward a *temporal* fulfillment may well be illusory. The crimes committed, deliberately or inadvertently, by means of expanded scientific control cannot be dissociated from the stifling of wisdom that has accompanied over-emphasis upon scientific knowledge. We cannot be sure that the threat of destruction will force men to undergo that conversion which would have to occur before science might be used predominantly for spiritually enriching purposes, instead of increasing the tempo toward depersonalization. If such a conversion can occur, it will require the renewal of a different sort of *knowledge* as well as a change of will.

Hence the starting point must be sought, not in some sort of program that we initiate, but in an opening of the self to the light which God sheds on temporal life. This does not mean that we attempt to leap outside the conditions of temporal life; rather, it means that we see how pervasively mankind is being assimilated into a schematization of things. This assimilation *is* spiritual destruction, and we must refuse all complicity in it. Rather, we must maintain that in so far as persons are not things, human life is embraced by a living reality incomparably more dynamic and free than we are. It is true, of course, that because of our derivative freedom we possess the dreadful power of withholding ourselves from divine reality, locking ourselves ever more tightly into the prison which we create for our minds and spirits. Yet temporal existence need not be a prison, provided we respond with openness and fidelity to those solicitations from the beyond which can transfigure it here and now. Thus human life may become a temple which enshrines a gracious Presence.

Either spirit is an excrescence in a world that is hostile to it, or nature, temporality, and the body find their authentic meaning as earthen vessels suited to hold their heavenly treasure. In so far as this latter possibility is realized, the mysterious takes precedence over the purely problematic. To move from the refusal of Being, or God, into the invocation of the ultimate Presence, is, according to Gabriel Marcel, the proper end of *homo viator*.

NOTES

1. See 'An Essay in Autobiography' in *The Philosophy of Existence* (New York: Philosophical Library, 1949), pp. 83f., from which most of the information here set forth is taken.
2. Published in the United States by Henry Regnery, Chicago, in 1951. Other works now available in English are *The Philosophy of Existence, A Metaphysical Journal* (Regnery, 1952), *Being and Having* (Boston:

Beacon, 1951), *Homo Viator* (Regnery, 1951), *Man Against Mass Society* (Regnery, 1952), *The Decline of Wisdom* (Regnery, 1955), as well as a group of Marcel's plays.

3. *The Philosophy of Existence,* p. 88.

4. Ibid. p. 92.

5. Ibid. p. 79.

6. As illustrative of the way in which Marcel's aesthetic and philosophical concerns are bound together, we may mention his song, 'The Double,' written to words by Jules Supervielle, printed at the end of the volume edited by Etienne Gilson entitled *Existentialisme Chrétien* (Paris, 1947), or the fact that his significant essay on the 'ontological mystery' first appeared in 1933 as a long postscript to his play *Le Monde Casse* ('The Broken World').

7. *The Philosophy of Existence,* pp. 93-6.

8. Cf. Roger Troisfontaines, *Existentialism and Christian Thought* (London: Black, 1950), p. 17.

9. *The Philosophy of Existence,* p. 1.

10. Ibid. p. 8.

11. Ibid. p. 9.

12. Ibid. p. 12.

13. Ibid. p. 12.

14. Ibid. p. 14.

15. Ibid. p. 15.

16. Ibid. p. 18.

17. Ibid. p. 19.

18. Ibid. p. 20.

19. Ibid. p. 20.

20. Ibid. p. 25.

21. Marcel's remarks here are applicable to psychoanalytic counseling. The psychoanalyst should be both participant and observer, but there is the constant danger that he will become mainly the latter. The prevailing assumptions concerning scientific work, one's own training, a heavy schedule of appointments, and many other factors, drive him toward detachment and routinization. See especially Frieda Fromm-Reichmann, *Principles of Intensive Psychotherapy.*

22. Marcel's book *Man Against Mass Society* deals at length with this corrective, as do *Le Declin de la Sagesse* (Paris, 1954) and *L'Homme Problématique* (Paris, 1955).

23. *The Mystery of Being,* vol. II, p. 95.

IN CONCLUSION

THE FOREGOING CHAPTERS constitute a kind of panoramic survey of the dominant stresses in existentialist philosophy, by passing in review the thought of some of its most influential spokesmen. Now, by way of conclusion, we return to the question with which we began this book. What claim does existentialism rightfully exert upon religious people and what should be the character of our response to it? Without presuming to give in these last few pages anything like a definitive appraisal of the movement as a whole, I wish to give as straightforward an answer as I can to this original question.

It is clear that believers in God have much to learn from existentialism; it should also be clear that Christian faith, in particular, has much to offer by way of corrective and complementing insights. It has already been shown, I trust, that either outright rejection or wholesale adoption of the existentialist perspective is scarcely possible for those who must make up their minds about it. Yet the survey we have been making will certainly facilitate a fair-minded response to this exciting challenge; and now we shall proceed to characterize such a response.

First, let us grant that existentialist modes of thinking can prove extremely salutary in warning us against the way in which an idolatrous attitude toward science leads us in the direction of dehumanization in our Western culture. All the thinkers we have been studying put forward this warning in measured and meaningful terms. Each in his own manner issues a solemn, even prophetic protest

333

against this undeniable drift, accentuated by the vast prestige of scientific methods and assumptions in the modern world. Whether the existentialist is religiously motivated or not, he is characteristically one who comes to the defense of human freedom, uniqueness, self-transcendence. Furthermore, he regards this defense as a sort of mission that is made urgently necessary by the threats of abstract rationalism and pragmatic functionalism which have their roots in the widespread and uncritical adulation of science.

Also, and in the same vein, existentialism embodies a deep-seated distrust of all efforts to compel religious belief through the devising of arguments or so-called 'proofs' for the reality of God. On this point believers stand together with agnostics and atheists. What existentialism suggests, on the contrary, is that in so far as one is a religious person he should not try to vindicate his position by running to scientists or philosophers for confirmation and support. Instead he ought to develop, deepen, and then articulate his conception of subjectivity or arbitrariness; but it can now be convincingly declared, thanks mainly to existentialism, that these risks are by no means as great as those of objectivization and problematization where the 'existing individual' is concerned.

In the present cultural situation, a Christian whose thinking has been strongly influenced by existentialism has perforce to spend much time and energy in combating the Draconian pretensions of science and secular philosophy. This, admittedly, is for the most part a negative task. And yet if circumstances should ever allow us to pass beyond this stage of corrective resistance, it is not impossible to see a more positive task taking shape. A Christian philosophy, once it has come to terms with what existentialism has to teach it, may well pay more sympathetic heed to the constructive role which science and objective reason are able to play in serving the truly spiritual ends of individual and communal living. We have cause for rejoicing that a number of thinkers, men like Heim and von Weiszäcker, for example, are already entering upon this more positive phase.

In the second place, the movement we have been reviewing has much to offer religious believers by way of a drastically realistic acquaintance with the stuff of which human existence is made. For it exposes and explores, just as depth-psychology has been doing, the full and often terrifying terrain of guilt, anxiety, despair, and nothingness. To be sure, a great many people are repelled by existentialism for this very reason. They regard its preoccupation with these somber themes as morbid and debilitating. This is perhaps especially true of American church members who are in the habit of taking up optimistic and activistic attitudes toward such matters. But Christianity is assuredly not a fair-weather religion which is reluctant to face the truth about man. In fact, its own analysis of the human plight has proved to be quite as trenchant, grave, and disquieting as anything existentialism has to offer.

What good can possibly come of turning away from these irrational and demonic forces which are menacing folk in our own time so savagely? Why should we be unwilling, or unable, to face squarely the life of man in all its vulnerability, edginess, and estrangement? And how may the healing powers of the Christian gospel ever come to grips with the dark forces of sin, despair, and death unless—and until—these forces are brought radically out into the open by our searching thought? Only if we acknowledge them for what they are can we make any effective answer to them. Here it seems that even the atheistic existentialists have a picture of man-in-the-world to share with us which we refuse to face only at grave peril to ourselves and our own message.

Our age, perhaps, is in the position of Job before God, except that our claims to righteousness are clearly not as strong as Job's were. We have suffered, and do not know why. We have become inured to crisis, numbed by catastrophe, until the very capacity to be sensitive and sympathetic has been largely lost. It is almost as if, beneath the comings and goings, the forced smile, the planning and programming of life, a fundamental distrust of Being were being expressed. Such a distrust can only be overcome if it is laid bare and looked at with sober realism. Indeed, we must be encouraged, like Job, to give full vent to our indictment of life. In the name of faith we must make our accusations against God. While one is scarcely able to accuse a being in whom one does not believe, such a possibility becomes altogether real when one is a believer.

We must also refuse to be put off with neat, trim theories about God, if we are going to find some 'happy issue' out of all our questionings and sufferings. For any genuine resolution is bound to emerge out of our very wrestling with God. It must come in the form of God's presence with us in the midst of every sort of tragedy. Moreover, in reaching such a resolution the work of existentialist thinkers will have great descriptive and clinical value for the Christian interpretation of life.

Thirdly, existentialism can contribute significantly to our understanding of the vexed relationship between faith and reason. The movement has been often criticized for bringing about a sharp and quite unnecessary cleavage between the believing and the thinking self. We have already seen, especially in connection with Kierkegaard, that there is some real point to this criticism. Yet it is wise to remember that Kierkegaard's own invective against philosophy was launched almost exclusively at Hegel, who was the high priest of rationalistic idealism in his own time. Most students of the history of philosophy would probably now agree that this criticism, no matter how intemperate in some respects, is well taken. What is more, Kierkegaard was not alone in making it; he was soon joined by such influential thinkers as Nietzsche, Bergson, James, Dewey, and Whitehead, to name but a few in a very long list.

According to existentialism, philosophy does not have to culminate in abstract speculation about Being itself. It may take other forms than those of rational structure, logical system, or universal meaning. And that is a perennially important declaration. In so far as existentialism can succeed in showing that metaphysics or ontology may speak inside the vivid, concrete, personal language of drama and poetry, it opens the way toward a concordat between faith and philosophic reason which Kierkegaard himself could scarcely have envisaged.

Here, for example, Jaspers and Marcel give us grounds for hope.

Out of their approaches may actually come a new and constructive form of Christian philosophy. This new point of view may well be liberated from the old rigidity and special pleading which have so often plagued dogmatic and systematic theology in the past. Yet it will almost certainly be shaped by images and categories which are closer to those of the Bible than to those typically used in contemporary idealisms, naturalisms, or positivisms. Such an enterprise, to quote Pascal, will effectively avoid each of two extremes: 'to exclude reason, and to admit reason only.' It will also agree with him in holding that 'the last proceeding of reason is to recognize that there is an infinity of things which are beyond it.'

Fourth, the movement reviewed in this volume can provide quite indispensable resources for the present-day Christian apologist. Any defense of the Christian faith calls for a penetrating analysis of the condition of unfaith, an analysis which is non-polemical in at least the first instance. It must be confessed, I think, that much Christian theology today either tries to convince modern man that he is already in despair without knowing it, or scolds him for not being sufficiently in despair. The method generally adopted is that of puncturing all the balloons of his hopes on the rather questionable assumption that if all the plausible answers can be demolished, then he may be willing to swallow the less plausible things in Christianity as a last resort.

Now it is true that there may be a great deal in the current theological de-bunking of Deweyism, Marxism, Freudianism, technology, et cetera, which can persuade men of their falsity and disvalue. But how can one avoid feeling that the 'Christian answer,' which is proffered in the place of these contemporary substitutes for God, does not stand up any better, at any rate in those forms in which it is being presented to us? All too often 'faith' is employed merely to keep the theologian going; it is a banner waved in a losing apologetic battle. It may even be adopted in the face of the Christian's unavowed, but also undisguised fear that there is no chance of giving a genuine, honest, relevant answer. One suspects that if his own critical weapons were turned upon himself, upon the paradoxes and

337

contradictions which he invites others to accept, he might not come off so very well either.

Instead of examining unfaith simply for the purpose of showing how superficial or inadequate it is, should not the Christian apologist who has been influenced by existentialism frankly recognize the extent to which he is himself in the same boat with those he attacks? These days, one seldom meets a theological refutation of 'secularism' which dares to leave Saul's armor behind. By 'Saul's armor' I mean the confident foreknowledge as to how one is going to demolish secular viewpoints by brandishing established Christian convictions. The point is just that an existentialist analysis of despair must always run the risk of entering into that despair. Any genuine act of faith must be really open to alternative possibilities, which involves the risk of seeing whether an answer *is* forthcoming from the side of faith. Such willingness, in fact, is demanded as a pledge of one's good faith by those whom he seeks to convince and convert. And this is emphatically not the same as tucking the answers up one's sleeve where they can be flashed out in an emergency.

There is a good reason why Christian efforts to deal with human meaninglessness do not impress many of our contemporaries. It is that they suspect the theologian of never having come enough out of his own shell of presuppositions to run the gauntlet, to be trapped himself in meaninglessness. Hence, much that goes on under the name of apologetics is criticized, by Barthians and atheists alike, because it only pretends to meet non-Christians on a common footing. From the Barthian standpoint, it is hypocritical to leave in abeyance the ultimate promise given to us by God in Christ if we indeed possess it. And from the atheistic standpoint, it is silly to make such a pretense of understanding the condition of the beliefless man when one has 'the Christian answer' (however paradoxical and tension-ridden) up his sleeve all along. The true apologist is one whose faith carries him to the point of self-identification with those to whom, after all, God is not a premise but a question or a target. And such faith comes to the defender of Christian truth in the very midst of, yet also in spite of, actual meaninglessness and utter nothingness. Only such a person can become a real link between the church and the world. Perhaps theologians might come much closer to being such links were it not for the fact that somehow we think it virtuous to overlook the degree to which we too are modern men for whom the world is broken and falling apart.

A fifth important point of contact between existentialism and religious belief concerns the question of human freedom. This is an issue on which every existentialist philosophy pivots, but which can only be resolved on terms provided by religious faith. The movement we have been surveying offers two opposite answers to the question. Atheistic existentialists typically equate freedom with human autonomy, insisting, as we have seen, that man's self-definition and self-realization are attained only as he learns to master his own destiny without looking to an illusory, invented God for outside help. In this vein Sartre declares that 'existentialism is humanism.' Religious existentialists, on the other hand, maintain that genuine human freedom is discovered only by relinquishing this egocentric effort to run life all by oneself, and by finding highest blessedness in rapport or communion with the living God.

It is at precisely this point that existentialism may become, in Roger Troisfontaine's words, either a religious philosophy in support of Christian faith or the most anti-Christian philosophy that can be conceived. From the Christian viewpoint, this ambiguity in existentialism is decidedly fortunate. It means that one does not have to take all of it or nothing, but may bring to it insights and resources of one's own as well as a willingness to be instructed and corrected by it.

Human freedom is open to another interpretation than that which atheistic thinkers like Sartre or agnostics like Jaspers put upon it. Instead of being boxed up in our freedom, or suspended in it, a Christian thinker in the existentialist mode declares freedom to be openness and disposability with respect to God. It should be plain that the Christian affirms the sheer fact of freedom every bit as eagerly as does the atheist or the agnostic. The issue is not whether there is freedom or no freedom. It is basically whether freedom as it

339

stands is ultimately a curse or a gift, a situation or in fact a relation. The issue, then, is not freedom versus something else, but freedom without God versus freedom with God.

The Christian understanding is that God first granted man his freedom and still cares more wisely and mightily for its fulfillment than any human being can ever do. We know this to be so because of God's self-disclosure of Himself in Jesus Christ. Instead of remaining aloof from the human race and moving us about at a distance in accordance with the dictates of an arbitrary yet omnipotent will, God has come to us and offered Himself in the only way that can actually win us through our freedom, not against it. In taking thus upon Himself the burden of our guilt in costly love, He seeks to break through every wall of selfishness and hard-heartedness.

What is basically wrong with us, according to this understanding, is that we try to become self-sufficient by making ourselves independent of God. Even as a definition of freedom, however, this is utterly negative; there is no good reason why self-affirmation should mean God-denial. Here men like Heidegger and Sartre appear to be victims of the same disease of modern man which they have done so much to diagnose. The true remedy for this sickness is just what it has always been—the giving of oneself into God's own leading and keeping. But it can happen only through decisive and perhaps shattering personal acceptance and appropriation of the divine power. Freedom can surely become misunderstood and misused; but such abuse and error ought not to be made normative in either thought or life. Rather, Christians should strive to find ways of presenting the remedy of faith in full accord with the fact of freedom, which may well inspire the profound prayer that we may be enabled to point our contemporaries through and beyond freedom to the Christ who died to make us free.

And finally, if we succeed in doing this we shall have passed the stage of using existentialism as a philosophical support for Christian faith. Instead of consciously borrowing existentialist terms and themes in order to elucidate our own beliefs regarding God, man, and Christ, we shall then be making existential explorations from a

Christian base. To a large extent, this may come about because the existentialist outlook will have become so much a part of us; but also because with its help we have been able to probe more sharply and closely to the heart of our own faith, so that our believing will no longer require this particular kind of structuring and buttressing.

Then it will once again be clear that Christianity is actually compatible with different types of philosophical approach, just as it is already plain that existentialism, as one such type, harbors within itself a fundamental cleavage which can only be bridged by the truth of faith. Of all the thinkers studied in this book, Gabriel Marcel is perhaps the most prophetic with regard to this more constructive possibility. The same thing might also be said of others not reviewed here, notably Martin Buber and Nicolas Berdyaev. Thinkers like these have demonstrated great capacity not only to learn from existentialism but also to bring to it a distinctively religious stress and shape.

The name to be given to such a possible development does not greatly matter. What does matter is that religious belief should now transcend existentialism precisely by including it. We who believe in God, now that we have seen the ultimate nature of faith as a decision between God and nothing, must make that decision ourselves. And having made it, we shall find that our commitment is deepened into conviction, and conviction broadened into comprehension of the strange ways of God, whose very absence is a kind of presence and whose silence is a mysterious mode of speaking to us.

341

BIBLIOGRAPHY

A Selected List of General Works on Existentialism in English

Allen, E. L. *Existentialism from Within.* New York: Macmillan, 1953.

Blackham, H. J. *Six Existentialist Thinkers.* London: Routledge & Kegan Paul, 1953.

Bobbio, N. *The Philosophy of Decadentism: A Study in Existentialism.* Oxford: Basil Blackwell, 1948.

Collins, James. *The Existentialists.* Chicago: Henry Regnery, 1952.

Grene, Marjorie. *Dreadful Freedom: A Critique of Existentialism.* Chicago: University of Chicago Press, 1948.

Harper, Ralph. *Existentialism: A Theory of Man.* Cambridge: Harvard University Press, 1948.

Heinemann, F. H. *Existentialism and the Modern Predicament.* New York: Harper, 1954.

Kuhn, Helmut. *Encounter with Nothingness: An Essay on Existentialism.* Chicago: Henry Regnery, 1949.

Michalson, Carl, editor. *Christianity and the Existentialists.* New York: Scribner's, 1956.

Mounier, Emmanuel. *Existentialist Philosophies.* London: Rockcliff, 1948.

Ruggiero, Guido de. *Existentialism.* London: Secker and Warburg, 1946.

Troisfontaines, Roger. *Existentialism and Christian Thought.* London: A. & C. Black, 1950.

Wahl, Jean. *A Short History of Existentialism.* New York: Philosophical Library, 1949.

Wild, John. *The Challenge of Existentialism.* Bloomington: Indiana University Press, 1955.

INDEX

Abraham, 70-71
Absolute, 79, 230-31
Abstraction, 285, 298, 309, 310
Absurdity, 224-5
Antigone, 66-7
Anxiety, 73-5, 153-4, 324-5
Aristotle, 17, 18
Atheism, 181-5, 202-3, 214-20, 224-5, 260-61, 320
Augustine, St., 15, 16, 22, 24, 30, 31, 35

Barth, Karl, 173
Being, 167, 172-3, 187-9, 250-53, 255-6, 283-5, 286-7
Bible, 53-6, 132-3
Body, 197, 211, 300-301, 311
Buber, Martin, 190, 200

Calvinism, 22, 29, 30
Camus, Albert, 206, 329
Casuistry, 26-7
Catholicism, Roman, 281-2
Choice, see Freedom
Christianity, 43, 53-6, 76, 90-92, 122-3, 134-8, 139, 208, 258-9, 264-5
Communication, 92, 240-42, 259-60
Conscience, see Responsibility
Consciousness, 165, 198-200, 203, 205, 224, 283
Cullmann, Oscar, 163-4

Death, 154-5, 247-8, 324-7
Decision, 67-9, 96; see also Freedom

Descartes, R., 48, 215, 235
Despair, 68, 116-23, 288, 289
Determinism, 85-7, 98, 210-12
Dualism, 198-9

Encounter, 200-201, 250-51
Epictetus, 21, 42, 43, 46
Essence, 216-17; see also Existence
Eternity, and time, 74-5, 245-6
Ethics (morality), 97, 220-22; see also Responsibility
Evil, 98-9, 285-6
Existence, 235-6, 310-12; see also Self

Faith, 84-5, 87, 130-31, 221-2, 247-8, 259-60, 314-16
Finitude, 118-19, 246
Freedom, 66-8, 73-5, 166-7, 177-8, 204, 209-14, 236-8, 260-61, 317-20, 339-40

God (theism), 48-9, 78-9, 108-9, 215-16, 312-13, 321-2, 329-30, 334
Grace, and freedom, 22-4, 29-34, 132, 318-20
Guilt, 114-16, 246-7

Hegel, G., 97
Heidegger, M., 147-90, 200, 204, 221, 249, 297
History (historicity), 86-9, 94, 141-2, 159-60, 244-5
Hope, 289, 290, 326-9

343